What People Are Saying About M. Taylor and This Book

"Taylor's folktales draw from his experiences with me and his times in Africa. They contain the stuff of folktales of old. They are a wonderful interpretation of African tradition."

— Grand Master Drummer Mamady Keïta

"Wow. This book is more than just about playing a drum. It is a powerful life story that teaches about community, connection to our ancestors, purpose for our youth, and overall meaning in life. Readers will have a multicultural experience that will take them to multiple continents and then back to themselves. Well done, Michael Taylor!"

— Patrick Snow, Publishing Coach and International Bestselling Author of *Creating Your Own Destiny* and *The Affluent Entrepreneur*

"Taylor, with gentle fierceness about his art, his craft, and his students, is brave enough to not hide behind his life—a rare courage. He's got good hands, too: tasteful, technically correct, deep, and controlled. He is also humble about his expertise; another rarity. There's a lot Taylor brings to the table to appreciate, and learn. We hope you get your chance. You will find it's worth it. I continue to be impressed."

— Sulé Greg Wilson, Author, Educator, Raconteur, and Musician

"In this powerful book, Taylor shares how playing the djembe not only creates captivating and versatile music but also inspires life changes beyond your imagination."

— Susan Friedmann, CSP and Bestselling Author of
Riches in Niches: How to Make It BIG in a small Market

"Passionate student, dedicated djembefola, loyal leader, dear life brother of mine! With his keen heart, generous smile, and that knowing glint in his eye, he both supports and cajoles one to extend just a little deeper into the landscape where heaven meets earth, where the known and unknown mingle; where the magic lives! To share in the wonders of Malinke culture with Taylor is to be led to the very heart of being in love with life. Your own life! His life! The life of djembe."

— Todd Tesen, Yoga Practitioner and Teacher

"In this powerful, thoughtful, far-reaching book, Taylor teaches how playing the djembe not only teaches discipline and creates incredible music, but can change your life. Reading his story was an unexpected treat that will stay with me for years to come."

— Tyler R. Tichelaar, PhD and Award-Winning Author
of *Kawbawgam: The Chief, The Legend, The Man* and *The Best Place*

"Taylor's account of the sound of the djembe echoing his life's calling is a remarkable saga of initiation, blending his inspired folk tales with African travel and pragmatic instruction. This is a book not only for drum enthusiasts, but seekers after ancestral wisdom."

— Dick Russell, Author of *My Mysterious Son: A Life-Changing Passage Between Schizophrenia and Shamanism*

"Acquiring knowledge in the world is a path one cannot avoid. However, seeking knowledge is a path traveled by choice and commitment. I consider myself fortunate for many reasons, not the least of which is that my chosen path intersected with Michael Taylor's. It is my sincere hope that everyone's chosen path is enhanced as mine has been by Taylor's humanity, friendship, life experience, and his commitment to seeking verified knowledge of the djembe and the culture therein."

— Matthew Henry, Music Professor and Professional Musician

"I love how in tune Taylor is with his African roots—a journey he went on to reconnect with his past. His love for djembe is inspiring, and the truths he shares about being of mixed race, and how we all need to reconnect with our cultures when we feel displaced will resonate with you whether you are a music lover or not. *Remembering Your Ancestral Fires* is a real and very pleasant surprise."

— Nicole Gabriel, Author of *Finding Your Inner Truth* and *Stepping Into Your Becoming*, Shaman, and Yoga Practitioner and Teacher

Praise for Taylor's DRUMeditation

"Taylor's DRUMeditation is a transformative experience. He sets a comfortable, inviting atmosphere and guides participants through meditation with incredible musicianship and storytelling. I left the session with a much lighter spirit. I look forward to attending again at the next possible opportunity!"

— Laura Dee Miller

"Taylor, how do you do that? Transport one down a river, over the hills and deep into a valley in two hours from my tiny office? Magical indeed— thank you for your abundant talent and generous delivery of drum genius. Was that you playing the entire time? Crazy! Your authenticity is the genuine article and the reason we come to replenish to the sound of the Master Taylor. Thanks for launching my sixty-sixth year!"

— Maureen

"Michael Taylor's DRUMeditation is a powerful experience that can be many different things, sometimes all at once. It is a way to get back in touch with your body and breath, to experience connection and community, and at its most illuminating, it can provide a deep spiritual journey. Taylor's relationship with the drum goes well beyond what you hear, and I am grateful he shares this medicine with such beautiful intent. Go for the drumming, leave with a better understanding of self."

— C. Ojeda

"Taylor's DRUMeditation was an experience unlike anything I've ever had. A truly mind-expansive, portal-opening, positive, beautiful experience I look forward to having again very soon."

— M. Matrejek, Creator of the Breathe Discovery Festival

"Taylor is a gifted drummer who brightens my Wednesdays with his improvisational skills in leading our morning yoga class. He's an amazingly talented drummer who reaches and moves everyone in the room in the most wonderful ways. And besides his amazing talents, he's a wonderful guy. Please don't miss a chance to hear his DRUMeditation!"

— C. Meredith, Ahimsa Yoga Studio

"I have been to many DRUMeditations; every one is different because we are never the same, always changing. Free your mind. Bathe in the sound of the drums, and release everything to Spirit. I use this energy to help rebalance myself in this heroic world. You feel the DRUMeditation in your body and it changes you! Blessings, Taylor!"

— D. Curtis, Oakwood Farms Retreat Center

REMEMBERING YOUR ANCESTRAL FIRE

A BI-RACIAL MAN'S UNLIKELY JOURNEY OF SELF-DISCOVERY, HEEDING THE CALL OF THE DJEMBE

M. TAYLOR

HOLY GOAT

REMEMBERING YOUR ANCESTRAL FIRE
A Biracial Man's Unlikely Journey of Self-Discovery, Heeding the Call of the Djembe

Copyright © 2023 by Michael John Taylor. All rights reserved.

Published by:
Holy Goat Percussion
418 South Taylor Avenue
Oak Park, IL 60302
(773) 909-8633
www.holygoat.com

All Rights Reserved. No part of this book may be used or reproduced in any manner whatsoever without the expressed written permission of the author.

Address all inquiries to:
Holy Goat Percussion
418 South Taylor Avenue
Oak Park, IL 60302
(773) 909-8633
www.holygoat.com

ISBN: 978-1-63618-164-6
Library of Congress Control Number: 2022910410

Editor: Tyler Tichelaar, Superior Book Productions
Cover Design: Nicole Gabriel, Angel Dog Productions
Interior Book Layout: Nicole Gabriel, Angel Dog Productions
Cover Photo Credit: Olina Dolly

Every attempt has been made to properly source all quotes.
Printed in the United States of America
Second Edition

3 4 5 6 7 8 9 10

DEDICATION

I dedicate this book to:

Grand Master Drummer Mamady Keïta
(August 1950—June 21, 2021)

Elder Master Dr. Malidoma Patrice Somé
(January 30, 1956—December 9, 2021)

My ancestors

Shango

The three spirits at Kurunin,
Baladugu Djomawagna, Guinea, West Africa

My teachers (many of whom are unaware that they fall into this category;
I'm referring here to anyone I've learned *anything* from, good, bad, etc.)

My adoptive parents, Sylvia and Wilbert Taylor

My biological parents, Audrey Clancy and David Day, Sr.

My students

And all of you who helped illuminate my path

Acknowledgments

Extra special thanks to Christa Ojeda, my bestest friend, for helping in the very early edits of this book and to Sulé Greg Wilson and Kimosha P. Murphy for helping to clarify and flesh-out very important aspects of certain very critical, potentially controversial, parts of this book. Thanks to those I consider family (you know who you are), Michael Stelnicki, Brian Ralston, BJ Levy, Jessica Weidenheimer, Family Friedrich, The Council, Patrick Snow for Sage guidance in getting this book out of my head, Tyler Tichelaar for expert editing, Matthew "BHC" Henry, Adam Rugo, Matt "Bona" Hanson, Ted Oppenheimer, the Oppenheimer Family Foundation, Famoudou Konate, Moussa "Bolokada" Conde, Abdoul Doumbia, Yaya Kabo, Idy Ciss, Djeli Morikeba Kouyate, Atiba Rorie, Josh Fox, Djali Amadou Kouyaté, Audrey Kindelspire, David Day, Sr., Audrey Clancy, Moungam "Kabinet" Camara, Michael Markus, Elizabeth Nuti, Sam Debell, Kurt Hill, Pauli Caldwell, Leah and the Ivory Family, Sylvia Taylor, Wilbert Taylor, Piper Lynn Taylor, John Yost, Michael Miles, Diane Patterson, Olivier Ledoux, Tony Webb, Leddie Garcia, Yo-Yo Ma, Vinx De'Jon Parrette, Michael "Choco" Criddell, Sean Rowbottom, David J. Wren, Kevin Folta, James Frale ("The Flying Squirrels"), Eric "T'Challa" Thomas, Kristopher Sanders, Jason "Wolfy" Wolf, Justin Hundreiser, Andrew Elbert, Scott Mosak, Greg Lundberg, Monette Marino, Mahiri "Fadjimba" Keïta-Edwards, William Scheidt, Hiroki Murai, Sam Debell, Kelvin Kew, Pierre "Dr. Djembe" Challian, Paul "PC" Cotton, Moustapha Bangoura, Lee Ann Perry, Jeffrey Amon, Dawn Curtis, Quinn Reisor, Russel Anderson, Steve Meyer, Toby Christiansen, Chris Pawola, Tara Tucker, Stark Raving Ensemble, Todd Tesen, Michael Stewart, Graeme Goodwin, Mike McElya, CJ Greenberg, Dr. Eric Charry, Professor Randy Hogencamp, Dr.

Rebecca Gearhart Mafazy, Ruth McElya-Lestrange and family, Whitfield Holmes, Jeremiah Glauser, Courtney Higgins, John Scalici, Tom Harris, Tom Taylor, Joanna Koblanska and Kai Chapinski, Greg Ince, Yaya Diallo, Madou Dembele, the Old Town School of Folk Music, my apprentices at After School Matters, Dick Russel, Elder Theresa Sykes Brittany, Tam Tam Mandingue International, Jeni Swerdlow, Arthur Hull, M'Bemba Bangoura, Amy Krutek, Aldo Mazza, Dr. Frank Suggs, Paul Swanson, Warren Denniston II, Dr. Bob Steinman, John Hires, Mr. Herzing, Doc Friedl, Dr. Max Culver, John FS Williams, Hamisi Lee, Brad Nardick, Kalani Das, Bill "Shoobooty" Brickey, Graham "Mojoharp" Nelson, Don Livingston, Mike Catuara, John Barry, Dave Villarreal, Susan Schraiber, Victoria Boateng, Victoria Halas, Rahul Sharma and my Funkadesi family, Diane Patterson and Sheba Love, Rich Logan, King Errisson, Derek Fredrickson, Terry Reimer, Jeremy Williams, Deb Peyton, Steve Proudman, Doug Brush, William Scheidt, Bob Garrett, Freddie Zental Weaver, Ashley Bertling, Greg Fundis, Robinlee Garber, Latisha Strong, Yuyi Guajardo, John McCracken, Christine Cipra, Dr. Djo Bi, Jaylen Green, Suzanne Satterfield, Robert Chappell, Baba Collins, Baba Luther Gray, Manu Walton, Cheikh Balla Samb, Olina Dolly and Danny Gutierrez.

CONTENTS

Acknowledgments		11
Introduction		19
Chapter 1	Why Am I Here?	23
	"The Jungle"	39
Chapter 2	The Tao of Djembe	45
	Journal Entries: 1997 My First Trip to Guinea, West Africa	55
Chapter 3	Ancestors	77
	Africanesque Folktale—Origin: anta and Daouda; the story of the women and the Numun . . . of the heartbeat, the original heartbeat of one ancient culture in Africa	85
	Journal Entries: 1998—Guinea Trip 2	95
Chapter 4	In the Beginning	103
Chapter 5	My Early Years	113
	Journal Entries: 2001—New York, Guinea, Madou Dembele, Mamady Keïta, Spider Dance	130
	Africanesque Folktale—Duality: Hand of the Master	158
Chapter 6	1994: The Beginnings Begin	163
	Africanesque Folktale: The Story of Djemebeyaya: You Can Be Whole and Be Alone	174
	Journal Entries: 2002—Rewiring the Self, Building the Road to Tam Tam Mandingue, Chicago	179

Chapter 7	First CD; First Teachers	199
	Journal Entries: 2003—San Diego, Chicago, and Ireland	209
	Africanesque Folktale—Plurality: The Story of Moribayassa—Mamady and Kadia	214
Chapter 8	RememberingHow to Drum	221
	Journal Entries: 2005—The Big Tests	228
Chapter 9	The Inclusive "OR"	239
	Journal Entries: 2007—Yo-Yo Ma and Performance Tour in the Birthplace of Mamady Keïta	242
Chapter 10	Silence, My Favorite Note	267
	Journal Entries: 2008-2009—Vinx and Japan	270
Chapter 11	Zen and the Art of Djembe Maintenance, Starring My Teacher and Nemesis, Rope	279
	Journal Entries: 2010-2011—China	283
Chapter 12	Drum Circles	293
Chapter 13	Paul Caldwell, Tulum, and Malidoma Somé	297
	Journal Entries: 2013-2014—Malidoma, KoSA	299
Chapter 14	Rhythm Revolution/Funkadesi/Old Town/ASM 1996-1999	313
Chapter 15	A Typical Work Week and Typical Gigs	323
A Final Note: The Beat Goes On		333

About the Author	337
Take Classes in the West African Djembe Drum with M. Taylor	341
Book M. Taylor for a DRUMeditation™!	345
Book M. Taylor for Storytelling	349
Book M. Taylor for Corporate Team Building	351
About M. Taylor Coaching	353
Book M. Taylor to Speak at Your Next Event	355

INTRODUCTION

This book is a collage of my experiences learning, playing, and teaching djembe, a goblet-shaped West African drum. It is not chronological, but it is thematic, focusing on various aspects of my life, including my trips to Guinea in West Africa and other places around the world to learn and share djembe, "Africanesque" folktales I have written, and hopefully, a few kernels of wisdom about music and life that will help you on your own journey. Journal entries and folktales are sprinkled throughout and are not always related to the chapter itself but add additional insight into my experiences.

My interest in djembe—a West African drum—is also an interest in people, culture, communication, and the meaning of life. That may sound overly philosophical, but I hope you'll see what I mean by the time you finish reading this book.

Here are a few facts about me that may be helpful to know before we continue. My full name is Michael Taylor, but I prefer to be called "Taylor." You'll see a few quotations in the book signed "Taylor." Those are mine. I am biracial and adopted, with a black father and white mother, which means much of my early life was spent trying to understand why I didn't fit in. Raised by mixed race parents, my skin looks white but my hair is a straight-up Afro; as I write this book, it is in two-foot long dreadlocks. I think djembe found me to bring me home to part of my ethnic lineage as well as to my purpose in this lifetime. There is nothing about my regular American upbringing that has obviously resulted in my being on this path. Learning djembe, for me, has been a search for identity, awareness, and connection. Perhaps you are attracted to music, art, certain foods, literature, or something else for similar reasons. Even if you have never heard or played djembe, I hope this book contains universal truths that will resonate with your own experiences. If nothing else, playing djembe all over the world has taught me that while we all have unique gifts and different experiences, we have far more in common. Some of us may march to the beat of a different drum, but we all have something beautiful and unique to add to the rhythm.

Enjoy and appreciate your journey! Now read about mine…

Mr Taylor

CHAPTER 1

WHY AM I HERE?

> "The way you are *painted* makes you the perfect secret
> agent for change between black and white."
>
> — from Taylor's first divination with Elder Dr. Malidoma Somé

Whenever I see someone perform, present, or facilitate, I feel it is important to know why they are where they are. So, in fairness, I put the question to myself: Why am I here? I want to know the answer to that because my greatest fear is getting it wrong. Even more, the fear of getting it wrong for an extended period of time. I am hopeful, confident, and have faith that sincerely trying to succeed in not getting it wrong is good. This morning, pulling out in haste, I smashed my bike helmet under the wheel of my car because I wasn't paying enough attention; it's gone forever because of my lack of attention and awareness. The lessons I have received as the result of inattention and lack of awareness include but are by no means limited to the demise of a marriage, financial loss, and near-death experiences.

I'm motivated to write this book because of the hidden potential I see in folks. Potential that can be released by awareness, clarity, and discipline. I hope that people reading my lessons, at times painfully and enlighteningly learned, might be inspired to unleash some of their own amazing, unrealized potential. Through decades of studying the djembe with my teachers, especially Grand Master Drummer Mamady Keïta, from the djembe itself, as well as my students, my yoga practice, and my African spiritual studies with Elder Master Dr. Malidoma Somé, I have learned and observed a lot about human nature. What keeps coming to the fore in my thoughts is the divide between what we think we are doing and what we actually are doing—the divide between subjective description and objective demonstration. As the result of years of pondering and observing this, I now feel called to state publicly that my path is to help guide people, including myself, to higher forms of awareness. Part of this guiding path includes creating environments conducive to summoning and manifesting one's divine gift to the village. There is a saying GIGO: garbage in, garbage out. No one wants decisions to be based on inaccurate observation. Such decisions can result in unforeseen, unsavory results in both life and relationships. Life is about relationships—to other people, things, and the self. Observation and proper action are key to forming and maintaining healthy relationships.

With Mamady at the 25th Anniversary of TTMDA in Monterrey, Mexico 2017

While I was writing this book, my djembe master, teacher, guru, friend, and father-figure, Mamady, transitioned to the realm of the ancestors on the Summer Solstice, June 21, 2021. Since meeting Mamady in 1999, my life has changed; it has grown into one of purpose-my own life's purpose deeply aligned with Mamady's mission to preserve the culture and sustain the legacy of the West African djembe drum. Mamady's and my relationship was the most profound, consistent, and deep student-guru relationship of my life. Mamady was a special person with unbelievable talent, drive, virtuosity, and intelligence. His spirit shone brightly through his smile, manner, and playing all over the world.

Mamady was born into the Malinke ethnic group, in his words, "in August of 1950." A prophecy at his birth said he would become world famous, which was a remarkable statement given that he came from the village of Balandugu Djomawagna in Guinea, West Africa, where very few become world famous or even leave their village. He began drumming on pots and pans with spoons at age five, resulting in his nickname "Nankama" ("born for it") in Malinké, the language and name of his ethnic group. Soon after, he was introduced to Karinkadjan Konde, the village djembefola (the person who plays djembe for the village). Mamady and Karinkadjan would play for the initiations of youths, many aspects of farming, for popular festivities, and many other occasions for many other reasons in service to their village.

In the 1950s and 1960s, newly independent African nations created, developed, and began touring multi-ethnic folkloric ensembles; African drum and dance ambassadors to the world. Mamady became so well known as a virtuoso djembe player at such a young age that the government sent representatives to his very remote village in northeast Guinea, near the Mali border. This would be when Mamady was recruited into the National

Ballet of Guinea, called the Ballet Djoliba, named after the mighty Djoliba River (known as the Niger River outside of Guinea). It is said that more than 500 people auditioned, and he was one of only five drummers who was accepted. The great touring ballets of West Africa (e.g., Les Ballets Africains, Ballet Djoliba, Ballet du Senegal, Ballet National du Mali, etc.) are multi-ethnic performing ensembles that incorporate dance, music, acting, staging, choreography, and costuming into a large-scale performance. (Think of big Broadway shows like *Oklahoma*, *Les Misérables*, and *Wicked*.) These ballets take the numerous ethnic groups' traditions and perform new works that have traditional rhythms and music for their creative seeds, but no longer represent the actual traditions. Djembe, in its traditional context, may be just a few drummers—one djembefola and some apprentices playing other parts. "Djembefola" is the title of the person who plays djembe for the village(s). The ballets had upwards of a dozen drummers, dozens of dancers, and all the other support roles you'd find in Broadway shows.

Musician/producer/actor/activist Harry Belafonte—a friend of the Guinean president, Sékou Touré, who took control of the country after the French pulled out in 1958—saw performing ensembles from Guinea and was inspired to create one. So with the aid and blessing of Touré, Belafonte arranged to have physical trainers come to Guinea to make the artists strong and fit; the training was like that of Olympic athletes. One day, Mamady saw all the Americans board a boat and leave Kassa, an island off the coast of Guinea, where the training took place. After that, it was Sékou Touré's group. The group was a huge success, touring the world over and over and sharing the magic of the cultures and peoples of the nation of Guinea.

Mamady spent twenty-two years in Ballet Djoliba, quickly becoming its lead soloist, and for his last seven years, he served as its artistic director. The company toured every continent except Antarctica, sometimes staying in one country for more than a year. During an extended stay in China, Mamady learned kung fu, a martial art at which he became highly proficient. Having come from village life, he was not only steeped in the knowledge of traditions, but he was also blessed in being incredibly creative in coming up with performance ideas, including what he called a "pyramid." A pyramid is a series of rhythms run together with at least one very long unison figure. Many of the pyramids I learned and performed with him were upwards of an hour long; truly amazing feats of composition! After Guinean President Sékou Touré died in 1984, Mamady became a member of Koteba, a performance group very much like Djoliba, based in the nearby West African country Côte d'Ivoire. His next major move was to Brussels, Belgium, where he opened his djembe school, Tam Tam Mandingue in 1992. Through that institution, Mamady had more than 300 students a week for over a decade. People would come from all corners of the globe to study with Mamady. Around this time, the documentary film *Djembefola* was released. It is about Mamady's return to his village after being gone for more than twenty-five years; he returned as the prophecy predicted, internationally famous.

When the West African djembe drum entered my life at the age of twenty-seven in 1994, it was as if my existence began again. I became interested in djembe because I didn't get cast as an actor in a play. After I was turned down for an acting role, the directors asked if I would join two other folks, Antje Gherken and E. Rawlings Thurman, to create the music for the play. I told them I had never done this before, but I'd be willing to try, so they invited me on. Their request to the musicians was that the music must be played live, not pre-recorded, and based mostly in "ethnic drumming." None of us had drums, so we improvised with found objects until about a month into pre-production when Mike McElya, one of the two directors, mentioned getting a couple of djembes. I had only heard that a djembe was an African drum, and I had a connection with someone who could get such exotic things; I made it so.

Having had a mystery heritage—I was adopted, after all—I would later do a DNA analysis, revealing that one-third of my ethic lineage is West African and two-thirds Northwestern European—literally the colonizer and the colonized embodied in one person. The irony of this balance is not lost on me. Where are my loyalties? My allegiances? My responsibilities? This opens up the bigger question of "Who are culture bearers?" My belief, born out of experience, is that if culture bearers are not of the culture, then they are the ones who show up to learn aspects of a culture. The bearers are the ones who care enough to make the sacrifices to bend, pick up, and move forward. For example, the Africans I have studied with and known are welcoming and open about sharing their culture with anyone who respectfully and reverentially wants to learn. African Americans, often without knowledge of African culture, in my experience, only occasionally exhibit this openness about the sharing of African culture. I'm not mad at them because I understand the African-American experience we receive today has come through the filter of centuries of intergenerational trauma. As Bob Marley said, "stolen from Africa; brought to America." What have African Americans had stolen from them/us? Their/our dignity, language, specific tribal/ethnic culture and traditions and, almost, our humanity.... Perhaps an easier question to hear the answer to would be: What *wasn't* stolen from these people—and, by blood and culture, *my* people? As I ponder this, I wonder what intergenerational trauma I'm carrying from my white side. Though it is rarely spoken, I know that perpetrators must leave markers of their violence and its justification/rationalization in their own cells for future generations to deal with, not just in their victims. Consider that for the United States, in particular, there is a lot of blood in the soil from lots of people of color (specifically Native Americans and enslaved Africans); this is soil on which we dig foundations for our living spaces, grow food, raise children, drink water, and live. When I think about all the violence (especially gun violence) in the US, thinking about the memory of the soil of this place puts things in perspective. My DNA feels like very old relatives who are majorly at odds with one another sitting at the same dinner table.... I shudder imagining the scene. The black side brimming with anger of such a horrible past of misdeeds against them; the white side at once afraid they will receive the same treatment if they give blacks equal everything and also largely oblivious to what equality actually means or looks like and unwilling to embrace their unwillingness (conscious and unconscious) to share wealth, opportunities, and power.

Me and my big bro Sulé Greg Wilson c. 2012

Since African Americans have direct recent lineage with Africans, overlaid with the horrible intergenerational trauma brought on by hundreds of years of terrorism inflicted up them, some African Americans have an attitude of their presumption of "ownership" of African culture. Since a lot of the time that's occurring almost in a vacuum of knowledge about how Africa really is, and was, such powerful emotional reactions can become confusing. I really wanted to articulate many ideas in this chapter in a good way, and it gets into some very delicate subject matter, so I asked my dear friend, older "brother" Sulé Greg Wilson, author of *The Drummer's Path: Moving the Spirit with Ritual and Traditional Drumming* to chime in. In regards to African Americans claiming ownership of all things African, he says African Americans:

> demand a certain kind of reverence, based on something they hardly know anything about. And that is part of the anger—they know that they would know—that they *should* know. And here we stand. Sometimes that ignorant rage at the trauma of rape, murder, subjugation, and captivity takes the form of fear: anger over what they perceive as "another white boy coming to learn/take our shit."

It can appear that my learning about African culture is actually taking something from them—it's a twisted form of scarcity mentality. I agree with the argument that can be made that socioeconomic issues (and not just the money, but also lack of job/life/educational opportunities, disrupted family continuity—look at my story!) stood in the way of *some* black folks paying to learn African folklore by going to classes in the US, Europe (even in their locale), or committing to taking that big trip to Africa. Yes, for many, cost is a huge factor, but that's not the whole story. I've heard stories of black folks in the US refusing to attend African drum and dance classes with African masters because there were white folks in the room too, and I get that; white folks have denied access to and taken so much from African Americans since they were brought to the US as enslaved people that it makes sense not to want to learn anything African alongside them. Sulé goes on to say:

> And it's not "reverse racism." Blacks come to African Masters not to learn a skill, gain a hobby, or experience exoticism. They come to make a spiritual connection with some aspect of their own sense of personal and multi-generational loss. And they know, from painful experience, that if there's a white person in the room, the dynamic changes. The "white folks" often—albeit unconsciously—get preferential treatment (we've all been brainwashed!); their agenda are different, and their presence certainly makes it uncomfortable for some black folks to "let their hair down" with a perceived distant relative—the African teacher—if there's a stranger (or an adversary) in the room. Think about it for a minute: How comfortable would you feel in a classroom, learning sensitive, even "triggering" material in the presence of your abuser? Many, if not most, black Americans carry that "victim" baggage and haven't learned to fight "the system" by helping what they see as its representatives—and themselves—grow and change, on a one-on-one basis. They're still too scared of so-called "white people"…well, scared of the centuries-long abuse of power that the (relatively) non-melanized represent to them. Hardly any of us have grown enough to understand that the 'white folks' are victims too—victims of much unacknowledged power (which can

make them even more dangerous!). It's complicated but not insurmountable. It would have been amazing if African Americans would have overcome their fear and overrun these classes, invoking their "ancestral connection" and taking their rightful place at the table, instead of shirking growth.

I would have loved that and it would have changed the dynamic for generations to come. However, be that as it may, the very valid reasons Black folks used when they didn't receive opportunities for learning from masters of African culture in the end could be characterized as cutting off your nose to spite your face. The culture bearers of djembe (and its associated culture) over the decades, beginning mainly in the 1990s, have become a very mixed lot of ethnicity, nationality, gender, and skin color. Africa is a continent with fifty-five countries (as of the publishing of this book if you ask the African Union; fifty-four if you ask the United Nations), nearly twelve million square miles with thousands of ethnic groups, and only a few of them are traditionally associated with cultures related to the djembe. They are all in West Africa and are historically connected to the Malian Empire, a confederation of states which is said to have existed c. 1200–1500

Map of Malian Empire - darker area represents origins of djembe within the larger empire. This map is from a combination of sources.

CE. It was brought into one kingdom under the rulership of the great king Sundjata Keïta. The main ethnic groups associated with djembe are the Bambara and Malinké; then there's a second tier of ethnic groups that "took on" the djembe, sometimes adapting rhythms played on other instruments to the djembe; they include the Susu, Guoro, Baga, Baoulè, Landouma, Kassonke, Manian, Toma, Senufo, Maraka, and a few others.

In 2017, I had a conversation with a peer in Chicago who said to me that African Americans are mostly comprised of descendants of the Malian Empire, making a point that the connection African Americans have to the djembe and its culture is very direct. Meaning that African Americans have a *right* to the djembe, more than other folks and certainly more than "white folks." Why do I share this story? For several reasons: 1) because not enough folks know enough about Africa to even have any idea if this is true or not; 2) because Africa is, in my opinion, a place that deserves to have its truth represented accurately and not left to be diluted; 3) because my guru Master Drummer Mamady Keïta charged me (and his other Tam Tam Mandingue Djembe Academy school directors around the world) to fight to preserve djembe tradition as it relates to his experience (referring to us as "Messengers of Tradition"); 4) because it was impressed upon me by the late Elder Master Dr. Malidoma Patrice Somé that, because I came to this world as a biracial person, it was incumbent upon me to do whatever I can to mend the divide between black and white people—bringing the fight is sometimes part of it; and 5) because if this person in Chicago actually believes this, it's likely others may as well. Okay! So let's have a conversation about that. Well, I knew what this person was saying wasn't true, but I also knew I couldn't cite the sources of my knowing. It's good to be curious and seek out relationships with folks who know more than me, so I reached out to Dr. Eric Charry, noted ethnomusicologist and author of *Mande Music* and the article "A Guide to the Jembe," published in *Percussive Notes*, the publication of the Percussive Arts Society in 1996.[1]

He confirmed what I thought and gave me references to back it up, including an animated map that shows that less than 4 percent of all Africans who suffered transportation across the Atlantic into slavery came to the United States. Four percent! He also shared statistics and research that demonstrate that the 4 percent who ended up in the United States were *not* mostly from the area of the Malian Empire.[2]

Dr. Charry also gave the following resources:

1. Klein, Herbert S. 1999. *The Atlantic Slave Trade*. Cambridge, Gr. Brit.: Cambridge University Press. Herbert covers the where from (in Africa) and where to (in the Americas), with maps, etc., and gives a solid historical background.

2. Curtin, Philip D. 1969. *The Atlantic Slave Trade: A Census*. Madison, WI: University of Wisconsin Press. This classic established the foundation for the above.

3. Hall, Gwendolyn Midlo. 1992. *Africans in Colonial Louisiana: The Development of Afro-Creole Culture in the Eighteenth Century*. Baton Rouge, LA: Louisiana State University Press. This book gives some sense of solid historical research in the US.

4. https://www.slavevoyages.org/assessment/estimates. He also suggested that this website has since become *the* authoritative source.

---

[1] http://echarry.web.wesleyan.edu/jembearticle/article.html
[2] http://www.slate.com/articles/life/the_history_of_american_slavery/2015/06/animated_interactive_of_the_history_of_the_atlantic_slave_trade.html?wpsrc=sh_all_tab_fb_top

Beginning circa 2005, after more than forty years of the djembe being taught and used in African American communities (thank you Papa Ladji Camara and Elder Mor Thiam) African masters and well-intentioned students of Masters and enthusiasts have been posting free online videos that teach the very things I paid—often and dearly for nearly a decade at that point—to learn. For the record, these can be great resources, but if possible, it is always better to learn from a reputable source in person. Point being, you no longer have to pay much or at all to learn just about anything, including African cultural traditions. Whereas, in the past, many African Americans who hadn't had ready access to source-material stayed in ignorance with the advent of the worldwide web and it's incredible resources, many took advantage of this new access to djembe knowledge. This was a boon in learning! Then add that before the 1990s, it was nearly impossible to get knowledge about many African traditions. Why? Because it was difficult to get to Africa, and there were very few masters/teachers traveling out of Africa to teach. The folks who were studying djembe early learned many things that were not representative. As stated above, there were hardly any teachers and no codified system of curriculum of learning. It was, shall we say, "folkloric." My first trip to Guinea in 1997 showed me that this had happened to me while learning djembe in the US. I had learned many things, but not nearly enough to know if my knowledge accurately represented traditions of djembe from whence they arose; I learned that most of my knowledge at that point did *not* represent accurately. So I got more quiet and began relearning in earnest. Studying this drum—known in some regions as "the healing drum"—and its cultural traditions in-depth has been a transformational experience for me. Deeply studying this instrument was like going deep into a cave, or underground river, with each tributary revealing new truths, all iterating and echoing ancient wisdom teachings. At their confluence, the tributaries merge to demonstrate they are all expressions of the same magical essence. This journey of wisdom and discovery would reveal truths far out of the purview of this instrument, this tool. My yoga and kettlebell (a cast iron or cast steel ball with a handle attached to the top, resembling a cannonball with a handle used to perform many types of exercises, including ballistic exercises that combine cardiovascular, strength, and flexibility training) practices have been partners on my path with the djembe.

The more I practice these disciplines, the more I realize there are many roads to the place of essences—of oneness, of truths. What you practice is far less important than having a conscious practice. It builds upon itself, deepening wisdom and understanding. Unconscious practice is something to avoid. What do I mean? How does a person know if they are practicing consciously or unconsciously? One way to know is to have a source outside the self like a guru. There must be a teacher. Teachers/gurus can take many forms, and feedback from them is necessary for real growth. Many gurus are not in human form, yet I learn from them if I open myself to their teachings. I consider my yoga practice, kettlebell practice, and rope (used in the construction of djembe drums) to be among the gurus in my life. But can the practice itself be your guru? Only after you've reached a certain advanced level, and even then, it is important to check in with a human guru or at least review your reference material (in my case recordings of my teachers) regularly. Quick karma is also a great teacher. I believe that negative consequences for bad technique are also important. In an age where so much is digital, it is easy to think you are able to do a thing just because you saw it in a video; you might say "I know this thing." You then go on and do your own version of what you *thought* you saw take place on the video. You may be deeply incorrect, but in the absence of a teacher for correction, how would you ever know? Having no guidance is equivalent to having no accountability to the essence of a thing. Doing it "wrong" will ultimately bring negative consequences. If I do yoga, kettlebells, or djembe improperly, I will experience discomfort; likely, I will outright get hurt. Some folks want their practice to have no accompanying physical, mental, and spiritual challenges; however, "no pain no gain" is sometimes the right mantra; discomfort is not always a bad thing; pain is different than discomfort. This mantra can be misplaced if your motivation beneath your practice is escape/avoidance/denial.

Mamady shared many stories with me of his time in Ballet Djoliba, times when the ensemble would rehearse until they were totally physically spent. "Akaran Iko Iko" means "learn again, again" in Malinké. He told me this was what they would say when rehearsing.

"THE JUNGLE"

This was the 2004 show at Old Town School - my biggest to date.

First conceived on November 7, 1994 and originally titled "The Dungeon," this piece came through me very strongly and suddenly, visually and aurally, with colors, shades, and shapes, sounds, silences, and voices. I included it because it was the first of many poems, stories, and performances that came through me after the djembe entered my life. It is a metaphor for traveling the catacombs of my mind. It is also a metaphor for the surprises you get when delving deeply into something. I have performed this piece numerous times over the years. As a solo piece, my favorite presentation of this one was when I performed it in a huge old creepy cargo elevator that seemed to moan as much as creak in motion, at what was then called the Split Apple Creative Coop in Chicago. This freight elevator was big enough to fit about thirty chairs, and as it descended, the Jungle came through my voices (mouth and drum). Since then I have performed this piece with many other artists (musicians, visual artists, actors, aerialists, fire spinners, etc.). To date, the largest shows were in 1999 and 2003 at the Old Town School of Folk Music in Chicago in their main auditorium, the Gary & Laura Maurer Concert Hall, involving more than twenty cast members (including stage managers and tech people) sometimes performing all together, sometimes individually or in small groups. I have had the great gift of involving many of my incredibly talented friends in this piece, including Tom Sharpe (Manheim Steamroller), Leddie Garcia (Santana, Chaka Khan, Arianna Grande, Lady Gaga, Sounds from the Vault, Oprah Winfrey), Kora Master Morikeba Kouyaté, Yaya Kabo, Master Drummer Madou Dembele, Bob Garret (*The Lion King*; Sting), Doug Brush (multi-percussionist extraordinaire), Barry Bennett (amazing sound traveler), Derek Fredrickson (amazing sound and visual artist), Olivier Ledoux (master wood carver), Jeff Amon (The Bridge Studio, NYC), Dahui Drum Ensemble, and many more. There is an audio version with an excerpt from "The Jungle" on my CD entitled *Silence*.

The Jungle - Art Forms From The Silent Din

In…to the Jungle
In to the Jungle I go

Why? I cannot say at this point that I know

Something draws me
Something draws me so

A tenuous seduction, as from the lover to the loved

Into the Jungle
nto the Jungle I go

It draws me not like a gun (abrupt sound hit here)
It draws me not like a stick figure
It draws me not like the blood from a vein
Or a call to come hither
But it draws me still…

In the Jungle may lurk beauty of all shapes and all kinds
In the Jungle may lurk chaos and indefinite time
In the Jungle may lurk reality; reality denied

(Crescendo – the cauldron boils)

It may be a boiling cauldron
It may be a sacred brew
Psychic jambalaya or a
Cosmic stew

What lurks in the fiery darkness?
The deep expanse of the hole
Some subconscious beckoning as if speaking only to my soul

A pocketful of chaos
A rumbling vat of nothing
But within it clearly an energy
Like a chemical reaction or something

"This is interesting," I think
And I took a step back and took a mental drink

Not knowing to listen for, a grunt or a word
I opened my mind and this is what I heard...

<< *Inter-jungle-performance #1 - all "inter-jungle-performances" could be any one thing or several things done by one or a group of artists of any discipline*>>

My mind's eye dilated
And for a moment the unknown was violated

I thought "this is unusual, kind of different
But I dig the vibe and I like the precedent"

At this point I begin to think
That I would do myself a disservice
Even to blink

When out of the muck did appear
Another thing at which I had to leer

<< *Inter-jungle-performance #2* >>

"What an odd little abode," I thought aloud
"I wonder if this place has its own zip code"

I feel as if I am at the tip of some enigmatic iceberg
A foggy deep abyss
As if the full breadth of the Jungle is yet to be seen
And this, my friends, one must not
Miss

So deeper into the Jungle
Deeper into the Jungle I go

Why? I am intrigued but still do not know

For something draws me
Something draws me so

A tenuous seduction as from the lover to the loved

Deeper and deeper and deeper and deeper and deeper into the Jungle I go....

CHAPTER 2

THE TAO OF DJEMBE

> "To attain knowledge, add things every day.
> To attain wisdom, remove things every day."
>
> — Lao Tzu

The way or "tao" of djembe has been one of my greatest teachers. One way the teaching and playing of djembe is unique is that instead of adding things until you get it, you take away things until you are doing it. Most of my students begin by doing too much, so my teaching focuses on doing less. So much of it is about allowing flow and being open to receiving; this is a key aspect of what I call the Tao of Djembe. Another is understanding (intellectually or non-intellectually) how your part relates to the other parts; the higher level of this journey is understanding how all parts fit together to make the desired outcome. This understanding requires combining musical awareness with awareness of circumstances in general. There is a difference between playing your part and playing the music. Perhaps the highest expression is speaking with your djembe in an intentional context with the other parts, while, as a soloist, communicating with dancers or other elements in the situation. Djembe is an instrument of service. No matter if the rhythm you're playing is for initiation, agriculture, fetishers (the caste of people who deal in the paranormal in Mande culture), or whatever, it exists to serve.

One typical example of what many students begin with is leaving their hand on the drum as they play, not allowing the skin to vibrate to make sound. If you don't bounce your hand off the drum, you are not opening yourself to receiving your energy back from the drum; it's about giving *and* receiving. Another example is holding your arms and shoulders in ways that work against relaxation. Other examples are playing the notes of your part inaccurately, playing with inaccurate handing, being intentionally connected to the music, or not playing in the feel of the music. Eventually, students end up doing less with their hands, less with their bodies, and realizing that, when they can begin to hear the interrelatedness of the parts, listening to more is somehow doing less.

A life-changing moment I had occurred when I was teaching an inner-city high schooler. I asked him to repeat a part on the drum that I had done. He repeated something that was not even close to what I had done. When I asked him if what he had done was what I did, he said it was. Now there is an argument to be made that we were both moving our hands, which I take as an opportunity to clarify the semantics of what I mean when I ask if they are doing what I'm doing. This almost always leads to a brief conversation about the definition of the word "semantics." This made me look constantly at how folks do not do the things they think they are doing. In my classes, I regularly survey who believes they are doing what I am asking them to do. The percentage of folks changes rapidly after I tell them what percentage is actually doing it. It's important not to tell them who was and wasn't doing it; I want them all to wonder if it was them so they will focus more deeply and see for themselves. I find myself humbled on a regular basis by how I still, sometimes, after all these years of "awareness study," find myself not doing what I think I am doing. It's a humbling experience, no doubt.

> "Accounting for one's weaknesses is a strength."
>
> — Taylor

Then I started to focus on the relationship between semantics and those folks who are actually not doing what they say and believe they are. How are we defining what "it" is? Are we understanding two different things very accurately, but different things? Do you believe we are talking about the same thing? Have you considered that two separate things may be going on?

> "The unexamined life is not worth living."
>
> — Socrates

A wise friend, Kurt Hill, once told me that the greatest barrier to communication is words. Language is the best we can do if we want to communicate with each other with words. Language is a tool to represent a commonly understood representation of things; words try to represent thoughts; it's how we translate thoughts into something we can share out loud or in writing. But as hard as words try, they are not thoughts, just as a notation written on a page is not "music." Notation is a language, created to commonly understand something called "music." Notation is not music. The map is not the territory.

So, when are you *looking* at the map and when are you *in* the territory? Are you sure you're doing what you think you're doing? So often I have seen folks say they are doing something they are not doing. It's not something I realized was so prevalent, so pervasive, before teaching djembe classes.

One thing I love about teaching djembe is that folks open up; they allow for vulnerability. People come to class from all walks of life with an unbelievably heterogeneous wealth of experience, intuition, talent, etc. They may bring issues of many kinds into the room relating to being in a classroom, being in a group, being male, being female, being non-binary, being insecure, being overly confident, being in a context where they may make a mistake in front of strangers, and many more. I've realized that if I open fully in every way to everything they are telling me (verbally, non-verbally, energetically, etc.), they tell me how to teach them. Early in my interactions with students, I'm studying them, trying to understand what each needs, what motivates them, and what affects them in this environment. They tell me how to teach them—the way to reach them—if I'm open enough to receiving the answers from them. So much of it is question-based—good old Socratic method. First, I ask questions about what was happening when we played together; for instance, I'll ask if we were all doing the same thing at the same time. This question usually leads to a lot of folks realizing they weren't really paying attention to their surroundings. Then I ask them to observe and answer questions based on what they are observing. Much is understood when a person sees that they weren't seeing.

Sometimes I get hard cases that, for whatever reason, believe they are doing something they are not, even after exhaustive examples. The way I resolve these situations is for me to come to where they are at; I will do exactly what they are doing, validating it; then, I will move to a different thing (the thing I was wanting them to know in the first place). The other thing is great; it's just different. Belief is an interesting concept. It is important to have faith in what we believe, but at the same time, the power of belief can confound perception. The placebo effect is real. Because we believe it to be, a sugar pill can have the same effect as a carefully crafted, very powerful drug or plant medicine. Measurable physiological changes can be observed in those taking a placebo, similar to those observed among people taking effective medications. The word "placebo" comes from Latin and means "I shall please." Belief, however, can also work in the reverse direction. If you think something is harmful to you, you can make that thing harmful to you even if it actually is not. That phenomenon is called the "nocebo effect" (from the Latin "I shall harm").

Then there is intuition and emotion. Like with belief, it is important to have faith in our intuition, our innate perceptive ability that manifests itself in the physio-emotional. Your intuition, your gut, tells you to make a certain decision. Your intuition can keep you out of danger or allow you to make a hard decision that you can't articulate or analyze. Separately, I interpret what the heart tells you as what your emotional self wants and hopes for. In your heart, you know something is the wrong decision, but your gut tells you it is the right decision. But, like with belief, intuition and emotion can lead to an inaccurate perception. Having one's intuition and/or emotions clouded by programming—programming often left over from previous life circumstances (or even previous lives)—can skew our intuition. Our beliefs, intuition, and emotions need updating every once in a while. Every year? Maybe. Every few years, probably. Every decade, I'd say certainly. Every way we have ever been was the result of a complex combination of factors that existed at the time; they served us well then. But maybe those same things need to be reevaluated to see if they are in balance with what's happening in the now.

There are different kinds of knowledge. I heard Michael Meade (renowned storyteller, author, and scholar of mythology, anthropology, and psychology) talk about "embodied knowledge." In ancient Greek, there was a level of knowing called "episteme"—information or knowledge about things on the surface, descriptive information that doesn't generate knowledge, only more information. The deeper kind of knowledge is "gnosis," which means "to know." To know it, not only in the mind, but in the body, bones, and heart. Many traditional cultures have embodied knowledge, and because of this they don't have to believe things because they know things on a much deeper level. Their ability to access this depth of connection to truth is unencumbered by many aspects of the modern world, like obsessive commercialism and "alternative facts."

> "Learning from your mistakes is smart; learning from other people's mistakes is wise."
>
> — Bill and Finn Scheidt

Being able to separate yourself from your thoughts, preferences, prejudices, and beliefs is vital. "I am not my [fill in the blank]." Witnessing yourself is the power to see why you think and believe the way you do. The power to say, "Oh, I see why I gravitate toward that kind of person," or "I see why I don't feel good about challenging situations." I frequently ask my drum students to broaden their focus until they can hear the one thing that is the combination of all the parts; to pull above and change their perception from the trees to the forest. This is witnessing—the ability to see the things themselves in context of other things *and* how the unique combination of things results in a given outcome. It is listening (perceiving) with all your senses.

Witnessing is especially useful when communicating with animals, particularly bipeds known as people. You might be talking to someone whose intuition and belief system have been compromised; maybe they are out-of-date or misinformed. You can see that, but you can also see that they do not see it. That person likely has more going on than they are aware of, resulting in an inaccurate experience of reality, which usually results in problems, like conspicuous patterns of unexpected negative outcomes. One thing I find challenging is when I see folks believing in a misrepresentation of reality and defending their idea of what's really happening. Arguing with them is an exercise in futility because it's arguing about things that are not the same; it helps if you're going to argue about something, to be at least talking about the same thing and defining things in the same way. Having any discussion like this becomes an exercise in attempting to articulate that we are not disagreeing about the same thing; in fact, we are not disagreeing at all. We are talking about different things altogether. I wonder when I am the person believing in a misrepresentation; I hope I have the awareness and humility to know. Either way, I will always try to do my best!

> "Always do your best."
>
> — Agreement 4 in Don Miguel Ruiz'
> *The Four Agreements*

Sometimes our words don't match our thoughts, our thoughts don't match our feelings, and our feelings don't match our intuition, and so goes a clusterfuck. It's no surprise miscommunication takes place more frequently than we may even know. Again, it makes me wonder how often I am that person not knowing I'm misunderstanding! It was truly life-changing when I began to seriously consider all the possible things happening during communication. I realized the only way to plug into such a broad spectrum is with love. How am I defining "love" here? Love is that feeling and perceptive ability that combines a wide range of senses (physical and otherwise), empathy, compassion, and intellectual/emotional intelligence to result in feeling. Then this feeling must be witnessed to really be understood. Without the ability to pull above the minutia and see the whole, we are largely without sight. What is our arc or sphere of understanding?

Awareness, belief, intuition, emotion.... Intentionally or not, as author Brené Brown puts it, is everyone just doing the best they can, given a wide range of influences? Can it be any other way? Is there an influence-less state of being? Maybe that's what enlightenment is.

When are you aware of your non-awareness?

What obscures our senses from perceiving what's really happening? When we *do* see the signs, that's awesome! Are those signs *the* signs? When we don't see the signs, why don't we see the signs that we aren't seeing them? Many answers to these questions involve socialization (what author Don Miguel Ruiz calls "domestication"), education, gender, race, socio-economic status, prejudices, etc.

What obscures our sight from what's really happening? When you look, do you see? When you are listening, are you hearing? If you see, what is it that you see? If you are listening, what is it that you are hearing?

And then there's something I learned from a drum student who is a psychotherapist, Dr. James A. Warner. I was talking to him about how frustrating it is when a recital contains musical catastrophes that were absent in rehearsals; he suggested it may have to do with "state dependent learning." State dependent learning is when knowledge has an unconscious connection to outside things, affecting one's access to their knowledge. For instance, if you rehearse in one physical arrangement in the room, changing that can change one's access to their knowledge. When the state of your audio and visual sight lines change, it can have an effect on one's access to their knowledge; for example, being in practice sessions where you are always facing a clock. Even being caffeinated when you study and not caffeinated during testing can affect memory recall. I learned not to study on my bed in college and now I realize it was also a form of state dependent learning; sleeping and studying should not be commingled in the mind. I had a sub for one of my djembe classes who didn't wear ankle bells, and my students could not do what I knew they knew. I had created a dependence on having the ankle bells keeping time! It was a good lesson, so now, halfway through multi-week teaching sessions, I intentionally stop wearing the ankle bells. Also, regarding recitals at the end of a multi-week session, the last week before the end, I set up the room to reflect exactly how the group will be performing. Once you get in the habit of looking for ways to confound state dependent learning, you see many examples of it in life. When learning something, change your surroundings, the way you sit, the direction of your chair, the room, etc. Then your knowledge will be more intact and less vulnerable to state dependent learning.

How is context related to how we define things? In the djembe world, when someone says they can play something, but the thing they are playing, while by itself correct, is not in the context in the intended way, it's not the thing. Djembe rhythms are like puzzles, where the parts need to fit together in the right way to get the intended result. Your puzzle piece can be perfect, but does it fit into the puzzle correctly? Two elements to "knowing" in the world of djembe (and other worlds) are: 1) what you do, and 2) how what you do relates to a given context. One without the other is not it; it's a different thing. So understanding some things has to do with a necessary awareness of a thing *and* its relation to a context, perhaps many parts of a context. It's not unlike a combination lock where several numbers need to be together to open the lock. To hear the one thing that is produced by all the constituent parts is lovely to behold. Being able to hear—no, *perceive* or *witness*—all the parts together as one is an essential practice to understanding the higher levels of interrelatedness in general.

Journal Entries: 1997
My First Trip to Guinea, West Africa

My first of six trips to Guinea, West Africa, left my life shifted, disrupted, and left me quiet in many ways.

1997 balcony overlooking Conakry.

This was my first trip crossing the Atlantic and my first time visiting the source of the African instrument that, for me, had become an obsession—something I at once didn't know and definitely somehow remembered. During each trip to Africa, I read at least one whole book; this year it was Layne Redmond's *When the Drummers Were Women*. Never having been on an international flight, I was blown away by how much good food and drink was available! The flight to Guinea began with an eight-hour flight from Chicago to Brussels, Belgium; then it's another six hours to Conakry, Guinea's capital. Being on a plane for that long was, in itself, mind-blowing. The many hours left a lot of time for reading, sleeping, eating, watching movies, and thinking.

By playing and studying an African instrument, I began to see the difference between people who have what I call "entitlement mentality" and those who do not. I am biracial, which in my case counts as light-skinned black. This idea of "entitlement mentality" came from my observation of some folks in the black community in the United States acting like they were African and presenting themselves as such, sometimes knowing nothing about African things (e.g., culture and music). One person I know in Chicago even took on an African name and outright pretended to be African, going so far as billing themselves online and in advertisements as African and saying they had direct blood-relations in Africa, even though they were born in the US and had never been to the motherland; the term "cognitive dissonance" comes to mind. What I observed was the mindset, "I am black; therefore, I am African, and I know all things African by virtue of my blackness. So I don't need to study or learn anything African because it's all in my DNA." This mindset was initially revealed to me when I realized that sometimes when I wouldn't get gigs, it was because a darker-skinned black drummer would get them, even though they had no idea what they were doing and were making up things, thereby doing a solid disservice to preserving the oral history of a place that is really keen on keeping its oral history accurate. I wouldn't want anyone to misrepresent my story either!

The djembe is not an African American drum; it is an African Drum! The African masters I study with say things like "Djembe is for everyone" and "The djembe knows no color, nationality, gender, or race." The djembe is not owned by African Americans, but sometimes, I see them taking this ownership. The djembe belongs to anyone with an open heart as exemplified by this quote from Djali Djimo Kouyate—"clean heart, clean hands." It is open to those who approach it with reverence and respect.

I started to see more and more black folks claiming this kind of entitlement to Africa. In one respect, I can understand that. I had the great honor to ask questions about this subject of some black elders in Chicago that I hold in high esteem, namely Babu Atiba (Muntu Dance Theatre in their prime years) and Kimosha Murphy (Muntu Dance Theatre c. 1975 and ALYO Children's Dance Theatre), who have made studying African drum and dance into their life's work. Something I learned from them I saw as entitlement mentality; black folks taking back their African-ness—could be more accurately related to "intergenerational trauma," trauma from hundreds of years of oppression, dehumanization, and enslavement. But what I can argue with is not making an effort to really know something about what you claim as your own. There is knowledge that we are born with, there is "embodied knowledge," and there is also factual knowledge. This begs a question about the semantics of knowing a thing. What makes me outright indignant is when I hear someone misrepresenting things about Africa, especially djembe music. If you want to represent a form of music, then learn it to represent it well. Where is the line between how oral traditions can drift a bit and outright misrepresentation? Well, I prefer to talk to the elders, especially those elders from Africa who are master musicians and teachers, to get my answers to these questions. This subject is ever-evolving and I welcome dialogue about it!

Among the cornucopia of shots, pills, and inoculations recommended or required to travel to Guinea, one was especially special: the antimalarial drug mefloquine hydrochloride, aka Lariam. Its potential side effects included dizziness, confusion, hallucinations (auditory/visual), delusions of grandeur, paranoia, lucid dreams, unusual behavior, depression, restlessness, confusion, convulsions or seizures, and vertigo. At the time, to combat the malaria strain in Guinea (the "nasty kind" remarked one pharmacist), Lariam was as good as it got. After beginning taking the pills, I experienced many of these side effects; I felt my previous experiences with hallucinogens were advantageous. Most of the effects I experienced were in the dream state. One time, I dreamed a rat bit my hand. I woke up startled, with my hand hurting, but with no evidence of an actual bite. Over several weeks, I had so many of these lucid dreams that I began to recognize within the dream that I was dreaming. I went so far as to dialogue with the characters in my dreams, letting them know I was on to them: "You can do whatever you want because I'm on to you—I know this is a dream." But if it was a nightmare, well, let's just say a few times after waking in terror, I would decide not to go back to sleep and just read for hours until daybreak.

After landing in Conakry, the plane taxied to the airport. Then I saw two burly military men walking hand in hand. Homosexuality is illegal in Guinea, but men holding hands is not a homosexual behavior in this culture. It would be the first of many revelations about my socialization to American cultural mores, and we hadn't even gotten off the plane yet. After deplaning onto the tarmac, I entered the chaos of Conakry's tiny airport. Many people and many languages equals much confusion. One useful bit of advice I had heard before arriving was not to give your passport to those who requested it, uniformed or not.

The study trip I was on was organized by Master Drummer M'Bemba Bangoura and Michael Markus. Michael was my very first djembe teacher. We met at the Drum and Dance Fest held at Oakwood Farm in Selma, Indiana, in August of 1995. The first time I heard him play, I was absolutely blown away. His clarity of sound was astonishing. The day I met him, I played dununs for him for twelve hours—two drum classes and two dance classes (all ninety minutes), a rehearsal for the evening show and the evening show. What a marathon!

Thankfully, Michael and his teacher M'bemba have a lot of experience dealing with getting foreigners through the Guinean airport and had handlers at the ready to help us out when we arrived. After traversing the airport and being pulled around by our handlers like escapees, we piled into the vehicle that would take us to our final destination. The vehicle looked as if it had been reclaimed from a junkyard and patched into working order. It was a very old sports utility vehicle. We piled the luggage of a dozen people onto the roof, packed about sixteen people in and on the vehicle, and then we were off into the warm, thick nighttime air of Conakry.

As we traveled up the road, it was clear from where I was sitting that the truck's joints were moving like a loosely assembled erector set. The streets were mostly filled with tiny yellow taxis; they seemed like car-rodents the way they moved. Magbanas were everywhere. A Magbana is when you take an old, pieced-together van/minivan, have the only seats be wooden benches that line the internal perimeter, and fit in as many bodies with no space between them as you can; most people are standing, crouching slightly due to the roof being so low. I couldn't believe I didn't see any accidents. It was a truly great example of ordered chaos. The amazing array of olfactory sensations, most of which made my face crinkle, was also new to me. The smells ranged from carbon monoxide and burning garbage to I-don't-what-I-just-smelled-that-made-me-gag. So warm and thick. One odor was omnipresent; perhaps it was the smell of this place.

"Find shade when you can; if there is shade, find it."

— Michael Markus, on the UV power
of near-equatorial rays

The house we stayed in was extremely nice, especially by Guinean standards. Many rooms, but one (count 'em, *one* for about fifteen folks) working bathroom. Our first dinner was excellent! M'bembas' sisters prepared a meal of grilled snapper (whole fish cooked and put on a mountain of rice), with sliced tomatoes, cucumbers, and potatoes, all with sauce over them. We ate heartily, then arranged our sleeping quarters. I decided to set up outside on the upstairs porch. The toughest part was figuring out the logistics of putting up the mosquito netting. We worked together to make it work. Eventually, I rested under African skies. Did I mention that the ocean was less than fifty feet from us? No need for one of those cheesy "ocean sounds" recordings to go to sleep; it's the real thing here in Africa.

In a short time, several mosquitos (*sasi*, as the Sousou, one of the main ethnic groups in Guinea, call them) were on the outside of the net; then many, many more. The stars vastly outnumbered my carnivorous insect friends. I saw two shooting stars that night; they told me to be in the moment and really absorb this experience; I would see more. The night seemed to last a whole day; sleep was broken. I was never really sure when mosquitoes were biting and when it was a Lariam-fueled hallucination. I saw lizards (smallish iguanas) all over the place. I also saw huge spiders. Later, I would see mudskippers when we went down to what is the water's edge when the tide was in—a snapshot of prehistory; primal ooze. A spider's life: wait, eat, wait, eat, shit, wait, eat, fuck, eat, wait, eat, wait, eat, shit, wait, give birth, eat, wait, eat, wait, eat, shit, wait. The building of the web is not to be underestimated, though.

The night's sleep did not come without a price. Our rigging of the mosquito nets was good for a first try, but needed refinement. In some areas, the net would touch your skin if you moved in the wrong way, opening the flesh to a mosquito-treat. My kneecap, which rested against the netting, got an indeterminate number of mosquito bites. There were so many I could no longer see individual bites. It was a good take for the mosquito population that night. I did my part in feeding untold numbers of wrigglers. Maybe they would mature in time to also have a go at me before I left…and the wheel keeps a'turnin'.

Time moves very differently in Guinea.

A good condition $100 bill is equivalent to 120,000FG (Guinea-Franc). Five twenties, you get less; bad condition $100 bill, you get less; travelers checks, you get waaaaay less.

An interesting phenomenon in Guinea is the ever-present haggle; it happens wherever you go, whatever you do. Whether it's going through the airport or trying to get a fishing boat, you deal with people who seem to feel like they must make your life difficult. A good example is the military here. When I first arrived at the airport, the folks wearing military uniforms appeared all-around clueless. They looked like they had all won their uniforms in a poker match. The Keystone Cops looked like professionals next to these folks. But with that uniform came the power of deniability. "In order to get from point A to point B, you have to get my approval. I hold the power, the power to which you are beholden. In achieving this goal, the goal of using my only power, I will maximize the number of mindless hoops you have to jump through in order to fully breathe into my power, for it is all I have." It's a game really that boils down to folks taking what they can get versus the folks who know damn well that they are dealing with folks who want to take what they can get. Anyway, you get the point....

On the boat to the island of Roume, Guinea, West Africa, c. 2001.

Wreckage on the way to Roume; just after this photo a family that was living in this vessel emerged, c. 1999.

We took a rickety dugout boat with a single outboard motor from a small port in Conakry about forty-five minutes into the Atlantic to the island of Roume. The tide had receded and the port was mostly mud-filled with rotting fish and vultures. We waded to the rickety boat and awkwardly climbed aboard. In the boat was a driver, with his hand on the motor, and a person with a big cup to scoop out the water constantly gathering in the bottom of the boat. As I looked down at him working, he looked up and smiled while methodically removing water. I wondered if he had a job title. En route to the island, we passed several enormous oil tankers. Conakry has a large tanker port. We also passed smaller ships, dead on their side, rusted out, and left over from when the French didn't know how to navigate the tides around the area decades earlier, before the shipping channels were dug. As we passed, a family emerged from one of the small ships, waving to us with big smiles. About ten minutes in, some folks were getting seasick while others were basking in the sun. In the water, we noticed tiny, tiny jellyfish. Looking closer, we saw the water was saturated

The island of Roume, Guinea, West Africa.

with these tiny little wonders. For the next half-hour, we glided over a bed of these amazing creatures. I wanted to touch them so bad because they were so cute. I wanted to eat them! I resisted the urge to put my hand in the water…just barely.

When we arrived at Roume, it reminded me of Gilligan's Island, minus the castaways. The trees, the rocks, and the sand so pure it squeaks beneath your feet. For the first time, I swam in the Atlantic Ocean. It was breathtaking. We swam, hiked, and ate until we left many hours later. The flora was how I imagined a jungle to be…. "Into the jungle, into the jungle I go…."

The first day I was there, I honestly didn't like it, what with all the travel—overnight travel with a thirteen-hour layover, other-planetary surroundings, mosquito nets, etc. But things quickly felt much better. I learned a great deal from the people I was with as well as the place…this place…Africa!

Our first day of class, we started at 8 a.m. with a breakfast consisting of a baguette, bananas, and tea. Oh, did I say the day started at eight? Well, what I actually meant was the day started *again* at eight since I had been woken several times in the dark morning hours by a rooster I think was on *East*-Africa time!

Our first lesson was usually at 9:00 a.m. with two drum classes and two dance classes, lasting until about 6 p.m. Good thing I had brought my cycling gloves because my hands hurt after the first few days of classes. Some days, we would go look at drums or go to the market during some of the class time.

The compound was surrounded by a ten-foot tall, one-foot wide cement wall with broken glass shards diabolically sticking out of the top. Within these walls was a large house with about four to six rooms, as well as a small house that the night watchman stayed in. The rooms in the main house had different configurations of bunkbeds. To enter the compound, you passed through a large metal door (designed to also let cars in). We would see locals and ask, "How are you?" but in French (ça va) or Susu (*innuole*). Lizards crawled on the walls surrounding some of the houses of the affluent. There is money in Guinea, but there is no real middle class. Guinea is one of the poorest nations in the world cash-wise, though it is mineral and culture rich. The lizards sometimes do this run and push-up move that just cracks me up.

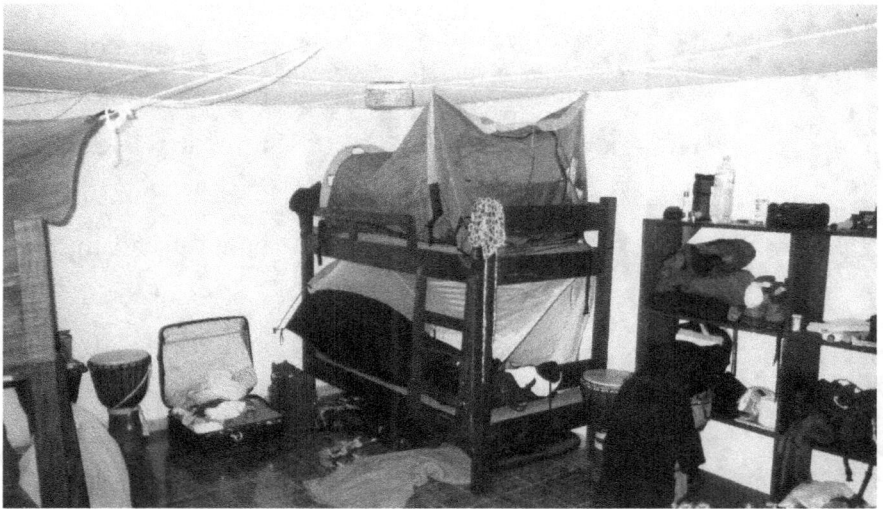

Multiple-occpancy living quarters, Conakry, Guinea, West Africa, 1998.

Most of the time, lunch was fish and rice; be careful with that *pilipili* (local hot sauce).

I got to play with some young djembe players for one of the dance classes. Unbelievable! Genius! Recalibrate the meters! Their names should, in my opinion, be known to the world, but may never be. But I'm working on it!

During some of our drum lessons, we were treated to a genuine, bona fide old school traditional djembe master. He had been in Les Ballets Africains for decades, taking over the lead drummer role after Grand Master Drummer Famoudou Konate left in 1987. He gave us a window into traditional (not ballet) rhythms and arrangements, and let us see what a lot of years of djembe playin' is all about. His name (*asunam*) was Master Drummer Gbanworo Keïta. Over the weeks, we took about half of all our lessons from him.

Taylor, John Yost and the great djembe master Gbanworo Keita, c. 1998.

A bunch of us made a trip to the airport to try to phone home; at that time, it was the only place in Guinea to call home. I had my first Coca-Cola on the way and realized I hadn't seen myself in a mirror for several days. After we got back to the compound, one of our Guinean friends asked if we would like to go downtown that night. I thought it would be good for my continuing research...yes, research, that's right!

At the club, I had a Guiluxe beer—Guinea's beer. It was interesting to see a Guinean club. I guess it shouldn't surprise me that it was more like one in Chicago than not. For me, the ride home was much more interesting. On the way home, we heard the sound of music and saw a small crowd so we stopped to check it out. A man in his twenties was singing and playing a Gongoma, a four-keyed m'bira on a large calabash semi-circle; broken hacksaw blades served as the keys. We were warmly invited into the group, and he sang a song for us. Soon after, it was time for another taxi. Before we had gone out for the evening, we had been told that because of the late hour, we should have our passports and yellow fever vaccination cards with us. At the first random checkpoint, soldiers took and held our papers for about thirty minutes, eventually returning them. At the second random checkpoint, they made us get out of the taxi. One soldier asked me for money. I told him I was an artist and artists in my country were poor. It worked; he left me alone. After we got back in the taxi, we learned that they ask for money to mess with you, but in reality, they wouldn't do anything. The movie version of that moment never would have gone down that way. At the third checkpoint, they had us show our passports, but this time they were satisfied that we had them and let us through.

As the mornings passed, either I developed an immunity to that son-of-a-bitch rooster or he was no longer cackling three hours before sunrise.

A few days into the trip, I went to take my first look at drums in Guinea. We went to the carver that does drums for the famous ensemble Les Ballets Africains, Kabinet "Moungam" Camara. I bought two for myself, one big and one small. The larger one would have the image of a happy goat on one side and my name on the other. I couldn't wait to get it—it was made of balafon-key wood and was ready in about a week. The price for these two drums was negotiated at $65 USD. Unbelievable!

When we returned to the compound, a performance was being held for a Japanese dignitary. As I watched the show, seeing our teacher, master drummer Gbanworo on stage, I realized I had seen him perform with Les Ballets Africains a few years before in Chicago. I also realized that he is the lead soloist on Les Ballets Africains' video (VHS) of their famous show titled *Heritage*.

Taylor and Kabinet "Moungam" Camara, drum carver extraordinaire! c. 2002

During my time there, the power would randomly go out and stay out for several hours; another lesson in how fortunate we are in the West where the power rarely goes out. Actually, that we had no power for over a day at one point had little effect on our daily lives, which was surprising.

Two of the young Guinean drummers, Joe and Alpha, were such amazingly beautiful people. Their level of expression on the drum and connection with the rhythm and dance was truly astonishing. The morning lesson was with Minto Camara, the current lead drummer for Les Ballets Africains. He was a beefy, good-looking young lad with wickedness in his hands. The afternoon lesson was with Laurent Camara, another senior master drummer with Les Ballets Africains.

The house contained no shelves, chests, drawers, etc. Hot water showers were a luxury I had left in the States. Every day, I took a coldish shower in an unfinished bathroom (like much of the house). Perhaps that was best in view of the circumstances since it served well to keep my libido at bay. The shower floor was not separate from the rest of the bathroom floor, so we'd squeegee regularly or else have a standing pool in the middle of the bathroom. I made sure always to brush my teeth with bottled water.

One night we went to a sabar, which, in this context, was a celebration usually held in conjunction with a marriage. It was held on the street. At one end of a square-like setup were the drummers/musicians. I likened it to a jambalaya of instruments; there was a drum set, two djun-djun, four djembes, a guitar, and occasionally a singer. The PA system was…hmm... how to say...the speakers looked like big boat horns, and feedback was omnipresent.

I met my first African teacher's teacher; Yaya Kabo's teacher was Lansana Diabate; it was interesting seeing a bit of my teacher's musical lineage.

As I was sitting watching the sabar, a child was leaning against my back. Africans are much less conscious of personal space than Americans—I earlier mentioned how men think nothing of holding hands. Perhaps being less concerned about personal space is one of the many lessons to be learned in Africa.

The lead djembe would be miked so close that it sounded like complete shit. The PA components were probably a mish-mash of throwaway pieces—it was hilariously terrible and very innovative. They also used a very bad reverb of some sort on the microphone—everything that went into that mic came out sounding like it (or you) was on acid. The scene was fairly chaotic. It passed being fairly chaotic when we were pulled up into the dancing—the crowd loved the crazy *fotays* (Susu for "white folks") and me.

The next day, while having a seemingly innocent conversation with one of the young Guinea drummers, I asked a question about the djun-djuns. He responded with a quizzical, confused look and asked what I was talking about. I gestured to what I knew as the djun-djun drums. He replied, "You mean the dunun?" I would go on to learn that the instrument I referred to as "djun djun" was not, in fact, called that where it came from. In fact, the word "djun djun" didn't exist in Malinké (Guinea) or Bambara (Mali), the two dominant ethnic groups in regards to djembe. It is called "dunun" or "dunum." Good to know. Perhaps the djun-djun is the month after May-May?

Magbana on Conarky Street c. 1999.

The first few days, I felt gross from constantly sweating and damp clothing. About a week in, though, I was much better adjusted. Soap and toilet paper were readily available by then, as was bottled water. My hand had also made a miraculously quick, full recovery by the second day of classes.

If it weren't for my journal, though, I would not always have known the day or date. At least once, I dosed on Lariam and felt kinda funky.

I had my first ride in a magbana, the ubiquitous van/taxis; I was sitting next to an African man who had a growth from his earlobe to the lower back of his head and over to his Adam's apple. The growth was the color of his bluish-black skin with the texture of large marbles within a fleshy vesicle. A mucous-like substance was between some of the peaks and valleys. I wanted desperately to show it to someone, ask about it, photograph it, even touch it, but it was not to be.

At the street (the dirt/rock road was about a quarter mile farther down from our compound), I could see taxis all over the place, magbanas, locals, and permanent vendors in shipping containers selling things like bread, sunglasses, oranges, and Coyah (local bottled water).

The landscape was broad and low. A carbon monoxide haze fills the air, as does the omnipresent stench of the open sewer channels that line the streets. The streets are paved, but the sides end randomly and sometimes jaggedly. There are no stop signs and no lines on the roads. None of the few stoplights I saw were functioning. African driving is like African negotiation—totally without rules and everyone taking what they can get. Horns blared regularly. I saw traffic acrobatics that reduced me to thankful laughter. The people were warm and welcoming, perhaps because almost everyone was selling something. "Ade" (AH-day) is the response to give when you don't want what they've got. It is illegal to photograph the military or their installations.

The streets had random garbage strewn on them, but were navigable. The business deals I did with drums were based on a handshake; only once did I have to write down specifics.

I began to ponder what life would be like when I got back to the other side of the pond. Should I go back to a life of comfort and regularity (at least by my standards), or uproot myself and give drumming the time it deserved? I needed to be able to sustain myself with my art; to work to the degree that I could obtain a reasonable livelihood with my art.

Four bloodthirsty *sasi* bastards got into my tent; they became lethargic with the weight of my own blood and were unable to escape because they were too swollen. They were like little dirigibles, slowly floating through the air.

Walking around the bay to one of the fishing ports, we heard the sound of music in the distance. Shortly thereafter, we found a ballet rehearsing in a warehouse. The leader was playing a krin, a kind of log drum, and appeared to be a member of the military. When the scene would change, he would pick up his leather whip and give a couple of lashes to a few he felt were in need; evidently, they had messed up a step or a line, and this was the way it was handled. The ballet was very good, and the performers seemed to be enjoying themselves, even in the face of the constant threat of physical harm. Maybe it wasn't as bad as it looked.

One of my last days there, I was sitting on the floor of my room when I saw one of the bloodsucking demons by the baseboard. I had really tried to keep it together when it came to the mosquitos, but now I was starting to take it personally. I'm sure the Lariam had a bit to do with my state of mind. I lit a candle and attempted to torch this scourge of human flesh. Some wax dropped on her, consuming over half of her wiry, proboscis-heavy body. Either the burning wax ended her life or the hardened wax did. Justice.

One evening, we were hanging with a young drummer named Jolia. He was one of the three youngest members of Les Ballets Africains and an amazing player with rich finesse. Anyway, it is customary for men to hold hands in Guinea. So he held my hand for, like two twenty-minute walks. Trippy. A hard, male, African, mega-calloused hand. My American socialization made me twitchy, even though I fought it, trying to find a deeper place than my social programming.

After three weeks in Guinea, I began to reflect on many things. I understood more each moment I was there, certain that I would always be infantile to a degree in my understanding. Each new moment carries with it infinite possibilities and infinite smallness, for a moment is but the inflection between the past and present.

It only took about 20FG each in bribes (20 Guinea-Franc equivalent to about $.002 USD)—there were six of us—to get us through the airport. The mosquitoes lingered in the night air as if to remind us we weren't gone just quite yet. We did the Vinx song "*Choosey Mama*" on the way over to the airport, a cappella. All my camera film was used up. I was immensely looking forward to the flight. Our goodbyes were great in number.

The first song I heard after I got seated on the plane was "White Christmas." Wait, *Christmas?*

As we took off, the map on the screen showed various countries around Guinea, including Burkina Faso, whose capital is Ouagadougou—without a doubt, my favorite place name!

2,955 miles to Brussels
6 hours to destination
-70F outside air temperature

I despised that smoking flights still existed in 1997. I had to walk through the smoking section to get to the lav, and it was *vile*! Just plain blue-faced wrong! I held my breath the whole time (during the walk, lavatory, and walk back), but still, it got in me!

After so many days of fish and rice, airplane food was quite good—especially on international flights.

After having been to Africa, I have a greater appreciation for many, many things, some trivial, some not:

- Hot water
- Potable tap water
- Food other than rice and fish
- Yaya Kabo, my first African djembe teacher in the US
- Rhythmic possibilities
- My own place in the world of drummers
- Shower with proper drainage/floor
- Mirrors
- Where rhythmic interpretation lies in the world of traditional rhythms
- Emissions standards

- Curbs
- Sidewalks
- The necessity of traffic signals and signs
- The rewards of hard work that comes from the heart
- Faith in one's calling
- People
- What is necessary
- Cold weather

Just south of Greenland, over the Atlantic with about 2,000 miles to go (about four hours), I was just finishing up Layne Redmond's book, *When the Drummers Were Women*. Passing over a massive section of Canada that seemed to take forever, I saw nothing but frozen tundra—lots and lots of frozen tundra—no roads, no houses, nothin'. At the one-hour point from home, we reached US land, which, at that altitude, didn't look much different from London or Casablanca. The last part before landing took us right over the spot deemed the Haunt of the Holy Goat, where we drum at Lake Michigan.

CHAPTER 3

ANCESTORS

"Your purpose in life is not something you find;
it's more like it finds you."

— Malidoma Somé

At the age of four, about 1960, West African writer and medicine man Dr. Malidoma Patrice Somé was abducted from his people, the Dagara, in Dano, a village in the West African country of what was then called Upper Volta, now called Burkina Faso. His abductor was a missionary who took him to a boarding school where Western, Catholic education was inflicted upon him. Somé endured sixteen years of physical, emotional, and sexual abuse from the priests, but after a physical altercation in which he struck a priest, he left the school at age twenty to return to the village of his birth. He had actually thrown the priest out a ground floor window and then took off, walking ten days back to his village.

Upon Somé's return, integration into his traditional tribal religion and customs was difficult, due to his long absence from his culture and his apparent indoctrination into Christianity and a "white man's world." Elders from the village believed Somé's ancestral spirit had withdrawn from his body and he had already undergone a type of rite of passage into manhood in the white world. Despite this, they agreed to let him undergo a belated manhood rite with a younger group. Having been raised outside of the culture and not speaking the language made the six-week-long, physically, mentally, and spiritually arduous ritual, believed to unite soul and body, more dangerous for him than for the culturally-indoctrinated Dagara youths also undergoing the rite.

In his first book, *Of Water and the Spirit*, Somé writes that each person is born with a destiny, a divine gift, and they are given a name that reflects that destiny. He explains that his culture's beliefs and very existence are based on a deep relationship with their ancestors. His name, Malidoma, means "friend of the enemy/stranger." It was Somé's destiny to come to Western audiences and promote an understanding between Western and African cultures. As the result of passing through the aforementioned ritual, his clarity of sight was such that he could tell what answers professors wanted on tests, so, while in university, he earned three master's degrees and two doctorates (from Brandeis University and the Sorbonne).

My first cowry shell divination from Malidoma revealed my purpose, which I was already living. In Dagara cosmology, I am a fire person; Malidoma is water. This reading was interpreting what the ancestors were saying about me, and Malidoma was the interpreter (diviner). Numerous unlikely experiences have led me to places I needed to be, to get where I needed to go, as if guided by an unseen influence. There was a time when I thought I was just lucky; now I see the larger picture. To what extent are we already living our purpose? To what extent are we aware of the extent to which we may already be living our purpose? Or maybe aspects of our purpose? 10 percent, 43 percent, 82 percent? How can you be sure you're doing the thing you should be doing? Intention and awareness of purpose are the fertilizer that help us deliver our highest level of genius to the village. Among the perspectives Somé opened to me are "initiatory experiences" and the importance of ritual. In the Western world, ritual and initiation receive little focus, though they do exist.

Some examples of initiations in the West are the Jewish bar/bat mitzvah. In Brazil, there is the Sateré-Mawé coming-of-age tradition: Bullet Ant Initiation. The Amish have their rumspringa. The Hispanic coming-of-age tradition for fifteen-year-old girls is quinceañera. Christians celebrate confirmation. But by and large, there is no broadly applicable tradition of initiation into adulthood and community life in the West. In practice, initiatory experiences delineate where you were from where you are. Sometimes this can mean your mental, emotional state from when you were a child to that when you are an adult. It may also mean from when you had a certain level of awareness to when you have a greater level of awareness physically, mentally, emotionally, spiritually, and/or psychologically. Part of the reason I feel like we have forty-year-old boys and fifty-three-year-old girls in Western culture is because of a lack of delineation between childhood and adulthood. If you never had an initiation that marked the end of childhood and beginning of adulthood, it's possible you never left the former.

Many experiences can be considered initiatory. What makes an experience so? What makes an experience initiatory vs. non-initiatory? The answer lies in what makes an initiation an initiation. Things typically found in initiations involve being separated from one world and being invited into another; some take this to mean death and rebirth of self. Initiations have aspects of discomfort, from minor discomfort to excruciating pain. They can involve dealing with stages of grief. They should involve learning new information. Some examples of initiatory experiences are a major divorce/breakup, some perceived or real existential threat (losing a job, death of a loved one, a near-death experience), etc. If we looked at these experiences as initiations, what would that mean? It would mean looking at yourself before the experience, reflecting on yourself while you were in the experience, and why/how you got yourself there, and then reflecting upon the ways you are different afterwards. It would also mean exploring what you learned from the experience, what you let go of, and what choices you might make going forward as a result, being mindful not to step back into old habits as if they should still be there; maybe their time is finished and it is time for new habits.

I've had experiences I can reflect back on to see very clearly that they were necessary steps to get to where I needed to be; they were initiatory experiences, and in the moment, they sucked supremely! Those experiences were necessary for a time; they served a purpose, but now the same circumstances that made them necessary no longer exist, so they are no longer necessary. A good friend who is a therapist, John FS Williams, told me that he saw his unborn son on a sonogram and he noticed that his son was clutching his hand as if gripping something. Seems humans are wired not to let go; letting go of things is something that, if not consciously practiced, will not happen. The default is not letting go of things.

Maybe it would serve us well to consider that we have gone through many initiations in our lives. Thinking about initiatory experiences going forward as you would about an initiation may reveal opportunities to break/

reevaluate any and all patterns. Do you put all the same stuff back in the room after you've experienced it empty?

In Malidoma's Dagara culture, it is assumed that you cannot be born into this world without a purpose; your very birth is evidence of which divine gifts you will bring to the village. Initiation can put you face-to-face with your purpose, pushing all else to the periphery. Western education largely obscures the relationship between what you *can* do and what you *should* do; what you are able to do and your purpose. Your divine genius is what *you* have brought to the village. There is little emphasis on individual divine gifts; instead, conforming to an education system is emphasized; this system is a model where the student needs to be taught what they should know. I prefer to think of students as already possessing knowledge that the teacher helps them uncover.

> "Ritual is the most functional means by which archetypal energies are dealt with. Indigenous people have been aware of that for eons. In the modern era, we focus too much on psychological counseling. There is a tendency for people to 'linger endlessly' in therapy without receiving significant help. The 'shadow' parts of our lives 'keep coming back.'"
>
> — Malidoma Somé

Malidoma believed that dealing with "the things we cannot escape" is best accomplished within the context of ritual.

For me, writing this book has been a way to make sense out of those things I cannot escape. It is the result of many years of experiences, sharing stories, and making observations. Experiences that, as a biracial person growing up in the 1970s, set me on a path with few precedents. I would learn later the positive impact upon youth when they see someone successful who looks like them; no one I knew or ever saw had Caucasian-looking skin and an Afro. My experiences taught me early on that many black and white folks didn't accept me because I was neither, and for them, this distinction was a necessary condition for acceptance. I always found it curious to put stipulations like that on acceptance. What assumptions were they making? What ideas did they have about me? What preconceived, indoctrinated notions were the lens through which they were seeing me? All of this was, and to a degree still is, a mystery to me.

In this book, I share stories about my time before the West African djembe entered my life, stories about *why* it entered my life, stories about my numerous trips to Africa, stories about the role of my ancestors (and ancestors who are significant in my life who are not in my lineage) and my life trajectory, stories about the unique perspective of being biracial, stories about how this African drum has changed my life and the lives of so many others, stories about the stories that we tell ourselves that frequently limit our perception and motivation to change.

In this book, I make observations on race, cultural appropriation, and the semantics of how folks define something they "know," on the human condition, on how folks understand the world within and around them, on how often perceptions about how we interact with those around us are so varied (intentional and unintentional), about one's perceived abilities (or lack thereof). My time as a teacher of the West African djembe drum has educated me most in ways of understanding how people understand. Sometimes this means what they *think* they understand, which may be different from what has been demonstrated. Sometimes, it means what I think they are thinking by way of what I am observing them saying and what they are demonstrating. Understanding communication as a receiver phenomenon has been instrumental in my understanding of how to teach and my effectiveness (or lack thereof) as a teacher/communicator. As I was playing *Pictionary*, I realized what a great example this game is of communication being a receiver phenomenon.

I am writing this book because of what the djembe, my life, my teachers, and my students have shown and taught me. This is not a book for those who are currently drummers, because although many of the stories and observations were facilitated by my time with this incredible instrument, the wisdom gleaned was not subject-specific. The practice of a practice (drumming, yoga, tai chi, meditation, martial arts, etc.) is incredibly important to reaching the deeper truths of existence, and those truths are within reach of all. Do I mean a "spiritual practice"? I think I do. To be clear, in my opinion, a spiritual practice (no matter what it is that you practice), should have some basic ingredients in order to be pursued legitimately: a guru (some person you check in with to see where you're at; the person just needs to be someone you trust who has gone farther down the path than you), conscious repetition, awareness, and execution of intentional technique that puts you in a practice of being in touch with the essence of a thing. This thing could be accounting, acting, ancestors, building, destroying, yoga, or many others—it all depends on how you practice it. You've probably heard about being in the present moment—that is a component of this. I have found that it is not a simple thing to keep my mind in the present moment. Only with lots of practice and experience am I able to sometimes (hopefully most of the time) be in this place.

Djembe has taught me so much about so many things. Sometimes, I vent these things out loud, usually in one of the numerous djembe classes I teach. It's as if the practice of djembe vibrates, calls, draws things to the surface. A particularly noteworthy observation happened when my students taught me there can be a schism between what we think we are doing and what we are actually doing; between what we think we know and what's actually happening. Not until I began saying these experiences, stories, and observations aloud did I begin to see their value to other people. Then came the thought to write some of them down. My greatest hope is that my experiences, stories, and observations will serve you as they have served me; perhaps they will kindle a spark in you to tell your own story. Maybe you will remember what gifts you are here to offer to the village.

The following is an original creation of mine. It is one of what I call my "Africanesque" folktales, all of which are my original compositions. Mamady Keïta said about them, "Taylor's folktales draw from his experiences with me and his times in Africa. They contain the stuff of folktales of old. They are a wonderful interpretation of African tradition."

All of them are sourced from my decades of study with the djembe, with my teachers, especially Mamady Keïta, and my numerous times traveling to West Africa. The names are based on actual people I've known or heard of; the places on actual places. I have written many of these Africanesque folktales, but there is a trilogy I created that represents origin, duality, and plurality; this one is the origin story of djembe. I am including it because I want you to know something about the origins of the djembe drum and its culture; how it began and why it is significant.

Africanesque Folktale—Origin:
Fanta and Daouda; the Story of the Women and the Numun ... of the Heartbeat, the Original Heartbeat of One Ancient Culture in Africa

In the beginning was the music, then the drum.

In the beginning among the Mande in West Africa, there was the music; *then* there was the djembe.

It was the twelfth century, in a place known as the Malian Empire in West Africa.

The sun peeked over the savannah as Fadjimba, master hunter, set out to the bush. He journeyed past a field where the farmer and his workers were just arriving.

He could hear Fanta singing and clapping music, encouraging the farmers to make their work more of a dance; the women of the village had realized that it was always better to work with music, so they had created rhythms by clapping their hands, making dance movements, and creating songs to sing for every occasion.

Fadjimba was a "simbon" or master hunter. When he was young, he learned how to track, hunt, and take down game. He was well-versed in medicinal plants, and he could understand the calls of the birds—what they would say to each other and what they would say *to* and *about* him. Simbon are not separate from nature; they are a seamless part of it. It is known by all animals when it is time to enter into a different part of the cycle. It is said that animals will freely offer themselves to the simbon when they know it is their time.

Daouda Kouruma was a "numun," a blacksmith, a caste of great physical and spiritual power; rightfully, numun are revered by all and feared by some.

Daouda was an exceptional blacksmith and medicine man. As such, he knew how to make tools for the farmer, weapons for the warriors, and knives for the cooks. But he also possessed secret knowledge about magic and otherworldly things; he was a fetisher. Frequently, he was called upon to make objects of power for the fetishers and sorcerers, using parts of animals, insects, plants, to create fetish objects and potions for rituals and incantations. People would come from all corners of the Wassolon, the region now separated by the Guinea-Mali border in West Africa, to meet with him.

One day when Daouda was making a mortar out of a log, his carving tool broke through the bottom of the bowl.

In this moment, he had a vision of a skin on the hollowed-out mortar. Swirling diffuse beams of various colors, light, and energy radiated from this image, sending ripples of sound that transformed into dancing images. The spirits that protect the village that dwell atop a small hill called Kurunin were awoken by this energetic shift, as were the ancestors, knowing an object of great power was now in the process of creation.

djembe
djembe
djembe
WAS ALL HE HEARD

He knew what he needed to do and the creation of this thing would involve the willful sacrifice of a tree and a skin. He took all of this as a clear sign that a channel between the spirit world and the physical world would be opened by this creation. He knew he would be creating a very powerful tool…and it would take the form of a drum.

The next day, he went in search of a tree that would allow itself to be party to making this drum. He went deep into the forest. Approaching a tree that seemed like a good candidate, he brought out his cowry shells and cola nuts. The cola nuts were an offering, a show of respect. The cowrie shells would be used to throw five times to see if the tree would allow itself to be used for the creation of a drum. He asked one tree—the tree said no. He asked another tree—it said no. He asked another tree—you know what it said? No! He visited eight trees before he got the right reading that said he could bring out his ax.

It is said that the djembe contains the spirit of the tree, the skin, and the carver.

After extracting the right piece of wood from the abiding tree, the next step would be carving the shell.

He waited until late at night, when the spirits, the *jina* [in Malinké culture, these are nature spirits] are most active, to begin.

He went to his special tools, passed along to him by his ancestors, imbued with many generations of blood, sweat, and *baraka* [spiritual power imbued in objects often associated with those used repetitively in ritual or artisan work]. With only the light of his forge, he carved the mortar. After a while, the mortar became more goblet-shaped, with a large hollow bowl on top and a narrow, hollow stem on the bottom. As he worked the form with his razor-sharp tools and master's touch, the goblet shape revealed feminine curves, and as the light of dawn crept into the night, *she* was finished. The mortar had blossomed into a smooth, shapely form that was waiting for its voice, its tongue, to sing.

Daouda knew the final step in the creation of his vision was the skin. He spoke to his good and respected friend, the master hunter Fadjimba, and asked him if he could find a skin for him. Fadjimba gave him a surprised look, then shared with Daouda a dream he had dreamed the night before. Douda's eyes widened and stared at him with wonder and curiosity.

"Last night I dreamed I was waiting in the bush with my bow and arrow, crouched, being still as nature herself. Suddenly, the ground disappeared and I began floating. Everything around me danced to an energy, a pulse."

djembe

djembe

djembe

WAS ALL HE HEARD

"Then an image of a white goat with bright green eyes glowing like candlelight trapped inside of an emerald appeared before me. It encircled a radiant goblet, as if made of dancing smoke. Like a snake, the spirit-goat wound around the goblet until it reached the top, then swirled down inside and out the bottom. Repeating this flow continuously, the two forms became one and vibrations of sound and light danced a joyous dance. Until the image came into focus as that of a goblet-shaped drum!"

Daouda then shared his vision when he broke through the mortar.

The two masters exchanged a look of ancient knowing. This would be a moment in history that the Djeli, the oral historians, court musicians, and advisors to kings would sing about. A great channel was opening to the spirit and ancestral world. The birth of a tool—an instrument of great power, joy, and healing—was imminent.

That day, Fadjimba set out to find a skin for Daouda. As dusk crept into the day, Fadjimba quietly navigated the grasses of the savannah, moving silently between bushes and trees. As night overtook dusk, Fadjimba's instinct, or perhaps the whisperings of ancestors, told him to crouch in meditation to open more fully to nature.

Closing his eyes, his other senses readjusted to sense sounds of the insects, near and far, the feel of the slow-moving air on his skin, and the moist smell of the earth, still clinging to the warmth of the day, cooling down.

After the songs of the creatures of the night were in full chorus, he heard movements in the distance.... Opening his eyes, he saw only darkness.... Continuing his meditation, he heard more slow movement, but saw nothing. Finally, two green orbs floating in space slowly came into focus. They were eyes, glowing brightly like candlelight trapped inside an emerald, looking right at him.... This was the creature from the dream.

As Fadjimba pulled an arrow from his quiver, the creature slowly drew nearer, never breaking eye contact. Fadjimba hesitated in putting the arrow on his bow because the creature kept slowly, gently approaching. The only light was a glowing green from the creature's eyes. Fadjimba realized he did not need his bow; the creature lay at his feet—it was the white goat.

They planned that evening to have a special feast, honoring the sacrifice of the mystical creature. Douda asked the women to prepare the bara, and he asked the *demesen*, the young men, to gather wood; tonight would be a feast for a very special occasion. This feast was not only to honor the goat's sacrifice, but to celebrate a thing that had not yet come to be. Douda had a very strong feeling that this would be a point in history that would change the direction of their culture. The fire filled the air with the scent of expectation; for where there is fire, there will soon be food! He asked the women to add some special spices that he had in the place where he kept magical things. The women's expert cooking skills, combined with Douda's very special seasonings, created an aroma that gave rise to much curiosity and anticipation in the village. Finally, the meal was ready. The village elder, Nankababa, who had recently celebrated his 112th journey around the sun, said that he had never tasted anything so incredible! It was as if he could taste the magic in the meal! He had not danced in the memory of the younger elders in the village, but that night, the drummers drummed and Nankababa tossed away his walking stick and danced as if possessed by the ancestors.

The next day, Fadjimba gave the skin to Daouda. He fashioned rope to hold her skin in place. He caressed the skin all around, checking and re-checking each angle. Then he put her in the savannah sun to dry.

Two days passed. He waited patiently for the right time for her to sing. The moon was full and the *jina* were restless in the bush. That night Daouda dreamed he was floating, connected to all things. Hands dancing, bouncing in an energy exchange of sound, movement, and music. In the rhythmic environment of his dreamscape,

djembe
djembe
djembe
WAS ALL HE HEARD

The day finally came when it was time for her to sing. Daouda looked carefully to make sure she was dry and ready to be finished. He pulled the ropes very tight with his numun strength and tools to open her voice fully. It was time.

He sat on a log in front of her. His hand bounced off the middle of the skin, producing an amazing DJEMMMM. This would be the first speech of djembe—a version of ohm, the first sound. In this area of the world, new sounds don't happen very often. Years, generations, centuries will pass without hearing a new sound. The sounds you hear are the same sounds that your parents heard, that their parents heard, that their parents' parents' parents heard! Nankababa remarked that in all his long years, he had never heard such a sound; he could not tell if it was fire, water, earth, mineral, or nature.

Everything in the village stopped. What was this new sound?

He did it again: DJEMMMM. The villagers began wondering what was making this sound and where this sound was coming from.

Then Daouda touched the drum near the edge and added a high sound—BAAAAY.

Then his hands began moving as if motivated by an unseen energy. He thought aloud, "I remember this!" But what could that mean? This instrument had not existed before this moment; he had never touched this instrument before!

DJEMMMM-BAY, was all he heard;
DJEMMMM-BAY, was all *Fanta* heard.
DJEMMMM-BAY, was all *anyone* heard.

As Daouda witnessed the spectacle of the hand dance happening in front of him, he wondered how his hands were moving in this way! Village members slowly drew nearer, not sure what to think of this sound that was clearly more than a sound. A deep energy, a vibration, a pulse....was this thing alive?

From far across the village, Fanta heard the sound, a sound the likes of which had never been heard. It was as if the village had a new heartbeat.

It seemed to come from all around. Fanta moved through the village following the sound. Soon, her movements became rhythmic as she danced her way with the sound, with the pulse ...

djembe
djembe
djembe
WAS ALL HE HEARD

As if drawn by a magnetic force, Fanta was being pulled almost off her feet until she stopped cold, seeing Daouda with a drum. As Daouda took notice of Fanta, her movements returned as if bubbling from some ancient depth. Her movements intensified, as did his hand dance. He created rhythms that inspired movement in Fanta. Fanta began spinning and leaping rhythmically while Daouda's drumming chased her, flowing with her every movement. The two began a conversation of sound and movement; soon they were finishing each other's sentences! As the energy between the two increased, so did the energy of the now large, moving, pulsing crowd.

djembe
djembe
djembe
WAS ALL HE HEARD

The village encircled them. Fanta and Daouda became the nucleus of a much larger entity that included Fadjimba, other animals (including humans) in the village, the *jina*, and of course, the spirits at Kurunin. All rejoiced together in bliss as movement and music became one. One of the villagers appeared out of the crowd and asked Daouda what this incredible instrument was called. Realizing he did not know, the instrument told him in a clear voice: DJEM-BE! DJEMBE!

Since that day, the name of this drum became "DJEMBE."

Since that day, the women gifted over the rhythms to the blacksmiths to play all the women's rhythms on the djembe.

Since that day, the djembe drum became part of every ritual, both secret and public, every celebration, every rite of passage, every naming ceremony. It became part of how the farmers worked their fields and harvested their bounty and much more.

Since that day, the ancestors had a portal to visit the manifest world, through the hands of the djembefola. The ancestors were the source of movement in Daouda's hands; he was unwittingly channeling them, with all their power, knowledge, and healing wisdom, through his playing. The moment he learned to give his hands over to the ancestors was the day he truly understood why he was doing what he was doing; his purpose had revealed itself.

Since that day, the djembe drum became an inseparable part of the fabric of Mande culture.

The End

Journal Entries: 1998—Guinea Trip 2

On the subject of dreams, just before leaving for Guinea, I had a dream that woke me up in a state of terror at 2:30 a.m. I was sitting with my head down on a table, facing sideways. A television was dropped on my head, picture tube facing down. As it impacted my head, I was hearing Chinese voices and my language/words began to change. After I woke up, I was so frightened—I also was confident that someone was in the room with me, so much so that I checked the entire apartment, leaving on the kitchen light. I also had to put on music so that random noises wouldn't make me jump.

Random polaroid of Taylor walking in Guinean market, 1998.

I returned to Guinea for a second trip in November to December 1998 to continue to study djembe. On this trip, the book I read was *Drum Circle Spirit* by Arthur Hull, the father of the modern drum circle. He reminds me to "follow [my] bliss" regularly. I was brought up with the idea that success was something that came via hard work. Enjoying what you do, or doing something you truly enjoy that feels right was never really in the equation. The problem with doing what feels right is you may not have a clear idea of what "feeling right" feels like. Modern public education doesn't foster a sense of purpose—of what we are called to do.

Just prior to the flight, I had heard on NPR that Kwame Ture (aka Stokely Carmichael) had recently died. He was a prominent organizer in the civil rights movement in the United States, who had been born in Trinidad. He moved to Guinea in 1969. He took the name Kwame Ture in 1978 to honor Kwame Nkrumah, Ghanian President, and Sékou Touré, Guinean President. A lot of American black folks made the pilgrimage to his funeral.

My travel partner, John Knecht, and I had a conversation with one of Ture's community. He called himself a revolutionary and said he had been in the business of being a "revolutionary" for more than thirty years. When he asked why we were going to Guinea, we told him "To study djembe." He replied, "You all don't understand" or something like that. He asked if we were going to the funeral. When I said he must be talking about Ture, he seemed to have a tiny bit of respect for us. We asked him to share details about Ture. He retrieved a folder of newspaper clippings and other info about Ture. Did I mention this man was sloppy-drunk? I thought, *Here is someone clearly attached to a past when the Black Panthers were a powerful force for good in their communities and a force for change in the civil rights movement.* I could sense the amazement in his voice at our ignorance about something that was clearly common knowledge. "I am a revolutionary." He prefaced his name with "Dr.," but I did not believe it to be true. Perhaps I needed to know more about this other famous Ture to understand what our acquaintance was really feeling.

We would also be in Guinea when elections were being held, which, in a military regime that has experienced coup attempts as recently as the 1990s, could mean many things not good for outsiders. It was recommended not to go outside two days prior and three days after the election. The election was on December 14. Our departing flight back to the US was December 12. During our time there, one of the Malinké opposition parties clashed with the military police at one of the marketplaces, inciting a riot. The government in power at the time was Susu. On the way to the airport, we had to go through a dangerous-looking mob—one of our cars was hit by rocks, but we made it through otherwise physically unscathed.

This trip was three weeks, which was long enough to get in two solid weeks of study/classes with one week of jet lag and acclimatization. The exchange rate this year was 141,500 FG per good condition $100 USD bill. I consistently attended three of the four classes per day. That's two djembe classes and one dance class, each ninety minutes long. Interestingly, this routine gave me too much energy, so I found it hard to sleep. Occasionally, we actually had air conditioning and hot shower water! Again, occasionally. Add to that list most-of-the-time electricity. But in a place where you didn't know these things were options at all, it's 100 percent better than nothing!

I either caught three tiny geckos or the same one three times in the span of three weeks. Looking back on it now, it seems like it could have been an attempt at communication from the spirit realm. It makes me think I was being guided to see something I could not see—maybe an animal/spirit guide—maybe something I was already looking at. We also had a black wasp in our room all the time. We didn't know if it was the same one or a different one each day; once there were two. The thing looked vicious enough to kill all of us, but we kinda took it on as a pet. We used to escort it gently out the balcony door, but it would come back the very next day. It always came back.

On these trips to Guinea, I used a few things as unique barometers to assess how I was doing. They included: solid shit (relatively), no injuries, not being sick, and feeling well rested. If all or most of those things were happening, I defined life as "all good."

On our way to get a grape Fanta (I never realized the depth of my sugar habit until my trips to Guinea, where my access to sugary things was almost completely eliminated), we heard drumming in the near distance. Investigating, we sought out the source. After rounding a few corners, we found the event—Gine Fare (woman's dance). The instrumentation was:

- 2 balafon (the predecessor of the xylophone/marimba with wooden keys, played with rubber-ended sticks)
- 1 djembe
- 2 botè with hand bells (botè is a Susu drum; a wooden bowl with a cow skin, played with a stick)

The botè provided the rhythm section with an absolutely smokin' dundunba-like rhythm. The djembe wasn't doing anything special, but was very effective nonetheless. This particular Gine Fare was for a wedding.

> "In the village, you must sweep your dirt."
>
> — Taylor

One particular morning, I found a small dirigible floating around in my tent. It was a *sasi* (Susu for "mosquito") with a full load of blood. A tiny blood barge with wings. It's an interesting trade-off for the sasi—extremely decreased performance with a full load. They soar slowly through the air, making them deliciously vulnerable to me. So a quick death is not necessary—I can actually enjoy this. It's come to that.

I apprehended the bloodsucker by grabbing it by its wing. "It's to the spiderweb for you," I said, taking her away. However, during the process of choosing which of my arachnid friends to feed, I lost my grip and the sasi escaped. She was unable to fly, so her escape was particularly admirable. I searched high and low, but I eventually had to accept that she had gotten away. Then I remembered a quote—I think it's from a Monty Python film—"the wounded mosquito is your worst enemy." If that is true, there is a sasi out there with a serious ax to grind with me. If this were a movie, we would now see how the sasi would go about exacting its revenge. I was up for it—let's play dirty—I'll get my lighter and can of Lysol.

I had the great honor and fortune to visit the village home of my dear friend and drum carver Kabinet "Mungam" Camara. He was supposed to be at the house by 8 a.m. so we could go to his village. He didn't arrive until 1:40 p.m. Then we prepared to leave, loading into a 1990s Toyota Land Cruiser. I was not even miffed—it worked out better because we had a new teacher that morning—Grand Master Famoudou Konate's eldest son Ibro.

In Guinea, "Let's leave now" means something like "Let's be on our way sometime today." "Let's leave now, now" is more immediate; occasionally, "Let's leave now, now, now" means imminent departure.

Once on our way, we passed a pineapple farm. I did not know pineapples were grown in the ground; somehow I thought they grew on trees like coconuts. At one point, we were driving between rice fields, and the smell of basmati was so thick in the air that I could taste it. Outside of the rice fields, we stopped for fried rice cakes that were about 12" in diameter, 1" thick, and very filling and tasty.

Intermittently, we would see mud huts. There seemed to be two ways of constructing them. One involved creating mud bricks, which were dried in the sun. The other involved placing balls of mud on a lattice of tree branches of different thickness. Other huts were all straw (whereas the mud huts had straw only for the roofing).

Mungam's village was much nicer than I had anticipated. His family owned a hotel/resort type of thing. It had a kitchen and a large indoor room with a stage and a PA system. The rooms they rented looked like stereotypical mud huts. They contained a large bed on a frame and had one bathroom per unit. We had a dinner of rice with Bonga fish (very tasty).

On our way home, we got some whole coconuts. We pierced them and drank the coconut water. I was very surprised by how much was inside a coconut; it seemed to be a gallon! After the water was gone, we ate the coconut meat. We got to the meat by smashing the coconuts together, breaking them. I hadn't eaten fresh coconut meat in a very long time, and fresh coconut meat from Africa—never.

Most Guineans are very proud to be Guinean; at the same time, they would leave if given the chance. Many Americans, if they know enough about their country's history, are not proud to be Americans; at the same time, they would not leave the US if given the chance. In Guinea, you have to work hard against an enemy, the government, who changes the rules arbitrarily in the process of getting a visa to leave the country. Then you have to come up with at least $1,000 USD for a plane ticket (some stats put the average annual income of Guineas at $2,000 USD). In America—you know, the place many do not want to leave—it is next to no effort at all to get a travel visa and our economy is such that, even if you are statistically unemployed, you can relatively easily earn enough money for a plane ticket. In Guinea, most people have a six-pack (abs that is) and the average drum is great. Their bodies and drums are naturally beautiful without effort. In America, most people want a six-pack (again, abs, that is) and the average drum is a piece of crap that some art dealer is selling who knows nothing about the drum or drumming. Our bodily appearance is of disproportionate importance and takes significant effort to make "beautiful." In Guinea, Guineans are always very well dressed, even if they have nothing to do (which is more often than not). Appearance for the Guinean is of major importance. In America, well, that's very different as well.

After each trip to Guinea, I wonder what the actual effects upon me will be; it's hard even to know *when* you will know how you may have changed.

CHAPTER 4
IN THE BEGINNING

> "Our souls do not like stagnation. Our souls aspire toward growth, that is, toward remembering all that we have forgotten due to our trip to this place, the earth."
>
> — Malidoma Somé

I was told I was adopted around the age of five; it was important to my adoptive parents, Sylvia and Wilbert Taylor, that I knew. My mother explained to me that I was put up for adoption because my birth parents would have been unable to adequately provide for me. The way I took it, it was a win-win—I got to be with folks who could take care of me very well, and those same folks got the child they wanted, to love and care for. I was a mixed/biracial baby adopted by a racially mixed

Left to right: Sylvia Taylor, me, Wilbert Taylor, Piper c. 1972

family. The French call it *métis*; I said, "mulatto," but in sixth grade, I was told that word was not okay. As of the writing of this book, there is no word or check box for me but "other."

It was always important to my mother that I would someday find my biological parents. She actually followed up on clues she had gathered from my adoption to try to find my biological mother. One day, we called a specialist in finding birth parents who kindly gave us this advice: "Contact the agency that facilitated the adoption and, when they don't respond, keep bothering them until they just want to get rid of you and will do the work." We did this and it worked! A letter was sent to my biological maternal grandmother, who contacted my mother. Shortly thereafter, we set up a meeting.

At the meeting was my wife at the time Suzann, my adoptive mother Sylvia Taylor, my biological mother Audrey Clancy, and myself. One of the

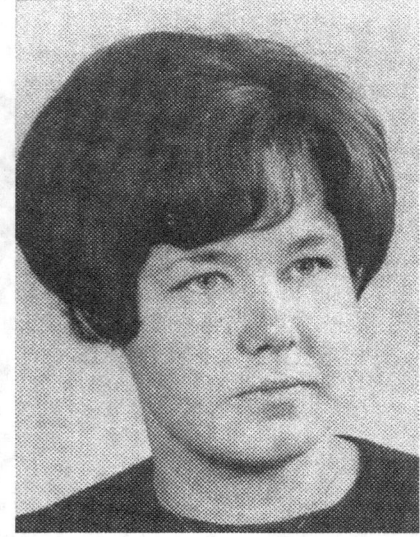

My biological mother Audrey Kindelspire (after marriage, Audrey Clancy) left 2023; right 1966.

My biological father, David Day, Sr, left c. 1984; right 1966.

first things I said to her after we sat down was "So, you are Jewish, right?" See, my mom (when I use this term, I will mean Sylvia, my adoptive mom) had asked lots of questions the numerous times she was with the social worker who facilitated my adoption. The conclusion she reached from the fragments of knowledge she received (the social worker couldn't legally say much about the biological parents) was that my biological mother was Jewish, so, by default, so was I. When Audrey answered "No," I heard it echo back as far as I had believed this—to maybe when I was five.

I learned from my biological mom that I was conceived in the St. Louis area in 1966 in the backseat of a car. My biological parents are Audrey Kindelspire, a young white woman with English and German ancestry, and David Day, a young black man of unrecorded ancestry. They were in their last year of high school when it was my time to transition from the non-manifest to the manifest realm, the earthly plane, the "10,000 things" in the words of Lau Tsu. (I'm a believer in reincarnation.) An interracial relationship in the South in the United States in 1966 was not only taboo, but could be downright dangerous for a black man. After I was conceived, my mother was sent to live with a family in a northern suburb near Chicago until I was born. She would be a nanny and live with the family until my birth. The social worker mentioned to my mom that I was from north of Chicago, which is what she based her Jewish hypothesis on. I would later find out my mother stayed with a Jewish family during her pregnancy. So began the learning about my blood relatives.

Audrey Kindelspire, my biological mother, was born May 23, 1948 in St. Charles, Missouri. She met my bio-father, David Day, during their junior year of high school, when they had a journalism class together; it was more like a club than a class, so they got to know each other there. They would get to school an hour early to hang out in the journalism room each morning. They also met secretly at the local park until someone saw them and reported it to Audrey's mother's cousin, who was the town sheriff. He told Audrey's parents he had seen them together, which caused a bit of a shitstorm.

Her parents' reaction didn't sit well with Audrey. In the era of Martin Luther King, Jr., rebellion was in air, and she was dialing into that vibration. In fact, as a senior in high school, she was already pregnant, but in denial of it until she had to take a physical for college. When she left the doctor's office after her physical, her parents were there to meet her; her mom had suspected she was pregnant. It was an indescribable moment. She was grounded. Lutheran Social Services was contacted. It had an arrangement in which unmarried pregnant girls would nanny for a host family; in this case, it was the McCarthys, who lived in Winnetka, Illinois. She stayed with them for the entire pregnancy and, after I was born, she stayed on for a few more months. Then she went to college in Cape Girardeau, Missouri, for general studies. About six months later, I had still not been adopted, so she was worried. She made a mental commitment to take possession of me if I wasn't adopted after nine months because she worried no one would want a mixed-race baby. However, I was adopted soon after. I have since learned that it was standard practice for newborns up for adoption to spend the first six months in a foster home; this information was never shared with her. She took a bus from college to Chicago, ended up at a bus station downtown, and found the courthouse and judge's chambers where she would sign over her rights to me. She told me the white male judge was a jerk who gave her a lecture.

Audrey went back to college in Missouri to finish that year, but she didn't want to continue school after that. A friend she had met in Chicago, who was in the same situation, said she was going to nanny back in Chicago, so they went back to Chicago together; Audrey stayed with the McCarthys. She had never before met anyone with as much money as the McCarthys, which was very eye-opening for her and provided her with an education about how to get around in the world.

After a while, Audrey's friend, Lynn Vanderloot, suggested they go back to college in Green Bay, Wisconsin, since Lynn was from a small town outside Green Bay. Audrey thought it was a good idea, so they went. They rented an apartment in an old house. There they met Ken Clancy, who was their downstairs neighbor. Ken was in business for himself flipping houses/apartments. He also built houses from scratch. He would later buy a small manufacturing company that made filing systems, desks, and metal office furniture. The Church of Jesus Christ of Latter-day Saints was his biggest customer. It had gigantic filing systems, as big as a room, filled with metal trays. He also sold to the North American Aerospace Defense Command (NORAD). Ken and Audrey started dating and eventually married. Meanwhile, rather than continue college, she got a job at Schneider National. She would work for Schneider for forty years, eventually retiring from this company. After some time, getting sick of Wisconsin winters, Audrey and Ken wanted to try living in the South, so they moved to Aiken, South Carolina, then to Charlotte, North Carolina, and then to Laurimburg, North Carolina. Schneider paid for all the moves, and they even paid for the house if it didn't sell.

While they lived in Laurimburg, Ken got uncharacteristically confused. One time, Audrey left for work when he was beginning to do the bills. She came home eight hours later to find he had not moved and nothing had been touched. Not long after, Ken's manufacturing company's factory went bankrupt, due to poor management. They used their personal money to keep the business afloat, declaring bankruptcy in 1998. He never worked again. The loss of his business traumatized Ken; he seemed incapacitated by it. In retrospect, the business' failure was likely due to the early onset of Alzheimer's. They moved back to Green Bay to be closer to family as Ken's condition worsened.

David Day, my biological father, was born on January 29, 1948 and died at the age of thirty-nine in 1987. It is said he had a heart condition. He was on Coumadin, and possibly steroids and cocaine (maybe crack) were involved when he dropped dead in the shower. It wasn't an overdose, but the blood clot that lodged in his brain may have been expedited by these factors. After I turned fifty, I learned I have a prolapsed mitral valve. Before then, I'd had no clue I had a potentially deadly heart condition. David was into sports and a bodybuilder and was loved by many. At times, he was loved by too many! Let's just say I've learned he was very charming and very much like me in many ways.

I made that first trip to St. Charles, Missouri, to meet the two sides of my family in 1998. They were literally separated by train tracks. My white grandparents' house was in a gated community; my black grandmother's house was on the poor side of town. The entire experience was very eye-opening in ways I wasn't even aware of. I bought a bunch of drums and percussion instruments to meet my white side—the Kindelspires (oddly, my name on my pre-adoption birth certificate is Ronald David Kindelspire—no joke). I had learned this side of the family had musical talent in their genes. Many of them were musicians, and they all had solid natural musical ability. I don't know what it must have been like emotionally for my biological maternal grandparents, being that they were the architects of my biological mom leaving the area before showing so no one would actually see her pregnant. It's not like anyone *didn't* know it had happened; the gossip mill kept all interested folks sated.

When I met my black side, they looked at me like they were seeing the ghost of my father. This side was where my athletic abilities came from. It seemed like I couldn't say one thing or make one gesture without someone saying, "Wow, it's just like David!" I have one sibling, Piper, six years older and the biological child of Wilbert and Sylvia Taylor (my adoptive parents). I have no biological siblings on my biological mother's side. I have two (known) half-siblings on my biological father's side—David Day, Jr., five years younger than me, born in Germany (his mom is a white German woman), and Dia Day, five years younger than him (her mom is black; they live in St. Charles, Missouri). There is wide speculation that I have more siblings around from David Day, Sr. When I met my biological paternal grandfather at a parade in St. Charles, I had to explain the timeline of who I was; he didn't know I had happened. He knew about David, Jr. and Dia, but not me.

It's hard to describe how I felt about being reunited with my blood family. Each side of my biological family welcomed me, a man of thirty-three years at the time, as if I had never been gone. Growing up, I was very different from my family. I can't say whether that is because I was adopted or just where the balance of nature vs. nurture fell with me. Did I feel any closer to my blood family? Not so much at the time or now. Did I feel close with my adopted family? I didn't know another family experience growing up, so I can say I always felt very different from them; it's hard to say if that is because I was adopted or just because I was different.

CHAPTER 5
MY EARLY YEARS

"Youth has no age."

— Pablo Picasso

Racist situations involving me being biracial have been an odd presence in my life. Only occasionally would the vitriol of racism rear its ugly head. Most white people didn't even notice, but some Puerto Ricans thought I was Puerto Rican and would speak to me in Spanish. Black women, especially elder black women, always knew. One said to me unprompted while walking through an airport, "And it was your mother that was white and the father black." Astonished and laughing at such a great and hilarious moment, I asked her how she knew. She said in her long years she had seen that if the mother was white, the skin tone was lighter.

Me in first grade, 1973.

Anyway, in my early years (until I was age six), on the South Side of Chicago in the early '70s, it was the wrong time and place to be a very light-skinned mixed male. There was a high-school-aged boy who was about my shade in my neighborhood who would regularly get beaten up. The one day I spent in first grade, someone picked at my hair, saying "nappy head." Interestingly, I didn't know enough to be angry; I was confused by what was happening and didn't know how to respond; my ignorance served me well for the first of many times. So, my mom moved us out of the city to what was then the country, Downers Grove, Illinois. There I found the racism to be verbal only.

Being called "nigger" had a few aspects. There was the fact that, yes, I had an African American parent. Yes, I had an Afro. Yes, my skin was straight-up Caucasian-looking, so I was the same skin color as them. Yes, it's clear some people are so passionate about being racist that they will pounce on any shred of blackness to find a reason to use the word "nigger." Yes, the perpetrators of this verbal absurdity were folks who smelled like urine, were always in trouble, and were, well, the type to say that kind of thing. Let me rephrase; they were the type who were *taught* such things. So, my reaction was that I couldn't take it seriously. That didn't make them stop entirely, but my thoughtful non-reaction with occasional comment illustrating that we, in fact, had the same skin color seemed to take the wind out of their racist comments. I guess I should thank both my sides for showing me that my path would be without much help from either. I must add that if someone asked me if I have benefitted from my light skin, knowing what I know now, the good, bad, and the ugly, I would have to say that I am sure I have. This is by no means a point of pride for me, only an observation.

My path would be one with few precedents, role models, or examples. "Hawkeye" Pierce, from the long-running TV show M*A*S*H was a childhood idol. I liked that his lack of seriousness never conflicted with his seriousness. He was the top surgeon, but also a total goofball. In seventh grade, I celebrated New Year's Eve by wearing a robe and cowboy hat, Hawkeye-style, and had my first experience drinking too much champagne. I was an overall positive kid, who did well in school, had friends, and was very active. However, in middle school, I attempted suicide. I took as much aspirin as I thought would kill me, but it didn't work. I never told anyone. I also used to chew on the insides of my gums; this behavior followed me into my college years. Sometimes, I would put salt on the wounds; sometimes, it would get bad enough I couldn't eat. No one ever knew. Looking back on it, I see it was not unlike cutting. A suicide attempt doesn't come without a reason(s), known or unknown. I thought I was okay. By all accounts, I was okay.

While growing up, it's hard to say to what degree I felt the bond of family. I can say my family life was a positive experience and I was allowed the freedom to pursue the things I liked. I had a lot of time to myself. Sometimes we ate dinner together as a family; mostly not. Sylvia and Wilbert both worked hard, long hours as a registered nurse and a brick mason respectively. They considered divorce at one point, but stayed together for me and Piper. My mother would tell me that my father loved me, but he didn't know how to show it. I can say now that he, like everyone, was doing the best he could. (Thank you, Brené Brown, for this one.) He did not have nice folks to raise him; he was raised by his older brother, who was not nice; I never knew how his parents fit into the picture, and I never met them or saw any photos of them. I learned via his obituary that he had a degree in teaching (which I found really surprising).

Sometimes my father would sit in the kitchen and watch as I did things, such as making a sandwich. He would criticize everything about the process as I was doing it. So I worked to a point where he wouldn't have anything to criticize. Problem solved. In my late teen years, more palpable tension existed between us, resulting in him blocking the door with a chair one time so I couldn't get into the house; another time, my mother ordered me out of the house because a physical altercation between my father and me was imminent. Before I left for college, I reached a realization of acceptance about the way he was and decided not to reflect back any negativity from him; that changed our relationship. I would not reciprocate the fight anymore.

After that, I worked as a laborer on his bricklaying crew the summer before I went to college. It was an amazing experience in so many ways. Getting to take a sledgehammer and break through the wall of a building so we could add an addition to a college dormitory was cathartic. I put all the stress of my life into destroying that wall. Dumping a wheelbarrow of mortar was educational; once it went past a very quick tipping point, my 165-pound frame was no match for that weight. As it tipped over slowly, I fought a losing battle. It took me down slowly like a martial artist.

Then there was the near-death experience four stories up on a rickety lativator (a somewhat makeshift external lift to get stuff to higher floors). I was on the landing and the other laborer was on the lativator platform with a full wheelbarrow of mortar. As he approached the top floor, the platform began to disconnect from the landing because of the excessive weight. The end of the wheelbarrow was on the landing and now and as the lativator platform slowly descended, the front of the wheelbarrow stayed on the landing. The wheelbarrow full of mortar was slowly tipping downward in a bad way. In a few brief moments, a lot of mortar would pour onto the other laborer, four stories up! My coworker, as he wrestled to keep control over the wheelbarrow, told me, "Jump down on the platform and pull the cord!" So, I jumped from safety onto a slowly descending platform four-stories up and grabbed the cord that controlled the lift motor so it would bring us back up to safety. This may have been my first near-death (or at least near-horrible-bodily-harm) moment.

When I was young, I thought I wasn't really all that special. I didn't feel I was lower than other people, but I just felt like almost everyone has the same potential so, in that way, I was not anything special. One thing that really changed my worldview shortly after leaving the South Side was the first time I saw two dogs close to one another in public. To that point in my life (on the South Side of Chicago), two dogs being in close proximity meant they would begin tearing each other apart; it was as sure as gravity. Well, the first time I saw two dogs nearing one another after we had moved, my stomach began to tighten because I knew bad carnage was imminent…but the two doggies just did the butt-smell and that was it. I couldn't believe what I was seeing. I realized I had assumed that *my* experience was *the* experience—the universal objective experience; there was no other way a thing could be.

My mind opened to the idea that anyone's experience at any time could be different. In fact, I realized it had to be the case that all experiences are different! How incredibly exciting! Perhaps if I were J. Krishnamurti, I would have posited "Truth is a pathless land"; I would learn this from his writings much later on, but it made sense in my life before I heard it from him. I would say it is a universal truth that all experiences are different beyond language, beyond words, and beyond semantics. I would argue that it is more important to have an awareness of what different beings all around you are experiencing.

What are the different stories happening around us all the time? If communication is a receiver phenomenon, what can being open to and listening to those stories tell us? Are we listening only with our ears, or are we listening to gestures, eye contact, and observations and questions, as well? Are we empathetically listening to energy and emotions? So many say so much more than they know! "Seek first to understand, then to be understood" (Stephen Covey, Habit 5 in *The Seven Habits of Highly Effective People*). I think about going into a crowd and yelling out some random name like "Bob!" and imagining what it means to everyone who hears it—someone's father who was amazing; someone's dog; the name of someone's friend who recently died, somebody's code name for weed, some horrible bully from high school, somebody's father who was abusive, etc. Everyone's reality is very much an iceberg; normally, we only interact with the tip of that iceberg.

The first books I really liked were about dinosaurs, reptiles, and amphibians. As early as the first grade, I wanted to be a herpetologist. I read early and was constantly curious. I was also fascinated with my mother's anatomy books. The giant green tome that was our *Gray's Anatomy* book was always open to some page. In second grade, I would listen to my teachers and think how ineffective their explanations and presentations were. How completely uninspired and dry…anything could be uninteresting under those circumstances. *Man, there are half-a-dozen better ways I could ex-*

plain that! I would think. *Why don't teachers ever ask if we know or what we know before they assume we don't know?* They assumed two things: 1) We didn't know what they were teaching, and 2) Their means of presentation was a good way; perhaps the best way. Wouldn't it be better if we were all invested in creating the path to knowledge? Aren't people born with the genius they have to contribute to the village already (as Malidoma Somé asks in *Of Water and the Spirit*)? Shouldn't we cultivate our children's innate talents to create a global village where all are infused by the passion of their purpose, living to their full potential? What is your calling? Clearly, it doesn't serve the larger community if we are not doing something we are particularly suited to do that serves the village.

In the third grade, I was in my first play. I had a paragraph-long monologue. I remember I played a farmer, but all other details are lost where all details go that get lost.

My second play was in fifth grade. I played an auctioneer:

"Twenty dolla, give me twenty. Who's gonna give me twenty? Who's gonna be the one? I wanna to see a twenty dolla bill!" said at light speed. I was totally into it, and remember joking to my friends, "Maybe I could make a living just talking in front of people!" I did athletics and piano lessons instead. The piano lessons began that same year and ended after two years; baseball was the next major focus, lasting through freshman year of high school. I got glasses in seventh grade. It was my first time seeing individual leaves on trees from a distance. Until then, I didn't realize that was possible. You can't miss something you don't know exists.

In eighth grade, my boyish awkwardness left and my physical self began to come together. My gym teacher wrote in my yearbook that I was the most improved student in all his classes. I was competing in gym exercises at the level of the school's top athletes. That year, the Flying Squirrels cycling team

Our cycling team the Flying Squirrels c. 1981. Left to right: Dave Wren, Kevin Folta, me, James Frale, Sean Rowbottom.

was formed by Kevin Folta, Dave Wren, Sean Rowbottom, Jim Frale, and me. Our mascot was Rocky, the flying squirrel from the old *Rocky and Bullwinkle* cartoons. We had shirts (uniforms), spandex biking shorts, helmets, racing cleats—the whole deal. We created our own criterium races in the undeveloped new neighborhoods—lots of roads with empty lots and half-built homes, perfect for our purposes. We would also do "century" (100-mile) bike rides, especially between Argonne Laboratories and Fermilab; I think we did that one six times over the years. Except for a few glimpses here and there, you don't actually see the Lab facilities from the parts of the trail that are actually on lab property; it's mostly through woods and ponds, with an occasional open field or stream crossing and, oh yes, bison. On one ride, while biking with no hands, my upper body gliding through the air with my legs on autopilot, I lost consciousness and passed out. My head hit the pavement like the ball on the end of a whip hitting its target. Fortunately, neither the skin nor the bones of my head gave way, since, for some reason, I was not wearing a helmet. After that ride, I wore my helmet around the house to protect my throbbing head for two weeks. I see now how incredibly lucky I was not to have received a much more severe injury. Lesson learned. To this day, I never, ever ride a bike without a helmet.

After one of these century rides, my mother and I dropped Kevin off at his house. Moments later, on our way out of the subdivision, we met an ambulance, police, and lots of chaos. We pulled over to see what was going on. The next thing I saw was Paul Frale, our friend and fellow Flying Squirrel, Jim Frale's brother. He was running down the sidewalk in distress. Soon after, I saw the paramedics were working on someone in the grass. As the stretcher passed us on the way into the ambulance, I saw Jim's familiar jean shorts. Something had happened to him. He hadn't gone on the ride with us that day because his knees were giving him problems. He had died as the result of a faulty wire on an electrical lawn edger. A short happened inside the wire casing, the casing melted through, and his left hand touched the live wire, sending a shock up his left arm and stopping his heart. Happening early in our freshman year in 1982, this was a very sobering lesson in the fragility of life. The Flying Squirrels created the James Gerard Frale bike-a-thon, raising money to help with our friends' burial. I rode 120 miles on the five-mile route.

Racquetball was my focus after baseball, then track, in my freshman year of high school. My best mile was 5:00 and my best half-mile was 2:19—very respectable for that age. Then, my sophomore year, motivated by the strong desire to meet girls, I tried out for a play. Well, it definitely worked—and, as it turned out, I really loved theater, too! It was my first love of art. In my time, I've enjoyed many life-altering experiences in English comedies, Neil Simon plays (getting the lead role of Peter Semyonich in *The*

Good Doctor was a highlight), Shakespeare, and many others. For more than three years, I was in a play with the next script in my back pocket being memorized. Playing Theseus, the Duke of Athens, in *A Midsummer Night's Dream* in 1984 at Downers Grove South High School was a pivotal moment in my life. I memorized the 250-plus lines of Elizabethan English, a dialect no one in high school could improvise with in the event someone dropped a line, so it was rote memorization. I told myself, "If you do this, you will be able to do anything." Fateful words that always stuck with me.

I loved the smell of the theater, dressing room, makeup, backstage, old costumes—the smell of theater folk; I had found my tribe! I loved breathing life into characters, really getting into understanding motivations, appreciating how, if you listen and understand the context, reacting to other characters was natural. Acting is reacting.... Acting *can be*, should be reacting.

Anyway, I graduated and got accepted at Illinois State University on a premed chemistry and theater track. ISU is serious about its theater; many ISU alums have been on television, in films, and involved with founding the Steppenwolf Theatre in Chicago. They didn't like that I was minoring, and I knew a major in theater was going to occupy too much of my time and prevent me from doing almost anything else. My major in chemistry ended with a defeat at the hands of an organic chemistry test my sophomore year. Most of the class, including me, scored in the high twenties to low thirties—brutal! A friend in the class broke the curve with a ninety-plus. When I asked him how he had scored so high, he replied, "I don't know; it's easy for me." Those words hit me to the core of my being. I was and had always been in a mindset that the more difficult thing must be the more rewarding; it had to be. If it was easy, well, it couldn't be a real, worthwhile thing!

All the while, I was realizing just how many different potential occupations I was being exposed to at college. So many different ways to make a living existed that I dropped my major and my minor and took a lot of interesting electives (including tap dance and tae kwon do) until I figured things out. This led me to think of where I would need to be if *I* were to say, "It's easy for me." This place would be a place where I could speak in front of people for a living, so I changed my major to communications and took a minor in philosophy. My philosophy minor was the gateway to coffee shops and coffee, reading three hours per day of John Locke, Plato/Socrates, Aristotle, and Bertrand Russell—intellectual thickness that broadened my ability to see things in very different ways simultaneously. One of my best papers was about Locke's idea of "substance." I solidly slammed the excessive verbosity that would often confuse simple concepts in philosophical writings. I feel like my appreciation of simplicity is very related to my time being overly wordy/thoughtful. Here is that paper's introduction:

> The corporeal consistency of the enigmatic configuration as assessed by the accompanying provincial protoplasmic synchromesh, exacerbated by a convoluted and obsequious sangfroid, undoubtedly has implications, albeit rudimentarily phosphorescent implications, of vertiginous verve. My point being, the difficulty in understanding philosophical ideas oftentimes lies not in the ideas themselves, but in the convoluted writing style philosophers often employ. Locke, me iudice, is guilty of this in his discussion of substance to a certain extent—not to the point of cognitive befuddlement, however (GADZOOKS! I think it's rubbing off on me!!)

I got an A.

I strongly believe everything—*everything*—in its natural state is simple. Complicated things make me suspicious. The best teachers can facilitate seeing the simplicity in just about anything. I can see now that this verbal-yoga/wordplay helped give me a strong foundation for public speaking and intellectual analysis.

My communications major was more challenging than I had anticipated, but my gift of gab and intellectual capacity served me well. It was easy for me, and it was okay that it was easy for me. For the first time, I embraced that idea. Between my major and minor, I wrote a lot. Later in my information technology mini-career, I learned how the corporate community's writing skills were abhorrent, especially those folks with corner offices. I'm thankful for so many things in/on my path. I attribute a bit of my success to my lack of planning how things would go down, while always moving to the next good thing. Another part of my success I attribute to one word: preparation. In *The Seven Habits of Highly Effective People*, Dr. Stephen Covey talks about the production/production-capacity balance. Your ability to produce anything is related to your capacity to produce. Many folks don't take the time to cultivate their capacity to produce. They have great, big ideas, but they can't bring them to life because they aren't prepared enough; their capacity to produce is weak. The great thing about preparation is that it's there when you need it, even if you didn't expect you'd need it. When I say "preparation," I mean physical, mental, intellectual, metaphysical, emotional, and spiritual preparation; they are all interrelated. I also mean being constantly curious. I find that I am more often concerned with truths than individual facts. To see the truths, it can help to study the facts, but not always; it's necessary but not sufficient. What is the "list of truths" of a thing? How many attributes can you shine a light upon that are true about a thing? Almost always, a fairly long list exists that can help you determine your own truth(s). For example, an apple is a fruit; it is also large (compared to an ant); it is also small (compared to a watermelon); it is also a very good projectile (harkening to my youth—no one was harmed), etc.

How often are we living the truths of others? How much of our worldview is inherited, programmed, domesticated—actually someone else's that was passed on to us unwittingly? Untangling yourself from others' ideas can be like peeling an onion; more layers exist where you didn't know there would be more layers. If you do the peeling, you will see how many people are living in someone else's truth or falsehood. Many aren't even aware that they are following someone else's idea of truth or reality. If you don't dig in and get inside of life, you'll just ride the outside of the bubble; be mindful that bubbles are known to pop. Often, people's true gifts to the village are obscured by Western education, by a lack of connection with where they are from ancestrally versus where they are today, by too many distractions, by social prejudices, by too much muchness, etc. (The list is too long.) The result is they are not doing the thing(s) they should be doing. My point is it can be hard to discover what your unique gift is in your village. I owe a great debt to the *I Ching* for providing a compass for me in the sometimes uncertain seas of life.

> "On its surface, the *I Ching* is merely a book. It is a very old book—one that has survived for thousands and thousands of years in many different forms—but it is just a book. It is also a very wise book—it is regarded as the foundation text of Chinese wisdom and philosophy, and was instrumental to sages such as Confucius, whose education and teachings were formed by it—but it is just a book.

"Beneath the surface, however, the *Book of Changes* is more than just a book. It is a living, breathing oracle, a patient and all-seeing teacher, an always-open spiritual school which can be relied upon for flawless counsel at every point in our lives. Those who approach the *I Ching* sincerely, consult it regularly, and embody in their lives the lessons it teaches inevitably experience the greatest riches that life has to offer: discernment, contentment, peace of mind."

— Brian Browne Walker

Around this same time, I decided to get back to playing piano/keyboards because three of my best friends with me at ISU were a drummer (Michael Criddell), a bassist (Dave Villarreal), and a guitarist (Don Livingston). All I needed to do was start playing again and I was automatically in a very good band. So a summer's worth of theory lessons and I was back in the saddle learning three-chord pop tunes. I realized I could sing and play, too! Our band was called In Colour, and we had a blast in the few years we did gigs at ISU. The first time I felt any degree of

In Colour, the band I was in in college - left to right me, Don Livingston, John Barry, Michael Criddell, c. 1990 on a break between sets at Illinois Wesleyan University.

fame was the first time we played at fraternity houses and they made the pledges carry our equipment. Awwwww yeeeea! We played clubs, fraternities, university functions, and many beer-soaked-floor basements. We did really great music; a lot of REM and Joe Jackson with occasional originals, Living Colour, Jimi Hendrix, Pink Floyd, and some TV themes. Some of the time, we used the roommate of one of the band members, Steve Meyer, to help us do sound for the band. He became one of our very close friends; little did either of us know we would be serious change-agents in each other's lives. One day when we were sitting around, I told Steve I thought he should get into acting, that it would be good for him; I strongly believed this. He ended up leaving ISU to get a theater degree from Columbia College in Chicago. There he met Michael Stewart and Mike McElya of the newly formed theater group Stark Raving Ensemble.

I graduated ISU in 1991 with a BS (major in communications, minor in philosophy). Anything in my degreed line of work paid a lot less than I could make as an assistant manager in a restaurant; it helped that I had worked as a fine-dining waiter three days a week while I was in school. Restaurant management should always be a temporary thing—a stepping stone to something less life-sucking.

After thirteen months, for the first and only time in my life, I quit my only job with no plan in place. It scared the shit out of me. I scoured the newspaper (yes, the newspaper), for job listings. When I found something that said (paraphrased) "Make lots of money and do very little," I figured, *What could happen?* I went to the group interview/presentation and signed on to be a salesperson of knock-off perfumes. I was supposed to be selling "only business to business," since that sounded more legit, but in actuality,

I'd walk into retail establishments and sell to the employees working at a business. I did it for four days, then quit.

Shortly thereafter, I saw another ad for manager trainee at Remco, Rent to Own. It seemed to include a lot of autonomy as the store manager with a pretty high salary. At the time, I didn't realize how sleazy the whole business model was (the company is not around anymore). My first assignment as a manager trainee was doing repossessions. That's right, I was a repo man. It was not nearly as cool as Emilio Estevez repossessing cars with Harry Dean Stanton. We did couches, microwaves, dining/table sets, and bedroom furniture. Here was the scene from one repossession of a stereo system:

> We show up at house.
>
> Wife answers door.
>
> "Well, what's he done this tiiiiiime?" she asks.
>
> "Ma'am," I say, "he's three months behind on his payments. We're gonna have to take the stereo."
>
> She lets us in; while we are loading it out, the phone rings and we hear the wife explaining to her husband what we are doing. He asks to speak to my trainer/partner. During the conversation, she looks like she knows the kind of venom coming through the phone, but my partner is calm. "Yes, sir. No, sir. Yes, sir. No, sir."
>
> He hands the phone back to her and says to me in a calm voice, "He's drunk and with a bunch of other drunk dudes. They have guns and they are coming here now."

We run to the van with components and stereo cables in tow. We screech away, not knowing where they are coming from, what car they are in, or what road they were on. We, however, were in a bright yellow REMCO van, so visible you could practically see it around corners.

Well, somehow, I'm here to tell the tale, so we made it back to the store that night. But that incident really put the fright in me. It was the reiteration of something I'd learned years earlier in rush hour traffic when I saw someone in a beautiful, spotless BMW cut off someone in a Bondoed, old Buick, with a different color door and more dents than I could count. The BMW driver didn't understand he was dealing with someone who probably didn't believe they had anything to lose. Someone who believes they have nothing to lose (regardless of the truth) is a most dangerous person. The clientele of this business were a lot of people who believed, for whatever reason, they had nothing to lose.

Journal Entries: 2001—
New York, Guinea, Madou Dembele, Mamady Keïta, Spider Dance

I began the year with my third month-long trip to Guinea and my first with Grand Master Drummer Mamady Keïta. One book I read on this trip was *The Hero With a Thousand Faces* by Joseph Campbell. This is the book George Lucas based the Star Wars film series on.

> "Fear leads to anger, anger leads to hate, hate leads to suffering."
>
> — Yoda, *Star Wars Episode I: The Phantom Menace*

Reading Campbell's book made me feel like I was witnessing myself in a maze from above. On my journey, I experienced cosmic unfolding and the opening of doors via intention, be it conscious or unconscious. It seemed I was not touching the knobs to the various doors—they simply opened.

This time, I departed from New York after spending some time with my first djembe teacher, Michael Markus, and one of my more recent teachers, Master Drummer Madou Dembele.

I met Michael in 1995, a meeting that was an inflection point in my life. I had gotten to sit in with his group "Magbana," rehearsing and staying up late watching djembe videos on a twelve-inch, black-and-white TV in the small apartment he shared with his wife Andrea. It was quite an amazing gift to have someone like him for my first djembe teacher—he was smart, funny, incredibly talented, and driven. When I close my eyes, I can't hear any difference between the greatest masters and Michael. As Markus and I watched the old Master Drummer Papa Ladji Camara tell stories on his djembe, we discussed, philosophized, and pontificated about what is important about the kind of drumming we do…there is something about the hand hitting skin—hitting it and sometimes hitting it hard—that is attractive to people.

Taylor and Michael Markus c. 1997, Chicago

I realized a disturbing parallel between drumming and the book/film *Fight Club*. Both share essential elements. The reality inherent in one's hand hitting the drum head is what hits people (pun intended)—what touches their soul. There is no gray area, no interpretation, no subjectivity in the striking of the head—it is totally, absolutely, viscerally, aurally, kinesthetically, visually, real; *direct* experience. *This* is your tone; *this* is your slap! Only a few situations exist when one can strike something as hard as possible with no legal repercussions. In whatever Fight Club is yours, the extreme reality of the thing is what makes it *your* Fight Club—the direct experience. In the United States, there is such a lack of substantive, absolute reality; so much indirect experience—too much ambiguity, too many masks, too much balderdash, interpretation, ballyhoo, so much subjectivity, brouhaha, double-speak, diatribe, and too much speciousness dulls the senses.

Before I left New York, I got a chance to visit the famous Djoniba Dance Center and take a class with the great Elder Master Papa Ladji Camara, the first African said to have brought djembe to the United States in 1959. When he walked into the room, I didn't recognize him since all the photos I had seen of him were decades old. I greeted him as djembe royalty, feeling honored to be in his presence. His style of playing was different and *loud*! I'm so glad our paths crossed before he transitioned.

Madou's place in Harlem was the perfect halfway house between Africa and the United States—a righteous acclimatization situation. I roughed it in an American-African kind of way here. He was living with several other Africans; I never got a handle on exactly how many. We visited an Ivorian restaurant that serves the type of African food I distinctly remembered from my previous trips to Guinea. One night, we stayed up until 3 a.m. I conferred with him about my dreadlocks, which I had started only a week or so earlier. He mentioned that he uses black soap and doesn't twist. Finding this very intriguing, I asked what he could do for my situation. Since I have some fote (aka Caucasian) hair mixed with my stuff, my hair could take some doing to get locked. Madou created a concoction of egg, sugar, black soap, and laundry detergent to put on my twists to hold them in place. I was worried, but he reassured me it was the thing to do. So, trusting him, I retwisted every twist, adding a bit of this concoction every time. I learned it's best not to wash your hair for a month during the initial locking stages. Going to Guinea was the perfect time to do this. Part of every day for one month would be having a head full of this concoction.

While twisting my locks, we watched videos of Madou's ensemble playing. When I asked Madou about the musical arrangements from the show, he told me the entire show was improvised! He said drummers from the

Ivory Coast can just do that. I guess I can understand that to a certain extent. I mean we can pull off gigs in Chicago with the right few folks because we share some common drum language. In fact, that is what this is all about—language! The more we speak the same language, the more we can effortlessly speak together. In a way, drum class is like a language class.

I found it amazing that my adoptive mother wanted me to bring home a walking stick *and* a djembe for her. This was quite the turnaround from our initial, contentious discussion about my

Me with Master Drummer Madou Dembele c. 2003 at Club Rhythm, Chicago performing with my group at the time Holy Goat Ensemble.

drum life. One such discussion led to a heated conversation that ended with my mother's racism coming solidly to the fore. Having me, a mixed-race child; being mixed race herself (she would be considered "high yellow" in old timey vernacular); and being born in 1934 had given her very good reasons to harbor ill will toward black *and* white folks. Maybe her request was a sign that she was beginning to see it is okay to have faith in the unknown. The unknown is not a place for just anyone to traverse; it takes courage and openness at minimum. I was pleased and surprised that she had found growth in my experiences with African culture, as I have.

Selflessness is necessary for success, or is that just a really comforting idea? There's certainly enough evidence to argue the opposite. What I truly know is what I feel. Interpreting what I know is another story. The semantics of what it is to know, epistemology—there's a lot in that idea. Then there's the timeliness of when knowledge opens itself to you. How many times have I "learned" something that was right in front of my senses for a long time? One day I look and finally see, listen and finally hear. "Now" is not always the right time for some knowledge. There's something to be said for "scaffolding theory" (an educational theory) whereby a sequence (ladder) should be adhered to in attaining knowledge. All that comes before builds on what is next. I can dig it.

Hope and fear commingle in a powerful way. I do not want fear in my life. Coming from a place of love is all I can feel when I am in the zone—it gushes forth, and it is all I can do not to cry in the presence of its overwhelming beauty. Selflessness is necessary to traverse the unknown—the void. The rhythm, when perfect, is the magic carpet that takes me away. I feel as though I am lifting/floating from my solar plexus; I feel as if I am transcending the flesh, and I understand a little bit more about the realm of the fleshless—the non-manifest. Transcending the confines of the flesh, that is what I seek; that is what this drumming experience is all about for me—it always has been. Visiting that place that I cannot yet explain, but yearn for—the place of oneness and absolute connection to all things.

I am a very, very lucky person. My college roommate and friend Ron Schankin would immediately say "external locus of control" any time the word "luck" was mentioned. Perhaps luck has nothing to do with all this, but it's the only word I can think of right now. I must say again how limited words can be in expressing ideas—I prefer speaking with djembe; I call it djembese! I would learn many years later that speaking djembese is how I connect and commune with ancestors; they have been the wizards behind the curtain of my life, guiding me benevolently through hard and soft times.

Love has its own gravity—I feel this deeply. We attract our future by the love we project. This goes for the people we attract into our lives as well. In *Scientific American*, I learned that very, very small particles that have antigravity may exist that could explain why the universe is said to be expanding. Maybe love is the energy that has gravity *and* antigravity. I can feel the cyclical result strongly—a whirlpool, a pull and push.

After eight hours in the air to Brussels from Chicago and another six from Brussels to Conakry (I won't even mention the layovers), we finally got set up in our room. With no knowledge of the time, food and sleep were all that was on our radar. Most people in camp spoke French. There were eight of us from the United States and one from Japan. Also represented were Canada, France, Israel, and Belgium. The smell of Guinea was so real. For that matter, smell is an underrated sense with Americans.

We didn't know what time it was since three of the Americans in the room forgot to bring clocks and the one who remembered lost his early on. Having no clock was actually a very liberating feeling—ours is such a time-bound society.

I regularly regard "the beginning" as when I began drumming in 1994. The beautiful dancing dulcimer in the song "Fortune Presents Gifts Not According to the Book" by Dead Can Dance echoed inside my mind, and I closed my eyes to savor its beauty. Lessons—the meat (or tofu) of this adventure—began the next day.

The first day of classes, my internal clock was still far afield; I woke before sunrise. After several attempts to get back to sleep, I realized it was not to be. So, I communed with Mr. Campbell and read until sunrise.

> "It is only when a man tames his own demons that he becomes the king of himself if not of the world."
>
> — Joseph Campbell, *The Hero With a Thousand Faces*

As I read the pages of this wonderful book, I saw myself reflected—death and birth—death of the old self only to be reborn anew. This had me wondering if my performance art piece entitled "The Jungle" is actually mythology.

I am thankful I mustered the discipline to keep a strict yoga and calisthenics workout routine throughout my time in Guinea. It kept me as balanced mentally, emotionally, and physically as I could reasonably be under the circumstances. The battle with mosquitos (*sasi*) continued—they are crafty! I would sometimes wake up with them in my tent, engorged in my blood; how did they get into my tent?

I cannot believe I made it through the first day of classes intact. At times, I would wake up while playing or walking around. Good thing I wasn't operating any heavy machinery! Regarding the classes, our weekdays were two, two-hour djembe classes and a two-hour dunun class each day; we could tape any classes we weren't able to attend.

I could feel the bias against the folks from the USA at the camp. We were, no doubt, walking in with all the stereotypes that come with that, true or not; sadly, mostly true. I had learned that an organizer for Mamady Keïta in Chicago had told him I wasn't serious about djembe; I could see

MY EARLY YEARS 137

Mamady was clearly interacting with me based on that statement. Unfortunate, but haters hate. Michael Markus gave me a great bit of information that when folks try to tear you down, it's because you're rising; keep rising and screw them! I had to establish who I truly was to Mamady, and I was in the perfect spot to do it.

I had no sex; no herb during this time—going without it (no matter what "it" is) is a good thing now and then. Campbell makes reference to the hero dying and being resurrected in a different form. How is the self dying and being reborn at any given time? I did not find his book; it found me when I was ready.

The next day of class, an unexpected visitor came to the compound, dressed in army fatigues, walking like someone important. Later, during a question/answer session, we learned he was the great djembe master Fadouba Oulare, the most senior of the commonly recognized "Big Three" djembe masters from Guinea; youngest to oldest, they were Mamady Keïta, Famoudou Konate, and Fadouba Oulare. Fadouba, who passed away in 2010, was the first lead drummer of the famed Les Ballets Africains, joining it at its inception in 1959. It toured many countries for many years and was the first ensemble to show the world outside of West Africa the djembe drum. Getting information from these luminaries was an incredible experience—accessing the tap root.

Campbell mentions in his book: "In our dreams...we may see reflected not only the whole picture of our present case, but also the clue to what we must do to be saved." Considering the frequency and lucidity of the dreams I was remembering, I found this noteworthy. It was hard to know how or whether Lariam was affecting my dream-state.

I murdered a large spider in our room. I felt terrible about it. He was easily several inches in diameter—smaller than my hand, but not by much. I thought of how long he must have lived in Guinea, only to have some punk-ass American squash him.

This is the spider 2001!

I found myself hoping to make it up somehow—to bring balance to this unfortunate circumstance.

Here's the scene leading up to this intentional killing: We saw this spider on the wall of our room. We got some Guineans to assess what to do. Their opinion was we definitely needed to kill it because it could be very dangerous. So, we went after it. This spider ran, twisted, leaped, and did some spider kung fu moves, almost mocking us, then disappeared into our room. Well, sleeping in the room with that thing was not an option, nor was sleeping outside the room. Luckily, it was early afternoon so we had time to develop a solution before bedtime. I sat in a half-lotus position in the middle of the room and, holding my book at the right height for maximum peripheral vision, I waited, reading. After about half an hour, I caught a glimpse of movement, pounced, and hit my target. It was more like stepping on a mouse than an arachnid (at least the type I'm used to). The murder had been committed. Was it self-defense? Perhaps, but I still didn't feel good about it.

Thought: When I was seventeen, I remember thinking, *Here I am*—that I had arrived at the person I was meant to be. That year I had three major roles on stage (Jack Chesney in *Charley's Aunt*; Theseus, Duke of Athens, in *A Midsummer Night's Dream*; and Peter Semyonich in *The Good Doctor*). I remember thinking for many years after that (in a good way) that I never progressed past seventeen. For the first time since I was seventeen, I now felt like my next chapter was imminent. Pretty sure some would call it my Saturn Return. That I was turning thirty-four during this trip, plus thirty-four being a multiple of seventeen, added to my perception of this time's significance.

The air was cool, the clouds hung lightly in the sky, the vultures soared, and life was beautiful.

A group of us took a trip to Roume one day; we played all day on the island. As dusk fell, after many toasts, Mamady left for the mainland. Several of us stayed behind for the night; I had not stayed overnight during my previous trips to the island. I looked up to see an incredibly bright entity in the sky—a star or planet, I'm assuming. The light at dusk was such that it was easier for me to see what I was writing if I didn't look directly at what I was writing. This wouldn't be the last time I experienced peripheral vision being clearer than central vision. Made me wonder if there was a metaphor hidden in there somewhere. My good friend Johnba (John David Knecht) and I decided to hike the island, and he asked me which way I thought we should go. I chose a direction, and soon thereafter, a large swarm of cackling fruit bats appeared; they mainly eat mangos. They were big as bats go; I could clearly see why some folks call them flying foxes. They gathered in a few trees intermittently, cackling loudly like so many talkative busybodies. We marveled at the sight of them for a good long time. I fucking love bats.

During our journey, we were joined by a nice doggie we had met earlier in the day. We decided to call her Sacajawea because she appeared to be showing us the way. She seemed happy to be hanging out with us. We got some advice from someone living on the island about how to get to its highest spot. We hiked there and found the view to be spectacular. We could see the tops of trees, the whole island, the surrounding islands, and Conakry. The climb left us tired, but well rewarded. The sounds of the forest as we reached the zenith were awesome—bats, birds, and whatever else, in chorus. We heard drums and a bala (a type of xylophone) in the distance calling to us. It was an awesome thing hearing what seemed to be the voice of the forest. We contemplated aloud what the colonizers a long time ago must have thought when they heard such sounds.

As darkness began to set in, we followed the sounds of music to a village that bore the same name as the island. Here we found lots of folks from all over the world, especially Sweden, taking part in a dununba. A dununba is at once the name of a type of drum, a family of rhythms, and a celebration. It was incredible to see so many types of humans celebrating together in this remote corner of the world. I had forgotten we had requested something to eat from the village folks. I remembered when I saw someone approaching us with a toothy fish, so big its tail was dragging the ground, held by its gills. It would be a couple of hours before it was properly cooked. It was so good, so pure, that even as I write this now, so many years later, my mouth begins to water.

After the dununba, Johnba and I did a ritual for the spider by the fire. Doing a tarantula-like dance, moving slowly, rhythmically with limbs outstretched doing the very best we could to channel spidery spirit. We meditated on the situation. Then we stood in the dark ocean and reflected on the meaning of the events that had led us to this place at this time. As the result of my experience with the spider I killed, I will act far more cautiously and slowly with things I do not understand, being mindful not to react, but to think (even though this spider situation is not the greatest example for this). We believe our ritual brought balance to the situation, as long as we don't forget what we learned from it. I will not forget.

I learned a valuable lesson another day from a crab that I had captured in some rocks at the water's edge—it was beautiful. Deep purple with nature, Escheresque designs in the shell, simply and naturally exquisite. It was too dark to take a photo; I appreciated it while it was with me. When I tried to capture another, I failed repeatedly. I could only savor the memory of what was; that had to be good enough—it was all I had. The here and now is all we ever really have.

I felt as if *The Hero With a Thousand Faces* was speaking directly to me, revealing to me the blueprint. Things I had only recently experienced were being explained to me in that book.

When we were headed back from Roume, we saw a butterfly headed out to sea. I thought, *For what purpose would a butterfly be headed out to sea?* This tiny, slow, awkward-flying creature is going in a direction where there is no place to land

This is an example of an upper-class toilet in urban Guinea. Photo from 2002 at Mamady's compound, Conakry.

for thousands of miles in any direction. I have no answer yet. Back on the mainland, back at the compound, the power went out again. Such a great reminder, another reminder, to cherish the fleeting moment.

About halfway through this trip, I was the victim of food poisoning. I puked violently three times and had the shits—it gave me the opportunity to use the outdoor commode (for better or worse); a ceramic in-ground structure/platform leading to a hole in the ground. A water spigot and a plastic water jug nearby—that's all. You definitely bring toilet paper to Guinea, and if you forget, well, do as the Guineans do and don't shake hands with your left hand.

I don't think I had gotten any significant sleep the night before. All day I was immobilized. Now I wonder how much of the pain in my muscles was caused by being wrenched past their limits from puking and retching. To add to the muscle issue, I injured my left lower back and upper back muscles doing yoga—a classic example of me pushing myself too hard. I felt like I had been beaten up; my energy was low, but I was still well enough to journal.

Several days later, I had my first post-sickness meal—albeit shaky. In all my writings during this journey, I woefully neglected to mention the magic of being in Mamady's kingdom. The prophets told his mother before he was born that he would be bigger than his village, region, or country. All corners of the world would know him. His mother asked, "How is this? Will he be a politician? A rich man?" She was told he would be known for having fun.

Being around Mamady is truly magical in a way that transcends description. His joy is boundless, as is his love and energy. Without doubt, he is a mythical character. One day, when people speak of the greatest master drummer who ever lived, they will mean Mamady Keïta. I know "greatest" is such a Western term. What do I mean by greatest? It begins with Mamady as a drummer, but it does not end there. His exuberant attachment to the essence of what djembe is all about is almost scary. He is the Bob Marley of djembe. He mentioned last night that he draws his energy from all living things around him—that explained a lot. Whoever acts in consort, in connection with nature, is also fed and sustained by nature. He knows so much; he cares so much; he is aware of so much that he inspires me on a mythical level. I am in the presence of a fleshy deity who is made godlike by his beauty emanating from within.

This trip was a major, unprecedented detox and recalibration in several ways:

- Emotionally—I have not been at "ground zero" in so many ways in my life in memory.
- Spiritually—reunderstanding how not in control I am.
- America-ally—remembering that there are two places—the United States and everyplace else (to be clear, I don't regard this as a good thing).
- Herbally—taking the normal sabbatical while I'm here from mother marijuana.
- Dietarily—this is debatable.
- Intellectually—getting back to reading.
- Physically—yoga five times per week with calisthenics.
- Lariamally—never underestimate its effects.

I have been through so much on this trip that I must be stronger; right now, I cannot tell.

Will desire cease when I hit bottom? I don't think I knew how dependent I had become on certain things until I wanted what I could not have. Will I stop needing when I hit bottom? Can I be sure of the difference between need and want? This difference seems to be more of a semantic, philosophical, or physiological issue. Will I know when I hit bottom? Have I already?

> "Have I slept? Have I been sleeping?"
>
> — Fight Club

Follow my heart and the rest will follow. Be sure it is the heart being followed—only through clarity can one be sure. Dysfunction, trauma, and habit can conspire to appear to be what the heart wants, but that is a terrible illusion. Absence of hope vs. hopelessness. The absence of hope is or can be a good thing—not unlike absence per se, the sobering void. Each day seems like eons. In just over two weeks, I traveled emotional, spiritual, physical, intellectual, etc., distances that defied any semblance of time. At such times, I need to remind myself I have every reason to believe everything will be great. I can say for sure that each non-warm shower I take brings me back to the here and now!

It felt like I was revisiting my past through my dreams so I could say goodbye. I threw away my water bottle that I'd had for about a decade—it was way past time to go. I did a ritual on Roume that was intended to sever my current self from my past self. I wonder sometimes if I am being tested. Then I realize that, even if it were true, even if I were aware I was being tested, would I be at a greater or lesser advantage? My only answer seems to be to listen, listen very, very carefully to my sounds, touch, words, energy, gestures, intonations, statements, questions, even my art, to see what the feeling is telling me. One of my roommates found a litter of dead baby mice in his clothes on a shelf that is low to the ground. Disgusting. What is that saying?

I took a class in Malinké language from one of Mamady's trusted people, Kalil. Here is some of what I learned:

Greetings

I soma	Good morning. (singular)
Aluni soma	Good morning. (pl)
Ayini soma	Good morning. (pl)
Ini tele	Good afternoon.
Aluni (or Ayina) tele	" " (pl)
Ini wura	Good evening.
Aluni (or Ayini) wuru	" " (pl)

(Alu or Ayi is the plural designation for a lot of words.)

Ini kay	Hi, or Thank you.
M'bah	You are welcome.
Tenaté	How are you?
Tenassité	I am fine.
Ee fanna nee kay	Very welcome.
M'bah	Okay, Yes.
Éé	No.
Oohoo	Yes.

Introductions

N'ne	Me
N'tole	My name is…
N'	I
I (long "e") toe dee	What's your name?
Y (long "e")	You
N'gne bola	I am coming from….
N'gne bola Chicago le	I'm from Chicago.
N'wato	I'm going….
N'wato Guinea	I'm going to Guinea.

Common phrases

N'wato nyen na	I am going to the bathroom.
Jelly é tay niyen jelly dee	How much does this cost?
Ah sonko belemon	This is too expensive.
Do ba ala	Lower your price.
Nye ye mé	Where's the bathroom?
Ala n'ye	Please.
Souman douman	The food is very good.
Gi	Water
Afo	Speak or play
N'so	Good (food)
Sin ma	Give me (object)
N'ya fry annye bara	I would like to work with you.
I doumanye	I love you.
Denih idoumanye	I love you, baby.

Me with the Grand Master Famoudou Konate c. 2010

Russell Schumsky, a Canadian friend, and I visited Famoudu Konate today at his compound in Simbaya. It was the lair of yet another of the djembe gods. We sat with Famoudou and shot the shit for a spell. He would be in Chicago in May that year. That made my schedule for pre-summer-Chicago: M'bemba Bangoura in April, Famoudou Konate in May, and Madou Dembele in June. It was an incredible gift to study with such titans of the art.

A little over halfway through this trip, I finished reading Campbell's *The Hero With a Thousand Faces*, perhaps the most influential and relevant book of my life. Now is the time to embrace the void; to stand strong with no crutches; to embrace what questions may come out of the darkness of the quiet mind—even questions for which I alone cannot provide answers.

> "...this is bat country."
>
> — Hunter S. Thompson

I took another trip to Roume, solo this time, to hike and do a particular ritual. I traversed the dense flora, looking up at about 200 bats, hanging out (literally and figuratively) in a palm tree about eighty feet up. I have a new appreciation for tidal pool ecology. I saw hundreds of tidal pools, and each one was its own little world. I never imagined sea anemones could be *so* tiny! The hike through the interior was, at times, treacherous in an Indiana Jones sort of way. At one point, I swung on a vine to get somewhere. I also came across a family of wild goats. The whole hike must have taken me several hours; it was incredibly tiring, but I felt elated when the journey was completed—all the way around the island, plus a good deal of internal scenery.

My releasing-of-my-former-self ritual took the form of capturing a small hermit crab, stating my intentions, and releasing them with my somewhat horrified hermit crab friend. As I stood in the waters of the Atlantic Ocean, I released those parts of me that needed to go as the result of all that had happened in my life over the past month or so. The Africa trip brought everything to a head as it thrashed me about, leaving me emotionally, spiritually, and physically so tired that I was faced with nothing but myself. It was time to get used to this—the real self—and not revert back to habits of the old self. Like I said earlier, this was the first time since I was seventeen that I felt I had changed as a person. I wanted to lick life. I wanted to embrace love. I wanted to commune with all that is pure and forge ahead with the power of my convictions. It was time to engage.

The moon was bright and the ocean spoke softly.

The previous year at this time, the cosmos had sent me a sign of no one even calling me on my birthday—it was as if I didn't exist. I could not remember what I did for my birthday then—a time of great darkness and growth. There was meaning in my life then, but it was not focused…not right. Low-level satisfaction with anything is dangerous because it is easy to become complacent, especially in the United States. Fuck complacency! It was time to go to warp-speed potential to see what this mother fucker was made of!

Sleep on the island never came because of my birthday and my releasing-of-my-former-self ritual. Another reason was the book I started reading, *The Color of Water* by James McBride. A therapist suggested I read it because it is about a biracial family. The book is incredible. Another reason I couldn't sleep was because I was on an island in paradise after having learned more about the craft of the West African djembe drum than ever before, and in just three-plus weeks from a grand master of the instrument. The last and perhaps most significant reason I was unable to sleep was some drunken Lebanese (I think) men were thrashing around on the beach. The sound of a generator could also be heard, keeping the lights on at a beachfront bar. Some nature scene.

I was looking forward to seeing what would change for me going forward and what would change after returning home. "I am so not in control." That is important to remember. "I am only in control to the extent I follow my path." Where is hope in this equation? David Mamet said, "Hope is a thing with feathers." I have never known what that means. I think he means hope is that sporting part of the human psyche that attempts to guess at what is to be. I say "sporting" because in sports, generally, you either win or lose; such is hope—either you get what you hope for or you don't. Getting what you hope for can add credence to what you believe your path to be, whereas not getting what you hope for can slap you in the head and prompt you to take notice, reflect, and move on in a different direction (or in a different way in the same direction).

As I was about to relieve myself off the trail, I saw unusual movements on the ground. I looked close and saw many skinks (lizards), small ones, about. Soon thereafter, I saw a snake that looked to be about three-feet long; it was brown with a small head. Figures—the one time I forgot my camera! It was the largest snake I've ever seen in the wild and the only one I've ever seen in Africa. So far, I've seen some very interesting birds, crabs, bats, hermit crabs, skinks, iguanas, a snake, numerous very cool fish in tidal pools, sea anemone, and wild goats.

My 2001 birthday was magical.

Back on the mainland, the day after my solo stint on Roume, I had a particularly noteworthy dream. Someone I didn't know was trying to lure me into something I did not want to do. At the same time, somehow I knew who he was and what his motives were—the jig was up and I shut him down. He was the specter of old habits—he was the ghost of those aspects that I cast away on Roume, attempting to weasel their way back in. These were his first attempts, but they would not be his last. I had to stay on guard.

One person in the workshop turned me on to the book *Total Freedom* by J. Krishnamurti. In the excerpts I read, he espouses not following any organized school of thought. His main thing (I am paraphrasing here) is to help individuals to be free—to be unencumbered by the perceived tethers of life. This sounds very, very familiar to me. It gives me a very warm feeling when something I've believed in so strongly for so long is iterated by someone who really seems to be knowin' sumpin' heavy.

> "Truth is a pathless land."
>
> — J. Krishnamurti

Getting through the Guinean airport was a comedy in bribes; good thing our handlers prepared us for the situation. Johnba and I were on the flight with Pierre Chaillan from Brussels—a workshop mate and tenured member of Mamady's extended drum family. He brought a rum concoction on board, and I took my third hit as the plane left the ground. Up and away we went!

Outside air temperature: -92F

39,000 ft altitude

4:30 local time at destination (Brussels)

C. 50 minutes to destination

Over Southern France

583 mph ground speed

As I looked out my window to my left, I was greeted by a very bright, few-days-from-full moon. I saw Casablanca on the map overhead and wondered if my drums were there in transit to me at home; then my gaze returned to the moon.

Love is not such a rare thing, if you are living with the right mindset; being *in* love is not such a rare thing either—being mutually in love is a very rare thing; being mutually equally in love, rarer still.

Balance and clarity in yourself—that is ultimately important.

On the leg home from Brussels, we each had a whole row to ourselves—it felt like a gift from the ancestors. We experienced a prolonged period of turbulence over the Atlantic. I was on the precipice of puking and later learned that Johnba was as well. I was nauseous for quite a while. If anyone would have ralphed, a chorus of puking would have ensued, I am sure. It would've almost been worth the story to have it happen!

I had read two books during this trip—by itself an unprecedented accomplishment in my life within a month's time. As I finished *The Color of Water*, I cried. This journey had me in despair and joy, the likes of which I've never experienced. I did more yoga than ever and more push-ups and sit-ups than I have done since college. I learned more about drumming—more than just rhythms (but a shitload of them as well), about the deeper aspect of bringing voice to my instrument, and about the spirit of Malinké tradition. With the aid of Joseph Campbell, I have exercised my intellect in ways I haven't felt since college. *The Hero With a Thousand Faces* seemed to find me right at the time in my life when I was ready for it; it was as if it were a literary interpretation of me and my life (and perhaps past lives).

My family has increased by one member—I gained a brother in Johnba (aka John David Knecht). We awakened our time together, albeit they were very different awakenings. We philosophized, hiked, worked out, drummed, ate, and read the same earth-shattering Joseph Campbell book (without knowing about it beforehand). I also achieved my mission of Mamady Keïta getting to know me better as a player and person.

I made many new friends from across the globe—Itzak, Pierre, Eran, Hiroki, Mahiri, Scott, Ben, etc. And I saw Africa in a totally new light. I had mystical experiences on Roume, communing with crabs, bats, birds, fish, lizards, and snakes. I ritually exorcized the "spider issue" and released my former self. I stripped away the layers of my physicality so I could become more accustomed to feeling the more refined *me*.

On the drive home from the airport, I didn't recognize the route and it took a long minute for me to remember what my house looked like. Seems I went so deep I couldn't remember where I lived. I can't help but think about how rebirth relates to this. A newborn can't tell you where they were born. A few days later, during my re-acclimatization, I came to the stark realization that I had hit financial bottom in my second year of djembe as a day job. I told myself not to worry. The money will come.

Some of the members of the first drum ensemble I was in, Dahui, Ensemble du Rhythm c. 2000, left to right me, John Yost, Rick Neuhaus, Bill Miller

What are the pros and cons of losing my fears concerning money?

- Pros: Clarity, no fearing loss, detachment from things I ought not to be attached to anyway, loving space, sans dis-ease.

- Cons: Taking a leap of faith.

There doesn't seem to be a downside.

In April of this year, I had the honor and privilege of performing for the great Babatunde Olatunji, who recorded the first work of African percussive music in 1959 on the album *Drums of Passion*. He is largely responsible for the world knowing African drum music and songs, at least initially.

Road tripping was the quintessential way to do this trip. As Dahui (John Yost, Rick Neuhaus, Amon, Bill Miller, Rich Similio, and me), we rocked!

I was honored to be asked by Arthur Hull to facilitate one of the drum circles for the Olatunji event. As it turns out, I was the first facilitator up. After an incredibly gracious introduction, Arthur let me have the circle, which was probably 200-plus strong. The love took over and dictated my every move, expression, and gesture. I recall few details; one was that I facilitated with a large songban (a cylindrical bass drum) I had strapped on. Arthur gave me huge kudos, especially on my modulating—putting rhythmic dialogue over a continuous rumble. He told me it was a very advanced facilitation technique—who knew? Lots of love from the participants; many mentioned how they really dug my teaching technique—that's interesting since I wasn't teaching in a normal sense. Feels like the stuff drummy dreams are made of. Our dreams become our reality to the extent *we* allow.

At the gig, backstage were:

- Giovanni Hidalgo—lots of love, totally cool.
- Baba Olatunji—lots of love and vibrations of the ancients.
- Mickey Hart—aloof, lost the love. Maybe he was just having a bad day. I learned he has terrible hearing.

- Gordy Ryan—Leon Latif's (2001 Guinea with Mamady) father and drummer on the groundbreaking 1959 Olatunji record *Drums of Passion*. So much love! He knew me from Leon and was very glad to finally meet me. What a trip—Gordy Ryan was glad to meet *me*!
- Innana—Fab-o women's percussion group. Lots of love—bought their CD.

Back to the drum circle….

After my facilitation experience, I felt the vibe, mood, and space of the circle and realized a pocket of dancers had developed on the circle's north end. Seeing a need in this place for a pulse injection/connection, my songban and I made our way over. When I arrived, I realized I was in the place to be—dancing is energy let loose in the whole body—a total expression of passion, mood, intention, and love via the whole physical self.

> "Our physical selves are a shadow
> of our non-physical selves."
>
> — Malidoma Somé

I felt like the nucleus to the dancers' electrons—a balance of Yin and Yang that formulated an energy loop that fed on itself, creating a pulsing, moving, undulating, gyrating, and rhythmic environment.

Late Saturday night, I turned my phone on to find four new messages that would tell the tale of my adoptive mother experiencing a heart attack a few hours earlier while we were performing. She was stable in the ICU now. My sister Piper was with her, but I was 1,000 miles away. This put an unintended and totally undefinable spin on the evening. So, the ingredients of the evening were: the drum circle, the full moon, the performance, my mom, and New York—I am surprised I didn't combust.

The journey home had us arriving Monday mid-morning with enough time to pick up master drummer M'Bemba Bangoura from the airport, clear my drums at customs (which were two-weeks late coming from Guinea), drop Bemba at my house, and go see my mom who was still in the ICU. Now it was also time for Sylvia Taylor to have an awakening. No more cigarettes. Near-death experiences tend to be very persuasive.

On Tuesday, September 11, 2001, I was stirred from a slumber with my partner Elizabeth by a call from my best friend telling me to turn on my TV. Many thousands of people had lost their lives; the World Trade Center in New York had disappeared; the Pentagon was broken. Something about this entire thing didn't surprise me. It horrified me, but it didn't surprise me. I checked in with all my NYC peeps; it took a long and nervous time, but they were all okay.

I was feeling stagnant in many ways. I believe I let my voicemails and emails back up so I would have some level of guilt. I know why I seek guilt—it is my status quo at this point. Guilt is an old senator whose time has passed—their influence waning, still cantankerous, but not dead just yet. After learning about the context in which I was conceived, I came to realize that guilt had been with me since conception.

I have had several holotropic breath sessions. (Holotropic breathing is a technique developed by Czech-born psychiatrist Dr. Stanislav Grof in the mid-1970s.) On my fourth, I finally "got it." I had an experience that whacked the crap out of me: I was in a crib in a hospital just after I was born. I was thinking, *Who are these people? Where am I? Why don't I feel any connection to any of you?* I felt angry, isolated, and sad, and I came to the realization that I have always felt this way.

This next Africanesque Folktale is the second in the trilogy of stories; this one represents duality and the understanding of self vs. other.

Africanesque Folktale—Duality: Hand of the Master

(It's not the drum. It's the drummer.)

Once upon a time, there was a young one who really loved djembe. But they could never find the sound of the master's hand in theirs.

So, they got frustrated and said, "Why can't I find the sound of the master's hand in mine? I want my hand to sound like the master's hand, and I can't figure it out! I play and play and play, but I can never find the sound of the master's hand in mine!" [Crappy playing here.] "I know," said the young one. "Since it can't be me, it must be my djembe! I will get a new djembe, and then I will find the sound of the master's hand in mine. So, what is it about this djembe that is not allowing me to have the sound of the master's hand in mine? This djembe must be, well…too short! That's the problem; this djembe is too short. I will get a djembe that is taller; then I will find the sound of the master's hand in mine!"

So, the young one set about to find a tall djembe and they found a tall djembe, so tall that they had to get a ladder to get to the top to play, and on that tall djembe they played and played and played. [Crappy playing here.] But alas, they did not find the sound of the master's hand in theirs. [Masterful playing here.]

So the young one said, "Okay, then this djembe must be *too* tall; I'm going to get a very short djembe, and that will give me the sound of the master's hand in mine."

So, the young one set about to find a short djembe, and they found a short djembe, so short that it was barely an ankle's height, and on that short djembe they played and played and played. [Crappy playing here.] But alas, they did not find the sound of the master's hand in theirs. [Masterful playing here.]

"Well, that short and that tall djembe didn't do the trick, but I am sure it must be the djembe that will not allow me to find the sound of the master's hand in mine! I know what!" they said. "This djembe is obviously too narrow; I will get the widest djembe I can find, and then I will be able to find the sound of the master's hand in mine!"

So, the young one set about to find a wide djembe and they found a wide djembe, easily thrice as wide as any normal djembe, and on this wide djembe they played and played and played. [Crappy playing here.] But alas, they did not find the sound of the master's hand in theirs. [Masterful playing here.]

"Well, that wide djembe didn't work, so I must need a narrow djembe; then I will find the sound of the master's hand in mine!" So, the young one set about to find a narrow djembe; in fact, it was the narrowest djembe in the village, and on that narrow djembe they played and played and played. [Crappy playing here.] But alas, they did not find the sound of the master's hand in theirs. [Masterful playing here.]

The young one had become frustrated more and more, so much so that their face scrunched up into a fist-face! After a long while of brooding, that young one had a very, very naughty thought. *I know, I will steal my master's djembe and try my master's djembe! Then I will find the sound of the master's hand in mine.* Waiting till late at night, when even the air itself was asleep, as quiet as a mouse, the young one snuck into their master's teebo (a mudbrick, thatch-roofed hut) and took their master's djembe. Scampering across the bara (the village center) going past the baobab tree, they hid behind the boulder, and played and played and played. [Crappy playing here.]

But alas, they did not find the sound of the master's hand in theirs.

At that moment, the master was suddenly awoken by the sound of his own djembe speaking in a voice, a language, that he did not understand. "How can this be?" He ran outside of his teebo to search out the sound. He crossed the bara and went past the baobab tree. Behind the boulder, he found the young one with the master's djembe.

The master asked the young one, "Why have you not asked me to play my djembe?"

"I'm sorry," said the young one, fighting back tears. "I'm so frustrated that I cannot find the sound of your hand in mine, no matter what I try—tall, short, narrow, wide. I thought that if I played *your* djembe, I would find the sound of your hand in mine."

"Did you find the sound of my hand in yours?" the master asked.

"No, I didn't," the young one said.

The master then went to his teebo and brought out a moth-eaten, dusty, tired, old, misshapen djembe. The master told the young one, "If you want to find the sound of my hand in yours, you will take this djembe and play only this djembe alone until you find the sound of my hand in yours."

The young one took the djembe and left the village. Time passed—many seasons, many naming ceremonies, many full moons, many harvests—

until one morning, so early the sun had not yet awoken, the master was startled from sleep in his teebo by the sound of his own hand! [Masterful playing here] He jumped up, startled. "How can this be?" he wondered, and he went to go find the sound.

Leaving his teebo, the master searched out the sound. He crossed the bara searching out the sound, went past the baobab tree searching out the sound, and looked behind the boulder finding nothing. But the moon had given the master a gift by providing just enough light to see a silhouette high on a hilltop; he could barely make out a young adult playing a moth-eaten, dusty, tired, old, misshapen djembe—this young person was the young one!

Approaching the young person, the master asked, "How is it that you have found the sound of my hand in yours?"

The young one said, "Many seasons have passed since you sent me on my journey to find the sound of your hand in mine; only after long years of practice did this djembe reveal the sound of the master's hand to me. Time has shown me the wisdom of patience and how knowledge and ability will reveal itself when the student is ready and not before. I see that practice, dedication, commitment, discipline, focus, perseverance, and patience, are the secrets to the sound of the hand of the master, not the djembe itself."

The master then went to his teebo to get his djembe and joined the young one, and they drummed together as the morning sun chased away the night.

The End

CHAPTER 6

1994: THE BEGINNINGS BEGIN

"The truth knocks on the door and you say, 'Go away,
I'm looking for the truth,' and so it goes away."

— Robert M. Pirsig, *Zen and the Art of Motorcycle Maintenance*

It was 1994, right around my birthday, when a trilogy of things conspired to put me on my true path:

- My first job in information technology
- The first time I auditioned for a role in a play and didn't get the part
- The first time I saw djembe
- My first interest in shamanism, vis-à-vis drumming
- My first practice of yoga

Okay, five things; counting was never my strong suit….

After about a month at REMCO and numerous repossession stories, I got a call from a college friend who told me the corporation where he worked had an opening at the help desk. I told him my only computer experience was taking BASIC 1 & 2 in high school and some desktop publishing on Macintosh computers in college. He told me I should apply, speak well in the interview, and say I knew WordPerfect, Lotus 1, 2, 3, and dBase. For those of you who know what those are, know that I, at the time, did not. So, I studied my lines, went into the interview, spoke well, and got the job! I was one of twelve support desk specialists. It's true that you learn a lot more, more quickly about things when they are broken. That, plus not asking the same coworker twice about anything, but one every twelve times, made it easy to stay disguised as someone who knew what was going on. Also, I realized if you speak less, you hear and learn a lot more—what an idea! Soon, I knew enough to really know what was going on.

The first time I saw djembe was on my birthday, February 4, 1994. Stuart Copeland, famously the drummer for the '80s power trio The Police, was doing a tour for the tenth anniversary of the release of his solo album *The Rhythmatist*. This tour would go to three cities—Los Angeles, Chicago, and New York—and it would feature vocalist/percussionist Vinx as emcee, Spanish flamenco guitarist Rene Heredia, the Brazilian ensemble Uakti, and the seven-member Les Percussions de Guinea. I still have the cassette bootleg from that show, and when I listen to it now, I can tell you what rhythms Les Percussions de Guinea played, but at the time, djembe didn't hook me. I was witnessing this incredible African instrument being played by some of the greatest masters of all time, yet it didn't hook me; it wasn't time for me to receive the truths of djembe just yet, but djembe was coming for me.

1994 - THE BEGINNINGS BEGIN

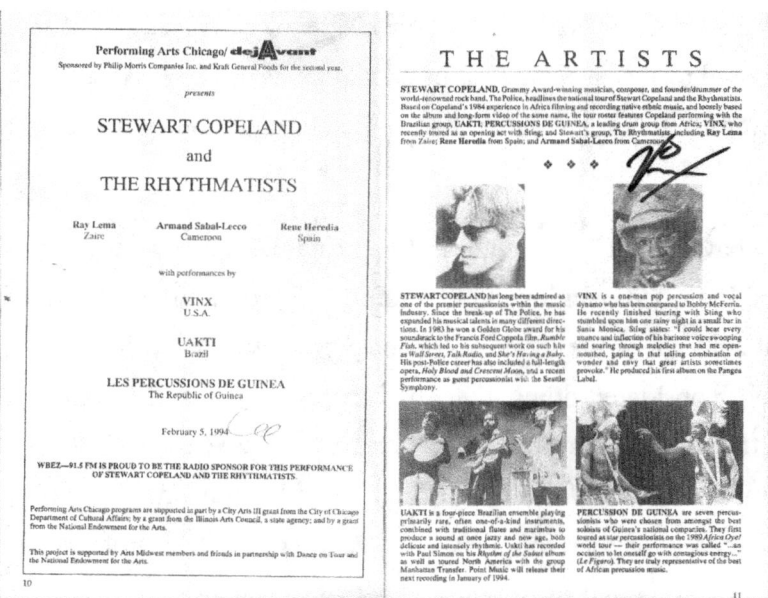

My first time I remember seeing djembe; the day after my birthday, 1994.

This was the play that began my rebirth in 1994. The poster for the show is shown in one of my altars with a hat that Malidoma Somé wore, his first book, and numerous stones from my worldly travels.

Around the same time, I started getting the jones to be in a play again. The people, the smell of the theater, the smell of theater people, digging deeply into a character, I missed all of it. So, through the former sound man for the band I was in in college, Steve Meyer, whom I had suggested go into theater some years back, I got word of an audition for the play *Light in the Village*, which was being put on by Stark Raving Ensemble. I learned so much at this audition. I read for a character; then after I was finished, I heard someone else, Paul Friedrich, read for the same character. I realized that not only were my acting chops out of shape, but he had really nailed it. I was beat and I knew it. This was the first time I had ever *not* gotten a role in a play. So, I left the audition with a new feeling: defeat.

In the days after, I got a call from the theater company. Seems my friend Steve Meyer had mentioned I had some background in music. Well, they asked me to help do the music for the play. It was something I had never done or considered doing, but I had the time, so I asked them if it was okay that I had never done this before. They were okay with it, so it was on! It was two other folks, Antje Gherkin and E. Rawlings Thurman, and me. They had degrees in music and were accomplished professional musicians; I had played music, but I wouldn't have considered myself a musician. To be clear, none of us were percussionists of any kind. They told us it needed to be percussion, played live (nothing prerecorded), and the setting was kinda like India. So, with no training in percussion and no percussion instruments, we embarked. Our rehearsals took place in an old building that used to house a sewing factory. It was across from a chocolate factory on the other side of the Chicago River, so memories of rehearsals are colored with chocolate air. Folks in the group donated various percussive instruments found around their homes, and we went forward until, about a month into pre-production, Mike McElya, one of the directors, mentioned a drum he had heard of called a djembe. He suggested we get a couple to see if they would add to the play's soundscape.

I knew just where to get a djembe. The person from whom I took half of my philosophy minor classes from at ISU, Professor Bob Steinman, had been fired for being a foul mouth in class. I loved taking classes from him because he was a raving lunatic philosophy genius and I learned a lot from him. And I thought his use of profanity was hilarious. Well, he sued the university, won, and opened a store that sold stuff from all over the world—he had djembes! So, I took a trip back to the land of my alma mater and met him at his store. As soon as I saw this two-foot-tall African drum with a foot-wide head, I was very intrigued. The moment I put hands on it, they began moving, as if animated by an unseen force. "Oh yes, I remember this" flashed in my mind. Then my conscious mind intervened to point out the absurdity that I could remember something I had never actually done (at least in this lifetime). That moment stopped me cold because I knew fully that something was happening unlike anything I had ever experienced. Or was it exactly like something I had experienced? At least it felt that way.

I got two djembes from Professor Steinman—one for me and one for McElya. The next rehearsal after I returned to Chicago, it was on! The rhythmic spigot was opened; the rhythms flowed. It was as if a great weight of water was behind a dam, with my hands being able to give voice to only a trickle at a time. Did djembe find me?

The play took about three months of rehearsals to create a one-month run in June of 1994. During that time, we took on another percussionist who was close to some of the ensemble members, a specialist in conga, Danny Guitierrez. Jose Aleman Sasieta was the set designer. We created the space to be mostly in the round. The main door to the space was basically a wall as wide as the space on ceiling rails that, when closed, created a total immersion in the situation. The set was mostly on the walls, starting at one side with a huge nest (think bird nest) with a bust of the Hindu deity Kali in the center. As the scenery traveled over the walls to the other side of the theater, nature slowly descended into a scene of post-nuclear apocalypse with images of bodies beneath soot and ash. We all participated in doing the body-castings for this which involved lots of nudity, Vaseline, and plaster of Paris; it's a story for another time. The play was very intense and the sonic environment was woven intimately within this fabric. By that point, I was playing only djembe. Other instruments included guitar, congas, various hand percussion, and m'bira. The play was a hit every night we performed it. The performance would run from 8-10 p.m. and the after party would inevitably run until 3 a.m. I think the play's intensity was the fuel for such a joyous, long release afterwards. We drummed, danced, communed with the audience, and enjoyed each other's energy. Indeed, it was a rare time in history.

Me with my breed indeed Todd Tesen c. 2018.

Around this time, my new and dear friend-brother Todd Tesen, who had done acting work with Stark Raving Ensemble before, put a book in my hand—Dr. Malidoma Somé's *Of Water and the Spirit*, which rocked my world, solidly introducing me to African spirituality via one of the greatest minds and diviners (some would call him a shaman) to come from the Motherland, Elder Master Dr. Malidoma Patrice Somé. I love the idea in Dagara culture that everyone is born a genius in some way and that cultivating one's individual genius is the greatest gift one can give to the village. After I read this book, I knew it was only a matter of time before Malidoma and I would drum together.

> "Tap source; it is where we are all part of the same essence; the same fabric of the universe."
>
> — Taylor

We rehearsed the play six days a week. The musicians played for hours per day. But that was not enough. On the seventh day, I drummed. On the lakefront, drumming by myself for hours on end, I began to realize that this drumming experience is about connecting to elemental consciousness—collective consciousness, to the One. Then, in the presence of other manifest beings, it is about relationships to manifest reality; what Lau Tsu calls the "10,000 things." It is about service in honoring the presence and contribution of self to/with/for other. Sometimes other members of Stark Raving would join me on the lakefront where we explored together in our innocent, blissful, rhythmic ignorance. We met some other drummers and flowed with them, but because at that point we didn't know the communication—the language of signals, starts, and stops—we were granted attitude from some other drummers. Until then, I had thought the drum world was devoid of mean people, but there they were, judging us for our lack of knowledge rather than helping us to see what we were missing. Many other experiences in drum circles happened, some great, some terrible, many in between.

Sometimes, I needed to be totally alone with the djembe. On Sundays, I went very early to the shore of Lake Michigan; I was sure no one else would be crazy enough to be there that early. So, I had the space all to myself. I remember returning to my waking, still-drumming body after astral travels. Out of body, I remembered the connection to the whole, the collective consciousness, to what I was sure some folks called "God." I felt my being dissolved into this other realm, only to return to a waking, moving, drumming being. This drum is clearly a key, a tool to reach the other side. To commune with the non-manifest side. So much remembering.

In 1994-95, I was reading Mickey Hart's book *Drumming at the Edge of Magic*. In it, he writes:

> Eliade calls shamans "technicians of ecstasy." What this means is that shamans are people who developed techniques that allow them to enter esoteric states of consciousness. In modern psychological jargon, they are individuals who have mastered lucid dreaming, clairvoyance, clairsentience, out-of-the-body travel—the whole spectrum of what psychiatrist Stan Grof calls "non-ordinary states of consciousness." Shamans can be thought of as individuals who have learned how to consciously enter some of these states and then bring back to this reality the information they obtain there.

So I thought I should look into what shamanism was really all about and how djembe could be involved. Dru Kristal, a shaman, in his book *Breath Was the First Drummer*, talks about "the way of the one note." You are always only ever doing one note at a time. I can dig that—give each note all the love as if there were no others! Each one! I loved the idea, but I still had questions regarding djembe and its role, or lack thereof, in shamanism.

I did a weekend immersion with someone who billed himself as a shaman and learned that the drumming that accompanies what shamans do is very basic, very methodical, and very much exactly what it needs to be. So my thing is a thing, but it's not *that* thing. I could feel I was reaching these other states of consciousness with what I was doing. I really wanted others to experience these states, so I thought of having one person lie down on the huge boulders at our normal haunt on the shore of Lake Michigan with drummers surrounding them. The right choices of boulders can be really comfy. The drummers were facing outward, like rays from the center; we called it a "baptism." I asked the drummers to be generous with their bass notes since those move the ultra-low frequencies. We would do a rhythmic journey, with all the dynamics of a powerful sea, sometimes for an hour straight. I was mindful to tell my drummers not to deviate in what they played; methodical, steady repetition is key for things like this; like a mantra when one meditates. Bass notes in succession make a continuous drone, ideal for inducing trance states. When we would stop, the person in the center of us would open their eyes. Many said they liked it when we sang together. We never sang. In their experience, where they were transported to, there was singing. So, this proved to me that our drumming was creating some portal to another place.

To bring this experience to even more folks, I created the DRUMeditation™. In the DRUMeditation™, I sculpt rhythmic environments to induce "ultra-conscious" states of consciousness; opening a portal to the ancestral realm with all its knowledge and healing power. Using djembe, dununs, the *tambin*, the three-holed Malinké flute, Tibetan singing bowls, ocean drum, tingsha bells, shakers of all kinds, etc., after a guided meditation with words, the guide begins to be the music, starting with the faint sound of a heartbeat coming from the djembe. The heartbeat turns to rhythmic percolation, ebbing and flowing as my ancestor-fueled hand-dance releases the music from the drums. I always keep the drumming portion of the DRUMeditation™ to at least one continuous hour; the entire experience is ideally two hours. This is the healing power of vibration.

Several folks mentioned that my ankle bells were one of the most memorable parts of the experience, with their metronomic, omnipresent regularity, as assuring as air itself—rhythmic air? One woman, a participant in a DRUMeditation™, had been nearly decapitated in a car accident by the trailer of an eighteen-wheeler. She had nightly nightmares. She had tried therapy and many other ways to find peace, but to no avail. After she did one DRUMeditation™, setting an intention to rid herself of these nightmares, they were gone. After many years doing these sessions, I started collecting testimonials, which are compiled on my website: https://www.holygoat.com/about/DRUMeditation/.

Also around the same time I was working at TransAmerica Commercial Finance Corporation, playing music for the play, and playing djembe, I started yoga at the suggestion of my good friend, the incredibly multi-talented artist and yogi Elizabeth Nuti (I would go on to collaborate with her on several artistic projects.) I had been an athlete in high

Me and Elizabeth Nuti in Old Town School advertisement c. 2001.

school and had made reasonable efforts to stay in shape ever since. My first year of yoga, I thought, *This is not torture. It will not always feel this horrible.* My soft-voiced yoga teacher would say things like "Don't push yourself if you're uncomfortable." Everything was uncomfortable! But I told myself, "It will not always be this way. It will not always be this uncomfortable." It reminded me of my first window into the difference between an intense sensation and pain and how I had forgotten this difference. The idea would come up later in martial arts, in the film *Fight Club*, and in observations I've made. I think part of the issue with the direction the modern world is going in is that we are removed from nature and interact via screens. Somehow, inactivity and numbness have resulted in believing any discomfort *is* pain. We have become so very pain-averse, or more accurately, discomfort-averse. Pain is a warning from our bodies that something is wrong. Discomfort requires a more subtle and layered look. When I was young, I was incredibly fortunate to have grown up in nature. We would wade waist-deep through ponds with fish, turtles, and frogs. There was a season when all these baby toads would appear. So many that, unfortunately, no matter in which direction we stepped, we would crush a footprint's worth.

We would wipe out on our bikes, fall into the water, and fall out of trees. As a result, we developed a sense of pain and, separately, discomfort. I credit my yoga practice with teaching me about the more subtle distinction of pain versus an intense sensation. Benevolent discomfort would be one of my greatest teachers.

Around this time, I met different folks who were selling djembes. I was introduced to Cheikh Balla Samb, a Senegalese art dealer, and bought a drum from him that sounded much better than mine. (I didn't even know mine actually sounded terrible.) If anyone asked me where to get a good djembe, I took them to Cheikh. That is until one day when he told me I should leave with several drums, pay him a discounted price for the lot, and then sell them myself instead of bringing folks to him. That is how I started selling djembes. One day at Cheikh's place, I saw an unusually dark wood djembe. I played one bass note; that is when I met Djembeyaya, the djembe that showed me what this incredible instrument really can sound like. I hadn't heard the bass of the djembe sing like that! Out of context, the norm can be difficult to know. I hadn't realized the depth of vibrational potential of djembe until this drum showed me. My first drum, nicknamed "Deadbeat," had a thumpy bass. Since I didn't know the difference, I accepted it as the way a djembe is supposed to sound. Djembeyaya's bass rattled the ancestors. Dense, dark dimba wood from Senegal, a thin, somewhat unforgiving bearing edge, and very heavy, its sound seemed like it was coming from all directions and all dimensions. She was my partner at a time when I was single and floating emotionally. This story is not part of the trilogy.

Africanesque Folktale:
The Story of Djemebeyaya:
You Can Be Whole and Be Alone

Djembeyaya was the first djembe I bonded with. Her name came from her being my "yaya" ("significant other.") She's not the first djembe I ever had, but she was the one who showed me many truths. Her sound was so resonant, her shell so thin and hard—dimba heartwood, hard as rock mixed with wood. The first time I heard her voice, it changed my reality forever. Before her, I had already fallen in love with djembe. I was in bliss in the beginnings of a profound remembering, with djembe as my guide.

Djembeyaya's amazing sound reset my entire world of djembe, and I became her devoted student. Seven days a week, we'd play together for hours. Out-of-body experiences on the lakefront, coming back into waking consciousness, having not missed a beat of playing. Before this djembe, I was having a great time; for me, Djembeyaya was like discovering a hidden door in the floor that leads to a much deeper place.

Then one day, as all djembe skins eventually do, her skin popped. Happy for the coming rebirth, sad for the loss, I put another skin on her. This skin broke prematurely; these things happen. A second skin rips almost immediately during the second attempt. Then a third, then a fourth, fifth, and sixth! At this point, I said to Djembeyaya, "I feel like you're trying to tell me something, but I can't yet see it. I'm going to think about what you are trying to tell me; when I think I've figured it out, I'll come back to you."

One dynamic in my life at that point was that in my relationships with women, I'd stay in unsavory situations instead of being alone. I would not feel whole unless in a relationship. My fear of abandonment and being alone were at the core of this soul dis-ease.

Several seasons passed. I reapproached Djembeyaya, feeling I had gotten to the message—had seen what Djembeyaya was trying to help me see. Her reskinning went perfectly, and this time, her skin did not break prematurely. Normally, a djembe skin will last 3-5 years. More than five years later, a small tear happened—a death null for most djembe skins. She lasted three more years with that tear.

What was it that Djembeyaya was telling me? I believe it was that I did not need anyone else to feel whole. My fear of being alone, my fear of abandonment, was an illusion that had been drummed into view, naked, unhidden to my sight. The greatest cure for darkness is light.

The end? The beginning.

***

At one point, the drumming folks from Stark Raving were talking about how this early Sunday morning drumming we were doing was our form of worship, so it needed a name, a designation. When my friend Pete Vojtik and I talked about this, he mentioned the word "haunt," meaning a regular meeting place. I loved this word and immediately connected it to another experience about ten years earlier when I had still been in high school. Understand that my knowledge of organized religion was limited to late night movies on Channel 9 in Chicago, where I saw Moses part the sea and Ben-Hur ride in his chariot; in both films (and all Bible-based films), there were goats everywhere. There were sandals, togas, long hair, lots of sand, and goats. So many goats that you could toss a pebble in any direction and hit one. Well, when I was talking to a friend about religion, I said "Yeah, it's like the Father, the Son, and the Holy Goat." After a long pause, my friend looked at me and said, "What?" I repeated it. My friend exclaimed, "It's *ghost*, man; what are you talking about?" I replied, "Wait, what? You mean it's always been that way?" After more than a few moments of pondering, it became clear to me how my misunderstanding had occurred. Or *was it* a misunderstanding? This place and time of our drumming on the lakefront would go on to be known as the Haunt of the Holy Goat.

I spent so much time at the Haunt, by myself, traversing rhythmic environments and coming back to consciousness while still playing, only knowing I had traveled because I had just come back! I would try to match the rhythm of helicopters as they passed. It's good speed/endurance training chasing the tempo of helicopter blades. Our first location was at Irving

Me and Stewart at the Haunt of the Holy Goat c. 1994.

Park Road on Lake Michigan in Chicago, on the boulders, just past the clock tower. The lakefront in this area had large, cubed boulders. They were great to hang out on when you could get good footing; they were also awesome to run on, and you could propel yourself off the angled sides of the huge, cubed stones. One day, I decided to get up on one of the more nicely cubed rocks—maybe a four-foot cube. With my djembe strapped on, I tried getting up on the rock. As I went up on the rock, I slipped and was thrown back. As I descended in slow motion, I saw the drum, still strapped to me. I knew I was going to get it in the face from this drum and in the back from a big, cubed boulder. Somehow, the back of my head did not hit the rock that my back slammed flatly on, even though my strapped-on drum hit my head like a bat hitting a baseball. I sprung up, got my footing, and was fine. Blood was dripping from my eyebrow, and folks were rushing toward me, already calling an ambulance, but I had somehow escaped terrible injury. I felt like benevolent spirits were watching over me.

Soon after the Haunt of the Holy Goat was established, Holy Goat Percussion was born in 1995. That year, I got a call from the Temple of the Four Winds, a pagan group who really liked my logo, the Holy Goat, and asked if we could drum with them for an evening. This was the first of many incarnations of the Holy Goat Ensemble, composed of me, Pete Vojtik, and my partner at the time, Suzann Robinson.

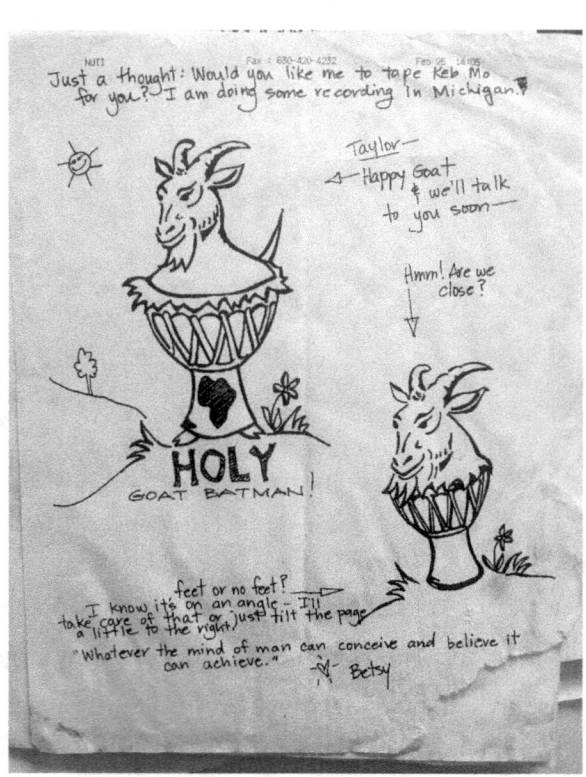

Initial sketches of the holy goat logo done by Elizabeth Nuti, c. 1994.

Journal Entries: 2002—Rewiring the Self, Building the Road to Tam Tam Mandingue, Chicago

> "If you become another person's needs answered you cease to be an object of their love; therefore, rendering yourself invisible. The psyche will not let you inviolate it."
>
> — Kurt Hill

In 2002, I was in the throes of the most emotionally crushing breakup of my life. "Gettin' real" can really mean a lot of things to a lot of people. While you are maturing, the semantics of your definitions of things can be moving targets. So much learned—do I think of it as an initiation?—now I do. It is part of who I am today, inextricably.

> "Where there is chaos, there is opportunity."
>
> — Chinese Proverb

I was walking around the hallways of the Old Town School of Folk Music, where I teach, when the concert promoter, Dayna Calderon, came up to me in a moderate panic. "What are you doing right now?" she asked. "Nuthin'!" I replied. Lucky for me because she had me take a van to pick up an artist at O'Hare Airport in Chicago. When I pulled up to get her, I found she had brought an African ensemble. When I mentioned I teach djembe at Old Town School, they immediately gave me the standard interview—shaking my hand to feel it for evidence that I was a real player. I passed their test. Later, I learned I had picked up Omou Sangare, one of the world's most revered Malian vocalists. I had the honor of playing with her during her show. Thank you, ancestors!

Many wise friends had been giving me advice that only then was I ready to hear. I didn't know my heart chakra was closed until my friend Kurt Hill opened it. (Chakra or cakra in Sanskrit, means "wheel" and refers to energy points in your body. They are thought to be spinning disks of energy that should stay "open" and aligned, as they correspond to bundles of nerves, major organs, and areas of our energetic body that affect our emotional and physical well-being.) Since he knew I was a skeptic of things unseen, he took out a pendulum and put it over each of my chakras to show me how it worked—it moved if the chakra was open. When he put it over my heart, it was still as a windless day. This chakra had been offline since I don't know when. He closed his eyes and concentrated as he put his hand on my chest, and as he lifted his hand, I could feel my chest rising, and afterward, the whole world appeared and felt different. Was that an initiatory experience? I definitely think so. Was I, in my rebirth, giving up the old paradigm and welcoming the new? I felt like I was going to the heart of the world so I could integrate my heart with its heart.

The incredible Kurt Hill http://holistichealthpractice.net/

It seems I chose to come into this world the way I did (an unconventional way) for a reason. The work Kurt did on me (removing a blockage over my heart) seemed to stir things up. Many realizations came to the fore: I was ready to handle what he called "the inconsistent immersive connection." My comfort level was/is consistency. I was in my birth stage, giving up the old paradigm and welcoming the new. The child is no longer the father of the man. The false self gives way to personal enlightenment. I am playing out the inconsistent immersion of my beginnings. We define our way by studying and defining what is *not* the way. We are the light that the darkness defines. What is the way? Everything that is not *not* the way.

While walking to a meeting in downtown Chicago, I felt more expanded than I have ever felt. Sleeplessness the previous night was simply part of the overwhelming feeling of self. On the Wabash Street Bridge, I viewed the awesome and massive Wacker Drive reconstruction and vibed on how many people's collective energy it would and had taken to do it. Later that day, it was time for my first dose of Lariam, to be taken a week before departure, for my next and fourth trip to Guinea, West Africa.

My reads for the 2002 trip were *Of Water and the Spirit* by Malidoma Somé (a reread, actually), and *Tao Te Ching* by Lau Tsu.

As I read *Of Water and the Spirit*, I was struck by the parallel between it and my own awakening/healing and my reacquaintance with my ancestry, which happened simultaneously. All of what was happening was part of a massive rebirth—a paradigm shift of ancestral proportions.

An hour before departure time, I finally sat in a space where I could do much, much less so that I might be a more open vessel to learn and understand much, much more. I had the overwhelming feeling that three weeks wouldn't be long enough. Then I heard the question, "Enough for what?" Good question. As the plane took off, I felt ascension—quite a theme. As we leveled off, I reflected on the most important single word in my life at that time: integration.

I mistook the light on the end of the wing for the moon. As the light came to an abrupt end, so the darkness began. Over water now, I saw a steward hang a baby carriage from the ceiling—a new one on me.

Each day holds new experiences in so many forms that it does not serve one to evaluate things based on belief systems from a different time and place. I felt childlike, and I felt love. I felt calm. I felt my breath. Yes, this year felt like a new plateau, a different space. Integration. The mantra of good words and thoughts manifesting. Fear losing its voice, truth singing praises, harmony resonating. Entrance—en trance. Yes, Friday, which means Lariam dose time and all the trippy side-effects that came with it.

If allowed, emotions tend to take over the inner conversation. Strength in other aspects of the self is essential for inner balance and peace. Strength. Worry not about answers. Key is the *strength* required to make the decision that feels right, even if that decision may cause temporary discomfort. If you know what you don't want, you can be more sure of what you do want. The more you know what you want, the more your dream manifests. And on the subject of "completion," it is very important to feel completion in different aspects of your life; by way of a degree, a project, fixing something, even something so simple as cleaning up a room. Some things are a *process* and are never done in a sense of ending or completed. There is something important about this that I've had a hard time articulating. I talk with my friends about how stressful it is that there are only twenty-four hours in a day and that so much is always left undone. It's very important to accept that some things will never be "done"; we, however, have ultimate power to govern at what stage of incompleteness things remain and to appreciate how different things are at different stages of completion. Part of this is accepting that you are doing your best (if you are, in fact, doing you best) and occasionally, importantly, feeling the bliss of completing something.

From very late 2001 until this trip, I felt like I had pummeled the well-fortified door of a secret room in my psyche to the point where it hung in suspended pieces from its hinges. Who, what, is behind this door? The image that comes to mind is the war room of Project Mayhem (*Fight Club*). It's the scene where "Jack" walks into the war room to see for the first time what has been festering in this metaphor of his sub, sub, sub, sub, subconscious. The people in the room are frozen with fear over what he might do in this place.

My attack of the door did three things for me: 1) It made me weary (if only temporarily), 2) It made me much stronger (*not* temporarily), 3) It allowed light to shine on the room's inhabitants—rays illuminating through cracks. The inhabitants were limitless in their power and influence under the veil of darkness. In the light, their limits were visible as was their actual degree of influence. Like the great Oz, behind his projection, their power was but an illusion.

I did not feel the need to fight them because their purpose was to show me what it takes to get through the layers of one's psyche. As this unfolded, questions arose: "Where did these layers come from? Why were all these doors and walls constructed?" As humans, we adjust to our circumstances physically, emotionally, spiritually, and mentally. Someone who seeks inner peace may strive to link behaviors to their origins. This may lead to opening doors—doors constructed long ago for very good reasons at the time. These defenses, however antiquated, served us well. But living is about change; it is not static. Because each day holds new experiences in so many forms, it does not serve us to evaluate things based on belief systems from a different time and place.

At one point, we had been over the Sahara for hours. As the ground began to turn from a shade of tan to a shade of red, I felt the nearness of Guinea. I was on a journey of emotional reconnection—heart reconnection while visiting the cradle of civilization, the heartbeat of the planet: Africa.

After a bit of confusion, we found ourselves making a brief stop in Mauritania. I was amazed to see people living in this desert. When we were approaching, I saw a very, very long straight road and other seemingly random buildings. Were some of them houses? Couldn't tell. None of them appeared to have access to the road.

My first night in Guinea, I slept the entire night with a rose quartz in my hand, on my heart. When I awoke, it felt like I had never left this place.

I spoke with my trusted friend Mahiri about what I needed to do to get the ball rolling on opening Tam Tam Mandingue Chicago (a branch of Mamady Keïta's TTM

DRTM logo created by Grand Master Mamady Keita in early 2000s.

Schools). He said first I should ask to use the DRTM logo, created by Mamady to represent that someone carrying this logo had demonstrated that they are upholding the musical traditions of the Mande (the area where the Malian Empire existed and the birthplace of the djembe drum). I had the conversation with Mamady and received his blessing to use the DRTM logo. Wow. Wow.

Drawing runes was one of the things I used to check in with Higher Powers (some say "the Universe") for advice. I just drew a rune—Thorisaz—gateway—place of non-action—the God Thor. Part of the reading said:

> Visualize yourself standing before a gateway on a hilltop. Your entire life lies behind you and below. Before you step through the gateway, pause and review the past: the learning and the joys; the victories and the sorrows—everything it took to bring you here. Observe it all; bless it all and release it all. For it is in the letting go of the past that you reclaim your power. Step through the gateway now.

Just after my rune reading, Olivia, a French woman on the trip from La Reunion (a tiny Francophile island nation just east of Madagascar in the Indian Ocean) appeared at our window, asking me to come talk to her outside about something I might be interested in. The interaction gave me a strange feeling. She and I talked about a proposition to acquire some hash for 6000FG. My heart loudly told me, "No!" But a tired part of me was intrigued by the whole scene. I felt more was going on than a discussion about hash. The right decision coursed through me and I listened. I was finally listening. It is clear this conversation needed to happen between me and me.

The magic of being here is waiting to be recognized—and it is being recognized.

I talked at length with three different folks who were Tam Tam Mandingue Professors in the United States—Michael Moonbear (Spokane, Washington), Beth Dyer (Santa Cruz, California), and Rusty Knorr (Seattle, Washington). Based on advice from these folks, I thought I would tell Mamady about my TTM intentions.

Dreams were so intense that sometimes I would only remember coming back into my body, like a cannonball coming back into its cannon. Definitely out of body; wherever I was, I was far into it. I began attempting to intentionally manifest dreams; my first was to commune with my ancestors in the dream realm.

That night, I became David Day, my biological father. I did not realize it until I remembered the entire dream.

I was in some sort of house. It was the 1950s. A friend from college was there; I kicked him out of the house because he was too messy when he ate. Some folks came by the back door to visit—they were friends of the family. We began socializing in one of the rear rooms of the house. As I was saying "Hi" to them, I mentioned that it was strange that I had moved in when everyone who lived there was gone. It was early December—the 8th comes to mind—and it was my family's house.

In the backyard was a tall tree of medium-thickness, maybe a pine, that broke near the middle and fell toward the house, landing on the back porch—it did not damage the house. While we were checking out the fallen tree, the porch slowly began to spin. I asked if anyone else noticed this.

It began spinning faster, eventually lifting into the air like a flying saucer! Sylvia, my adoptive mother, was with the folks in the rear room, who were Lithuanians with very thick accents. I did not know their names, but I believe they were aunts of some sort and all women. Sylvia had Lithuanian ancestry.

Anyway, the back porch took off like a flying saucer. It slowly soared above a playground where I saw the faces of all of my known natural relatives—only they looked like their brothers, sisters, mothers, and fathers, and it was the 1950s. I believe this was my first glimpse of my ancestors.

At some point earlier in the dream, I went up an escalator—a futuristic escalator. By the time I realized I was seeing my ancestors, I rushed back, running down the futuristic escalator. Remembering the entire experience, I would realize I was in some way David Day (especially given the dream's period).

As I discussed this dream with Marc (Sandrolini, a drum student, friend, Holy Goat Ensemble member, and psychiatrist), I understood more about more things. It occurred to me that my understanding of things is greater than my awareness of my understanding of things.

I told Marc reading *Of Water and the Spirit* was important for me at this time because Somé talks about how one need never feel alone, abandoned, or without community if one is in touch with one's ancestry. I told Marc it was my perception that my lineage goes back about six-inches, so not very far. I could feel that, as I got to know my blood family better, my sense of ancestry and lineage was slowly forming.

One highlight of this trip was washing myself under the huge waterfall in Kindia. I washed myself of the past so I could embrace the future more fully. I felt myself coming into me, slowly but surely coming into focus. I requested a dream to speak to—actually have a dialogue with—my ancestors, so I might draw on their wisdom and perspective.

I felt myself healing, then breaking a bit, then healing again. Things moved more into proportion in terms of how my emotional energy was used.

As I read *Of Water and the Spirit*, I found it ironic to be reading about the author's relationship to a tree since I had recently undertaken such a relationship myself. I performed a ritual where I buried some objects in the soil at the base of the tree in Mamady's compound; I did it late at night because it was important that no one see this ritual; it is a secret only the tree and I share. The same chapter was about Malidoma's return to being a bush person, and I felt the parallel strongly. I felt and believed I was on the path to clarity, wholeness, and true humanity.

Each night I slept with the rose quartz. It gave great comfort to me and my healing heart; it became part of my altar at home. I felt a gushing love and connectedness to all things that made me overwhelmingly happy and sad at once.

Olivia from La Reunion was acting strangely. I had heard she was often up late, keeping her three roommates awake. One morning, I learned she had been up pretty much all night. She'd had some kind of mental breakdown scene in the front courtyard which also kept up folks in some other rooms. I don't know exactly what happened, but Olivia and her roommates were not in class that day.

The latest word on Olivia's condition was that she was suffering from some kind of manic depression or other mania. Perhaps it was related to a pre-existing condition. She was not on Lariam. It turns out no one in her family knew she was in Guinea. She was sedated and would go home a week early.

While having a conversation with my good friend Johnba, I spied an unusual-looking creature. When I got closer, I saw it was a gecko, lightly colored with spots. I thought something didn't look quite right about it. A moment later, I turned my head and it disappeared. In searching for it, I found its broken-off tail, still twitching nervously. I don't know how it broke off, but that explained what was off about it. Fascinated, I brought it to the others to see. When some of the African children saw what I had, they warned me to wash my hands because they would swell up from touching part of this lizard. I decided to take their word for it, although I had my doubts. A few minutes later, in one of the outdoor lavatories, I saw another of the same kind of gecko—a possibly poisonous lizard. Then while looking for a candle in my room, I hit my knee very hard on the bed. I take all of these incidents as signs to me of a regression to old habits threatening. Signs heeded.

More tests involved a young Fula woman named Rugie. While at Mamady's, Amon and I mentioned to a small group of the folks at the workshop about our imminent trip to Roume. Most in the group were not into the idea and some were on the

2002 at Mamady's compound with Amon. Photo taken by Peter Schaupp.

fence. Rugie, who was not in the group I was addressing, said yes; she is the sister of one of the cooks and had been flirting with a few of the males at the camp, myself included. Doing the math on this unexpected development, I came to conclusions that were undesirable on many levels. So Amon and I left earlier than we said we would to eliminate this unwanted and unexpected guest. Getting a boat was fairly nightmarish; we eventually would hitch a ride with a Lebanese family. After arriving on Roume, our first order of business was arranging for dinner at the Susu village on the island. At the village, we discovered a funeral was taking place. This meant every fish that would otherwise be available for consumption was not.

Alternatives were limited to canned corned beef. Let me say again—canned corned beef. So Amon and I sat on Roume, the island paradise in the Atlantic, off the coast of Guinea, West Africa, eating canned corned beef on a baguette and listening to a Liberian radio station play British Metallica-ripoff music—what a scene.

After our meal, we headed back down the path to the beach. There is no light on this island, no electricity, and the night sky was lightless. On the path, we serendipitously bumped into none other than Rugie and a friend of hers.

The plot thickens.

So now we went to the beach with two unwanted visitors. As we walked up on the beach (on the rough wave side), crabs were everywhere—totally cool!

We made a fire and sang songs because we didn't know what else to do. We didn't speak Fula, and they didn't speak English. Soon after, some friends of friends showed up and saved the day by diluting the social situation to a very acceptable level. We took a dip (skinny) in the ocean with our new friends and had a great time.

Bedtime was when unbalancing and rebalancing needed to occur. Rugie, in broken English, confessed her "love" for me and wanted to seal the deal. This was so far from reality for me that it was only an issue of making reality—*my* reality—the most important thing. My reality was I would not let this situation reach critical mass or even come close. I felt a bit sad for her, because if she had met me at a different moment in my life, things would have gone her way, but my dominant feeling was happiness and peace for myself. I was happy because I was not stressed about the situation; I was clear about what I wanted with myself. No problem; no stress. I felt this was a kind of final exam for me before my return, and I'm very happy to say I passed. Here's to listening.

The next day, Amon and I awoke at sunrise, took a brief swim, and prepped for an island hike. Rugie was down for the first part of the hike; then we dropped her off in the Susu village and continued on. The second half was the real hike. Roume's interior was nicely dangerous and beautiful. The tide pools were always a surprise, teeming with beautiful aquatic life.

The hike around the island left us tired and sated. Being in nature recharges the batteries of the deepest self, but sometimes rest is part of being reborn. We had enough energy to arrange to get a boat back to the mainland and a magbana ride later. Then we were back at the compound for a well-earned evening of rest.

The lessons of the drumming experience are all encompassing. In the *Tao Te Ching*, detachment is big, and via dununba, a deceptively complicated family of rhythms, I was seeing yet another example of the harmony of detachment. To truly understand these rhythms, one must be able to detach from any particular part of the music and witness it as a whole. I'd say this is true for all djembe rhythms, but dununba rhythms come with a much higher level of understanding, awareness, and detachment.

Drumming is my *Tao Te Ching* in a way. As I understand what it is to understand the process of understanding dununba, this too glows with the Tao. I was myself with these things, having faith that I was *integrating* them. *Demystification and integration.* This was my current current. Odd the similarity to mastication and insalivation (i.e., chewing) since it is also a form of integration.

The recital at the end of the workshops went off extraordinarily. Amon and I hit a tasty arrangement perfectly. The entire workshop group celebrated last night after we performed and enjoyed an exceptional performance by Ballet Djoliba. We celebrated several things: my thirty-fifth birthday, the end of the workshop, and the evening's performance. We drank mango and pineapple-laced rum and bissap (hibiscus) and enjoyed our time together until very late in the evening.

There has been a death in my family—the family of me. I feel no need for celebration; the calm feeling is my celebration. Integration is next. This does not sound daunting to me because I know my barometer is stress and my teacher is degree-of-suffering.

Demystification. Integration. Manifestation.

By the end of this, my fourth trip to Guinea, I finished reading *Of Water and the Spirit*. As with *The Hero With a Thousand Faces* in 2001, it felt like I had read this book at exactly the right time in my life.

On my birthday, I dreamed I was dead. I was dead and only a few people could hear me speak, among them Amon. The dream felt very, very real. So much so that I remember worrying if it was a dream. Then one of the fans in our room let out an earth-shattering clatter, bringing me back to reality in fight-or-flight mode.

So my 2002 Guinea trip was over. As the Tao taught me how cleverness is a form of manipulation, we came in for a landing at Paris' Charles-de-Gaulle Airport, 2,900 miles from Conakry.

Sitting on the tarmac, we awaited the motion that would take us over the ocean. The flight was very empty, so we had a good space to expand physically and mentally. I was definitely wired.

As I read the words of Lau Tsu and looked at the stratification of clouds, the ripples on the ocean, and the shadow cast by the clouds on the water, I realized again that true beauty and majesty are taught by example via nature. Nature is always showing us the look, feel, smell, sight, and sounds of harmony. The clouds look like mountains, a close up of skin in black and white, continuous white water, cauliflower, and clouds.

I finished my first reading of Lao Tsu's *Tao Te Ching* and felt lighter. I felt the obviousness of the search for simplicity and calmness, serenity. When things get complicated, this is a sign—a beacon that things are clouding over, becoming less clear and need to be recleared.

Ignorance is blissful because it reminds us again and again how much more we have to look forward to. I can't help but smile as I think of that. If you don't understand what you have, you can't understand the potential implications of losing it. This is good sometimes; sometimes not.

As we descended over Lake Michigan, I reminded myself to reflect on this experience that was Africa 2002 so I could go forward as the person I was now, as the result of the experience, and not as the person I was prior to this journey.

John FS Williams; so glad he's part of my tribe!

I felt like I was running from brilliance. Why? Because perhaps on some level I still didn't think I deserved it. I knew that I did this, knowing, believing in it—it was my programming.

Back at home, after lunch with my good friend and counselor, the sage John FS Williams, I walked away with a few gems:

> "People risk their lives for stuff they want and hurt themselves by depriving themselves of what they need."
>
> — John FS Williams

"When you bury your emotions, you bury them alive."

— Mary Jane Yule via John FS Williams

"Build it and they will come."

— *Field of Dreams*

"Seek the feeling."

— John FS Williams

"Learn about my six-year-old self from observing actual six-year-olds."

— John FS Williams

"In the end, no one will sell you what you need."

— John FS Williams

I took a walk of several hours, during which time many things surfaced. "Most people fail when on the verge of success." "You can lead a horse to water, but you cannot make him drink." Well, I am *drinking*. When I said this aloud during my walk, my entire energy changed. I was in a place where I needed to remind myself of who and what I am. The person who came back to this country only a few months ago, who is he again? He is the one who exercises his inner strength.

INTEGRATION

I turned on the TV at the exact time the movie *Little Buddha* was beginning—my first taste of Siddhartha. It gave me a lot of good reminders of where I am on my path to source. I remembered something I heard while walking in a crowd some time earlier this year. A father was saying to his child, "Ya gotta get to where you are going; then you can do what you wanna do."

In *Ritual* by Malidoma Somé, I read that the journey to ourselves is a process of remembering. *Remembering. Re-membering.* Becoming a member again?

This year was the most transformative of my life (to date). What did I know now as the result of this year? How strong I actually am. How correctness brings peace. How adopting the counsel of the sage (vis-à-vis the I Ching) reminds us of what we really are. *We are all remembering.* I do love life; I am ever so blessed.

CHAPTER 7

FIRST CD; FIRST TEACHERS

"Learning is finding out what you already know. Doing is demonstrating that you know it. Teaching is reminding others that they know just as well as you.

You are all learners, doers, teachers."

— Richard Bach

I started playing djembe in March 1994. Six months later, I was in the recording studio with one of my life-long best friends, Chris Pawola. When we were in high school, we'd talk about how when we were able to have a recording studio, we would do whatever we wanted in it! Well, his path took him to music composition and performance degrees from Northern Illinois University, then to he and I playing in his basement studio. We let the tape run as we traveled the rhythmic environments. You'd never know from listening to it that it was recorded on analog 4-track, but it was. We did as much as we could with what

Left Chris Pawola, right me and our family of instruments on our first CD A Touch of Chaos in the Rhythmic Soup c.1995.

we had, and we did a lot. With one tune, we accidentally recorded several tracks at the wrong speed. When it was at normal speed, it sounded like drum-chipmunk music, but it was all tight and good. So on our overdubs, we played in time to it in real time. Problem? There is no problem, only an interpretation of things. We learned so much during the recording process, which took more than a year because Chris lived about an hour away from me and we were both working full time. When all was said and done, the distillation of more than 300 minutes of tape would give rise to *A Touch of Chaos in the Rhythmic Soup*. It is a pretty rare thing to be proud of your early work, and I'm glad I can still be proud of this one.

Soon after, in August 1995, I met Michael Markus at the 2nd Annual Midwest Drum and Dance Fest at Oakwood Farm, Selma, Indiana, a fest where I would go on to teach with Michael ten-plus years after my first year as a participant. He was my first djembe teacher. Hearing Michael's sound was disarming, inspirational, and amazing. I had never before heard such a sound and virtuosity—*language*—coming from a djembe. Michael and I stayed in touch, and John Yost and I brought him to Chicago to teach djembe workshops. Michael and his teacher M'Bemba Bangoura, a master drummer from Guinea, West Africa, had been doing organized djembe/dunun/dance study trips to Guinea. In 1997, I went to their camp for the first of six month-long trips over ten years in Guinea. Michael once taught a class without speaking at all! This required students to listen on all levels, especially non-verbal. The experience was so very village, without the slap on the head when you didn't get the part!

He was way ahead of the curve when it came to playing and teaching djembe. Having graduated with a Bachelor of Fine Arts in percussion with an emphasis on conga from Ithaca College, his conga teacher was also his kung fu teacher. When he met djembe, he was in an ideal learning space. To get free classes, he used to sweep the floors at the famous Fareta School in New York City where such djembe luminaries as Papa Ladji Camara taught. He would practice dunun parts with the broom as he swept. He is, without a doubt, one of my most influential teachers. He would go on to establish the Magbana Drum and Dance Ensemble. In 2005, he founded the company Wula Drum, which is debatably the biggest and best djembe maker and importer in the world.

I would later reflect on what great preparation I received by studying with Michael—especially that non-speaking class because later when I was in class with African Master drummers who spoke only their indigenous language (sometimes there was no translator), I was ready.

It was 1996/97, and around this time, I was being asked to teach. Folks who would hear me play would ask me to teach them. I offered to show them what I was doing, but I was reluctant to say I was teaching since what I was doing was improvised—just part of the flow. After going to a djembe workshop with Paolo Mattioli (he produced the very first djembe instructional VHS tape) at Guitar Center in Chicago, the drum shop manager, Felix, told me I could do a workshop there. I replied, "You'd let me do that?" Then it was on. Close to 100 folks came to the workshop. Among them was Jeff Bodony, master instrument maker from Washington state. He knew Morikeba Kouyate, a Jali (the caste of oral historians and advisors to kings), and master of the 21-24 stringed African harp called the kora. He was part of an 800-year-old Jali lineage. Morikeba had come to Chicago as part of the Senegalese performing ensemble (commonly called "ballet"), "Les Ballets de Silimbo du Sénégal." After the workshop, Jeff asked me if I was looking for an African djembe teacher. My response was that it was a great idea! To that point, I had not realized that Africans were teaching this art form—and in Chicago. So, I got one phone number and two names: Morikeba Kouyate and Yaya Kabo.

When Morikeba answered the phone, I told him I had gotten his number from Jeff Bodony—he was pleased. I asked him if he taught djembe. He replied in an accent steeped in the many languages he

One of my many workshops at Guitar Center in Chicago (at the time located near Clark and Belmont) c. 1997.

speaks, "No, I don't'a' teach'a djembe; I play kora." So I asked him if Yaya Kabo taught djembe, and he said he did. So I set up a private lesson with Yaya. Yaya, Morikeba, Idy Ciss (dancer) and many other Senegalese had come over to the USA in 1991 on a performance tour with the Ballet du Silimbo du Senegal. When they arrived at the Chicago airport, no one was there to meet them, despite what the contract said. It was the dead of winter in Chicago, but they arrived dressed in clothes suitable for the sunny heat of Western Senegal. Yaya led a group revolt that resulted in them defecting. Well, somehow, a few years later, they ended up at 6950 S. May St. in Chicago, which became known as "Africa House" for many years. By the time I arrived for my first lesson, I had heard that Yaya was planning to put together a drum and dance ensemble; I wanted to be part of it.

Jali and Kora Master and my dear friend/family Morikeba Kouyate.

When I went to my first lesson, Yaya answered the door wearing a brown turtleneck shirt with some of the stitching undone, having just woken from a nap. We headed downstairs to a basement where there were "rooms" divided off by hanging sheets on criss-crossing clotheslines. When we sat down, he taught me a traditional djembe rhythm called Yankadi. When he played, his sound was amazing! So clear, so pure. The lesson was going well. This was the first time I had learned from an African djembe teacher. When he took a short break to go upstairs, I blasted into a djembe flow that I hoped would impress him. After all, when playing accompaniment in traditional djembe rhythms, you can only show a small bit of your potential! He came back downstairs, gave me a look, and we continued on with the lesson. I am pleased to say that at the end of that first lesson, he asked me to play in his new ensemble.

As the lessons continued, Yaya would take me around with him to his various dance classes and gigs. We never rehearsed once, and we played hundreds of dance classes and gigs together. Part of learning from Yaya was keeping an open and agile mind. I loved it—we weren't in Africa, but I was learning in a very, very African style. The first dance classes we played were at the South Shore Cultural Center in 1995 for Kimosha Murphy, a former principal dancer with the famous Muntu Dance Theater, the founder of ALYO Children's Dance Theater, and an overall awesome human. Like many places where I would show up, the question "Who's the pale face with Yaya?" would burble up. Years later, I heard from my friends in the African American drum and dance community in Chicago that many, many people who are my friends now wondered back then, "Who does this white boy think he is?" In my time with Yaya, the prejudice directed at me was largely lost in my blissful ignorance of it and my blissful

Yaya Kabo and me c. 1997 from a recording session at WTTW, Chicago studios.

drumming with Yaya. Frequently, it would be just me and him playing for dance class. Playing dununs with Yaya was like trying to be a very strong, but flexible tree in a bizarre rhythmic storm, winds changing unexpectedly and drastically. Yaya was always dead-on with his musical timing, but his version of being "on time" challenged other players to be stronger. Being in that space with him alone was a path that was perfect for my development. Sometimes he would make me play djembe; he would grab the dunun sticks out of my hands, thrust his djembe in front of me, and make me give breaks (musical signals to start, stop, and change) for the dancers and play accompaniment and solo—a tall order! Here I learned about the dancers' wrath if the drummer doesn't deliver on what they are there to do. They are there to serve the dancer. Getting the stink-eye from the dance teacher is serious medicine for a drummer—or should be. You learn that you do not want the stink-eye; it's the dance teacher's house, and you are there to give them what they need in the music to do what they are there to do.

This particular lesson really hit home about how djembe is an instrument of service. Whenever you play djembe, it should be of service. Of service to a dancer, other drummers, to the ritual, for the farmers, for women, for other folks who have no choice but to hear you because you live in an apartment, etc. To intentionally serve the moment you are in is a very good thing. One main ingredient of service is the awareness of what is necessary, which begins with awareness of your surroundings.

No substitute exists for what you get from drumming for a dance class as a drummer. Here is where you get your power and stamina, hone your chops, and really get inside the music. Music is never separate from movement—or shouldn't be! Playing the same simple part at light speed for an indeterminate period of time is a humbling thing. The unfathomable amount of repetition where the music disappears and melds into a singularity is like being in a trance. It is a great, humbling thing. No drum class can get you what dance classes get you. I am so humbled to call Yaya Kabo, Morikeba Kouyate, and Idy Ciss my family—the first of my extended African family.

I vividly remember the first time I touched Yaya's djembe without asking. After seeing me do this, he calmly said to me, "I'm sorry." I was immediately very confused, but this kind of confusion between him and me wasn't entirely without precedent. So I asked him what he meant. He told me he had a curse put on his djembe by the person who had made it in Senegal. The curse was: "If you touch Yaya's djembe without asking, there will be a curse on you." He was apologizing because he doesn't know how to take the curse away. Two things came from this experience: I never again touched his, or anyone's, djembe without asking first, and I use this same story when folks touch my djembe without asking.

From 1994 until 2000, I worked several information technology jobs for several companies—Transamerica Commercial Finance Corporation, Comdisco, Wheels Inc., and Gateway computers. I learned a lot about how businesses work and how to get things done in organizations, i.e. facilitating good outcomes with people. I went from being on a help desk to being a computer trainer to being an independent consultant. I learned a couple of very important things in my time in IT that stay with me to this day. One is how to get people to do what you need or want them to do. Important in this understanding is how best to come to a win-win and to seek first to understand, then be understood (Habits 4 and 5 respectively from Stephen Covey's *The Seven Habits of Highly Effective People*). The second important thing I carry with me from my IT days is this sequence of how to change situations:

1. Current state analysis—where are things right now?
2. Future state analysis—where do you want to be?
3. Gap analysis—how to get from 1 to 2.

In 2000, I quit my day job in IT to do djembe full time.

Six months later, my marriage ended. I was barely making enough money to pay the mortgage and eat. Then I got a call from Jeff Amon, who was looking to learn traditional djembe. Amon was already a drummer, but he really hadn't tapped into the root of traditional djembe. We met and it was on. I had a very talented padawan, in *Star Wars* lingo. Soon I convinced Amon to move into my house. This really saved my ass. Rent-wise, it was a lateral move for him, and now we could train and study all the time. Amon was a great chapter in my life. We needed each other to get to the next level, and we did it and remained family. After two years, Amon moved out and I supported my home alone and still do.

I met Kurt Hill at the 2001 Drum, Dance, Trance Weekend at the Nuti Farm in Sawyer, Michigan. This was an event dreamed up by Elizabeth Nuti (who also hand-drew my Holygoat logo, did the artwork for two of my CDs, and always has a special place in my heart) and me. The trance part of the evening was facilitated by Kurt. Kurt is a vibrational and energy healer, medical intuitive, spiritual counselor, modernity's version of a thaumaturge, and what I would consider a modern-day shaman. After the trance experience at the Nuti Farm, he and I knew we needed to continue working together somehow. He wouldn't let me drum in his workshops with his own patients and students until he was good and sure I was "clean" as he said it, so we had many sessions together, exfoliating my mental, physical, and spiritual selves. Eventually, I drummed for his Advanced Psychosomatic Character Therapy students, which was an otherworldly experience.

Journal Entries: 2003—
San Diego, Chicago, and Ireland

The year 2003 began with an unbelievable number of reunions between me and numerous friends. It was a truly amazing union of folks from my childhood, PD (pre-drumming) years, and DD (during-drumming) years. All eras represented. This journey of reunions began when I was attending a professional-level workshop taught by Mamady Keïta in San Diego. It turned into a trip down memory lane with many worlds beautifully colliding. Numerous *I Ching* readings guided my path; I finished Malidoma Somé's book *Ritual* on this trip. I felt like I was in training. As I write this in 2020, I'm guided to reflect on why I need to remember these details now. Did the ancestors set the trajectory of that experience and this revisitation for some self-evolutionary purpose? I have a healthy and reverential distrust of the now because the now will change. Whatever *now* appears to be may just be a ruse, and it will change when it changes.

> "You will give yourself peace of mind if you perform every act of your life as if it were your last."
>
> — Marcus Aurelius

A week after the incredible San Diego journey, I hosted Mamady in Chicago. After successful workshops, it was a lovely birthday weekend for me. I could feel shifts afoot. My wise friend Kurt Hill said I was going through an initiation. This reminded me of something Malidoma Somé says about initiation: that initiation can take place outside of the normal idea of initiation. Experiences, if they contain elements of what can make an experience an initiation, can be initiatory. Could it also be said that any experience you are able to witness and learn from is kind of that way?

Obviously, some experiences are a lot more intense, and I think they're important, but the smaller ones are also important. In fact, I'm thinking my own life has shown me that if I have an extremely intense experience, it's likely because I wasn't paying close enough attention and missed many preceding less intense signs.

Me with Leddie Garcia in "Batterie" c. 2003.

What experiences from your own life would you think of as "initiatory"? Experiences that shifted you from the person you are to the next person you were to be because you were brave and aware enough to take the committed step? Maybe you're already totally dialed in to trying to understand the messages in adversity and suffering; for me, it took a long minute to get up on the surfboard of trying to listen to and look for messages/guidance in everyday life. "What am I supposed to learn from this situation?" can be a difficult question to ponder if the answer to that question is sometimes hundreds of years and many lifetimes in the making. The more I learn, the more I appreciate how little I know, and the more I appreciate how elusive knowledge is. I get the lesson because I ask for it. (Be careful what you ask for.) This place of truth was still very new to me, but as familiar as the most ancient of things.

This year, I hosted the great master drummer from Mali/Côte d'Ivoire Madou Dembele in Chicago for a month. He lived with me while teaching in the Chicago area; my house was very much an African village during this time! I was invited to join a small trio that Leddie Garcia put together called "Batterie"—percussion, percussion, and DJ. I traveled to the University of Northern Iowa for a residency related to the Percussive Arts Society—thank you Professor Randy Hogencamp for that one! My CD of music for yoga and meditation, *Silence in the Rhythmic Soup*, got completed, as was my first instructional DVD, *Remembering How to Drum*. I staged my performance art piece, *The Jungle*, for the second time at the Old Town School of Folk Music in Chicago—fifteen performers were involved this time. I met more of the Day side (the biological-paternal side) of my family and got the first pedicure in my life. I was also hired to be the djembe player for a very forward-thinking choir director, Paul Caldwell.

Silence in the Rhythmic Soup *(music for Yoga and Meditation)*, my third CD. Original artwork by E. Nuti; manipulation of original artwork by P. Vojtik.

Paul came into my life because Jubilate Children's Choir in the suburbs north of Chicago was searching nationally for a new musical director and found him. He had had some experience with the West African djembe drum and wanted a djembe player for the choir. He tried one person's djembe class, seeing if they would be a good fit; they were not. Next, he reached out to me. I thought it would be great, so I agreed to do a gig with them. I received a three-ring binder with sheet music and a CD with audio. I met him at our first gig together with the choir—he must have had a good feeling about me, doing our first gig together without rehearsing! From there on, we had many moments of magic, and I'm forever thankful for the experiences I had performing with Paul and Jubilate.

Me with the Jubilate Children's Choir, Director, Paul Caldwell c. 2008.

My first trip to Europe—Ireland specifically—happened in 2003 on a performance tour with the incredible Jubilate Children's choir, under Paul's direction. I was one of two musicians (the other a pianist, Mark Thomas) on the tour across the middle of the country, east to west, performing a work entitled *Adiemus*. It was a great challenge for me to provide such an intricate percussive environment, replicating as much as I could from the original recordings/score by myself. I was also tasked with being a chaperone of six youth in the choir; we named our group "The Goats." The book I brought along to read was *Heart of Darkness* by Joseph Conrad (the movie *Apocalypse Now* is loosely based on it). We were in two large buses—performers in one bus and parents/family in the other. At one point, one of the kids puked on the bus. It became known as the "puke bus" and was relegated to the parents. Even with deep cleaning, that smell was never extinguished.

On our off times, we drummed and played guitar together. It was a beautiful thing. Paul said when he saw it, he almost cried. At one point, I had rich, sometimes heated discussions with several folks about my view that Western notation is not music—it's a representation of music. How does one (or one culture for that matter) express the essence of a thing? We can only use the tools at our disposal, which don't exist in the same place as essence/(Platonic) form. Expressing essence. Expressions of essence. Breathing life into expression to animate it, giving life to the essential—bringing essence forward. Should not the mode of expression have as its goal to channel whatever essence as purely as possible?

Our tour guide explained all the places we passed, rehearsed in, and/or performed at. We were regularly in places that dated back to the twelfth century, equivalent to the time of the Malian Empire in West Africa and about the time the djembe was being born. We learned about things like Trim Castle (Caisléan Bhaile Atha Troim in Gaelic), where *Braveheart* was filmed, Clonmacnoise, the crossroads of Ireland, and unsavory truths about the actual Blarney Stone (and why you should dispense with all ideas related to kissing it). Our last performance was for World Refugee Day in Limerick. I am thankful I brought my journal and *I Ching* on the trip for regular check-ins.

The following Africanesque folktale is the third in the trilogy. It is about one's relationship to a wider context of plurality.

Africanesque Folktale—Plurality: The Story of Moribayassa—Mamady and Kadia

Once there was a girl named Kadia; she lived in a small village in Upper Guinea, West Africa called Balandugu Djomawagna. One day in August 1950, it was a day that seemed like any other day. The Tubaninlu Könölu kukoo'd (a type of bird) and the rhythm of the kolon kokalan, the mortar and pestle used to prepare foodstuffs, colored the morning air. But this was the day when one of the greatest djembe masters the world would ever know would be born. This would be Balandugu's first meeting with Kadia's last-born brother, Mamady Keïta. Kurunin, where the three spirits that protect Balandugu live, had already known Mamady, for it is from the spirit world that new babies arrive into this/manifest reality. The spirits at Kurunin saw in Mamady the spirit of the great Malinké King Sundjata Keïta, the king of kings, Mansa Baa ("big king" translated from Malinké), from the original Malian Empire circa the twelfth century. But instead of defending the culture of the Malian Empire with a bow, spear, and sword, Mamady would use other means to defend his culture.

Moribayassa, AY, Moribayassa Afo
Moribayassa AY, Moribayassa Yzo So Ya Sa

Everyone noticed that Mamady cried incredibly hard at birth. The village fetisher (the caste of people who deal in the paranormal in Mande culture) told the parents not to worry—this child had a great future ahead of him. Furthermore, the fetisher prophesied:

"This child will be known not only to his village, but all surrounding villages; he will be known in all of his country; his name will be known all over the continent of Africa; the entire world will know his greatness...but his parents will not taste the fruit of his fame."

Moribayassa, AY, Moribayassa Afo
Moribayassa AY, Moribayassa Yo So Ya Sa

Mamady began drumming on pots and pans as soon as he could pick up a wooden spoon. His mother said, "This boy will be a great djembeföla." The djembeföla's job is to accompany the work, rituals, and celebrations that would happen in the village; the djembeföla's job is to make the djembe speak. Soon, around age five, Mamady was taken to the village djembeföla, Karinkadjan Conde, to be initiated into the seven secrets of the djembe. Because Mamady was such a naturally gifted drummer, he was given the nickname "Nankama" ("born for it" in Malinké).

Mamady and Karinkadjan would drum for the tilling of the soil, for the planting of the seeds, for the naming ceremonies and initiations. They would play for the full moon, for important people, masks, fetishers, and, of course, for celebration.

Moribayassa, AY, Moribayassa Afo
Moribayassa AY, Moribayassa Yo So Ya Sa

One day, Kadia was called out to the fields to help with harvesting. When she returned to the village, she went looking for Mamady to help her bring water from the well. Mamady was nowhere to be found. As Kadia looked around, she noticed the feeling in the village had become distressed; she saw many worried, confused expressions on many faces! Soon she heard her brother, Mamady, was no longer there. Some people from the government had shown up in an army Jeep, asked for Mamady, then he was gone.

This was a day Kadia would never forget. She wondered aloud, frightened and astonished, "Why would they take Mamady away? Why would they take my little brother away!" She wondered if she'd ever see him again.

The year was 1964 and the government of Guinea, West Africa, was putting together a national performance ensemble as part of celebrating its independence from French colonization six years earlier, in 1958. They wanted to put together a group of the most gifted traditional artists—the best dancers, best djeli (the caste of oral historians), best koredjuga (the caste of comedians), best stilt-walkers, best actors, best writers, and, of course, best drummers in all the land. As the government searched for the best and brightest, the name Mamady Keïta was heard.

Mamady had become so well known as a great drummer in his region that, at age thirteen, he was taken from his village by the government to be in the national performing ensemble, the Ballet Djoliba, so named after the mighty Niger River. This was at once a great honor, a blessing, and a great curse. Because of his amazing talent, Mamady entered the national limelight, but it also meant he was taken away from his village, the only place with the only people and family he had ever known.

Days passed, then weeks, then seasons, then years. During this time, Mamady toured the world, earning a reputation as the greatest African drummer the world had ever seen.

But back at home in the village, Kadia would pray each day at Kurunin, to the protective and wise spirits, that her little brother would return. So many years passed—more than ten, then fifteen, then twenty! Eventually, Kadia took the vow to dance Moribayassa if her prayers for her brother to return were granted. The vow to dance Moribayassa is very serious, and it can only be taken once in the life of a woman in Malinké villages. In this dance only done by women, one wears clothes and shoes that are not their own. The dance is chaotic, without form. Frequently, objects are knocked down as the woman circles the village five to seven times. Folks pick up after her because everyone knows what she is doing and why. After the dance, she changes back into her normal clothes and buries the old clothes under a particular mango tree. In Mamady's village, Balandugu Djomawagna, one mango tree is named the Moribayassa Tree because of all the Moribayassa dances it had seen over many centuries. Kadia vowed, additionally, that she would wash Mamady's feet, the feet that had carried Mamady away so long ago, and drink the water upon his return.

Twenty-five long years passed. Over the years, rumors came to Balandugu of Mamady's visits to places far and wide, outside of Guinea, outside of Africa. Rumor said he had won the "Best Drummer in Africa" award at the age of nineteen in a place called Algeria, that he had taught people with different colored skin than his, that he had performed for kings and presidents of foreign lands, and so many other incredible stories.

Children became adults, then parents; Mamady's parents passed, as did his oldest brother, Nankaba, so named for the founder of the village, Nankababa, who established Balandugu Djomawanya during the time of the great Malinké King Sundjata Keïta in the twelfth century.

The year was now 1990, and on a particularly hot day, Kadia felt an unusual feeling—a familiar feeling from long ago—one she could not explain, but one that felt like a distant dream or memory.

On the horizon, Kadia heard an unusual roar coming from across the savannah; it wasn't quite a lion; it wasn't quite a hippopotamus; it wasn't quite a buffalo. As the sound became louder, the entire village began to take notice, all gathering together under the protection of the mighty dubalen tree, the tree under which all the important events in the village happened, the tree that was witness to Mamady's earliest days drumming. In the distance, Kadia could see a dust cloud moving toward the village like a herd of wild beasts! As it got closer, she could make out the image of something with round feet and no legs, moving very fast! *How can this be? How can this creature move so fast with round feet and no legs!* she thought. *What is this strange creature and what does it want? Why is it coming to our small village?* As it slowed down, it's billowy dust tail closed in around it, eventually to reveal an old army Jeep, something the village had not seen or perhaps did not remember.

As it came to a stop and the dust cloud engulfing the Jeep began to fade, a gasp went through the entire village as a figure emerged as if passing from the spirit realm to the manifest.... The image of an adult Mamady came into view. As the village prophets had predicted, he had, in fact, become a master drummer whose reputation reached all corners of the earth, whose parents transitioned to the ancestral realm before they could bask in the glow of his fame.

Kadia's eyes grew wide and her heart danced with joy! Her prayers had finally been answered! Her little brother, Mamady, had returned! After she greeted her brother with tears in both of their eyes, Kadia rejoiced; the spirits at Kurunin rejoiced; Balandugu Djomawanya rejoiced; Mamady had returned.

Later, Kadia washed his feet and drank the water. Then she summoned the drummers and they provided her the rhythmic bed for her to ecstatically dance Moribayassa, fulfilling her vow, for her prayer for her brother to return was answered.

Moribayassa, AY, Moribayassa Afo
Moribayassa AY, Moribayassa Yo So Ya Sa

The End

CHAPTER 8
REMEMBERING HOW TO DRUM

"Healing comes when the individual remembers his or her identity—the purpose chosen in the world of ancestral wisdom—and reconnects with that world of spirit."

— Malidoma Somé

bout 2001, Jeremy Williams, a student in one of my classes at the Old Town School, started a small video production company, Blue7 Media. One day, he asked if I'd be interested in doing a DVD project. I could see in his eyes that he expected I would say yes. As I pondered what I could offer in this way, I thought, *Who would want to learn a rhythm from me on a DVD when they could do the same from Mamady Keïta?* Mamady had already produced instructional videos for djembe, so there was no way I was going to do something he had already done. I just didn't think it would offer anything that wasn't already being covered, and it could possibly infringe on Mamady's profits and my relationship with him. So, I said, "No thanks." After a short while, though,

I began thinking about my own path and its teachings. About how *djembe* was my first djembe teacher. About creating and traveling conscious and unconscious, improvised rhythmic environments; about how even when improvising, some things clearly made sense, while others did not. About what naturally came about, unencumbered by thought or knowledge. At that point, I had been teaching djembe for about five years. I think the process of learning djembe is a process of *un*doing, until djembe invites you in. When you begin letting go, she begins opening up.

I had read Pirsig's *Zen and the Art of Motorcycle Maintenance* a few times. One thing I had taken away from it was a deeper appreciation for "quality."

> "Art is anything you can do well;
> anything you can do with quality."
>
> — Robert M. Pirsig, *NPR* interview, July 12, 1974

Quality is what separates a djembe player from someone who plays on djembe, a violinist from someone who plays on violin, and a pianist from someone who plays on piano. Because djembe primarily entered the Western world through drum circles, first in the 1980s in Europe, then in the 1990s in the United States, it had a stigma attached to it as a layperson's instrument. The djembe's approachability and potential for instant gratification are both good and bad. Good because djembe is so awesome; bad because some folks get so much joy while scratching the surface that sometimes they bash unmusically, unwittingly creating noise. Many never dig deeper and really don't touch the experience's greater potential. Djembe didn't become widely popular as a traditional instrument with the whys and hows that come with most other respected musical instruments in many places in the United States until two djembe grand masters came to teach classes. Grand Master Famoudou Konate did some teaching work in Germany in the 1980s, and shortly thereafter, Mamady began teaching in Belgium. Neither taught in the United States until the late 1990s. The first class I took from Mamady Keïta was in 1999. At that time, he said, "I've cleaned up my tradition in Europe. Now I'm here to clean it up in the US!"

Something I have learned from writing technical instructions as an IT person is you need to consider what folks are *inclined* to do, regardless of what you *intend* them to do, if you want them to do what you intend! Have someone try out your instructions and they will demonstrate if you've been successful. I've learned never to take a wordy explanation over a demonstration. As I learned from my communications major in college, communication is a receiver phenomenon. No matter what we intended to communicate, no matter how well we think we crafted our communication, whatever was *received* is what was communicated.

Bob Steinman, my philosophy teacher, used to tell us when we were discussing complicated philosophical ideas: "You think you understand? Explain it to your mother." By saying this, the level of knowing, of explanation he proposed was much deeper than I had ever considered before. Between Bob's anecdote and Pirsig's book, the idea that communication was a receiver phenomenon was constantly in my mind.

I realized I could do a whole DVD project and never cross over into Mamady's DVD world. In fact, my project could enhance the experience of someone studying traditional djembe. So, I proposed my idea to Jeremy and said I thought the title should be *Remembering How to Drum* because everyone has a heartbeat and I believe the heartbeat is our first drumming

Remembering How to Drum DVD, 2003.

experience; some just don't remember—*I* didn't remember until it was time for me to remember. We began filming soon after. I created the chapters from a lot of things I had observed while teaching djembe. Some of it involved stepping stones or exercises I felt would really serve in rhythms that would come later, if you continued studying traditional djembe. The entire DVD resulted from what was important on my path and what I saw as important to others' paths. Another of my students at the time, Derek Fredrickson (artist, musician, filmmaker), did the graphic design. He wanted to help me out because he found my project interesting. He would spend half of the year doing uninteresting things that paid well, then the other half of the year doing interesting stuff practically pro bono (I paid him in Belgian ale; good thing, because, not even knowing what he would have charged, I knew I couldn't have afforded him). I quickly learned how talented he is; he brought a truly astonishing beauty to my DVDs. Today, he has moved on to TV and major motion pictures. Derek also designed my website and is a great friend. Jeremy did the filming, authoring and sculpting how the DVD would function; Derek sculpted the look of the DVD. It was finished in 2003 and has since sold thousands of copies worldwide. It has been moved to a digital download as of the writing of this book. It's a path, a practice, so it will never go out of date.

Djembe is taught in the village with little or no explanation. Demonstrate, repeat, get it; don't get it, repeat. Then you eventually get it. As Stephen Covey says, "Begin with the end in mind" (Habit #2 of *The Seven Habits of Highly Effective People*). The traditional way of teaching djembe has yielded amazing results from folks who didn't know what they already knew. Teaching my students taught me that asking if someone can do something is not a good way to know if they can. Instead, it needs to be demonstrated. I also realized many folks didn't know they were doing what they intended to do.

> "They didn't have sufficient awareness of the thing they were doing to see what they were doing."
>
> — Taylor

After a student demonstrates something, I usually don't say that they did or didn't do it correctly because I want them to know the answer to that question for themselves. A typical question from me is: "Is that it? Did you show me what I showed you?" Then "Are you sure?" (It's important to ask this even when they are correct, or they'll always think they are not doing it when you ask; it's very important to have the confidence of knowing you know something.) Then I say, "Explain to me how you know. Where and how does your part connect with something else in the music?" If they can't explain, then we set about together to find linkages in the parts of the music.

Starting with little or no explanation when teaching djembe is not only very authentic in its delivery, but it serves as a current state analysis, and it doesn't assume students won't get it by visual, aural, or kinesthetic observation.

> "Don't make assumptions."
>
> — Agreement #3 in Don Miguel Ruiz'
> *The Four Agreements*

By teaching this way, I never start at zero with my students. They tell me what they need through how I see them observe—how they are sitting, their facial expression, posture, and their balance between what they think they are doing and what they actually are doing. Shouldn't being of service involve asking what someone or a situation needs? Without assumptions or presuppositions? I let my students tell me what they need from me, mainly via nonverbal communication; I'm looking for clues all the time. The dancer (or the dununs, if there is no dancer) tells me through their movement what they need from me as a soloist because I'm listening and looking for the communication.

I have removed the words "right" and "wrong" from my teaching vocabulary. As I see it, either you demonstrate or answer in a way that is what I am asking for *or* you do something that is different. The different thing is still a thing; it's just not the thing for this moment, in this situation, for this context. I'll usually say, "That's something different," or sometimes "That's not it" or, one of my favorites, "There is truth in that." I like the last one especially because I am always trying to honor correctness, even if there is correctness within something that is otherwise different. By not using right and wrong, I realized that almost every conversation I had was the same way—the words "right" and "wrong" were being misused. Those words do have a place, but not as often as I see/hear them being used. Their psychological impact is potentially significant, attaching to memories of being told you were wrong by a teacher or parent. On the other hand, it can be problematic when someone is seeking to be right instead of seeking to understand the truth in the context.

Journal Entries: 2005—The Big Tests

In 2005, I returned again to Guinea. This trip's readings were *Siddhartha* by Herman Hesse and *Journey to Ixtlan* by Carlos Casteneda. At sunrise, I saw a beautiful orange ribbon between blue-gray earth and sky as I arrived in Paris, more than halfway to Guinea.

This journey had its roots back in 2002 when I had told Mamady I wanted to do what it took to be the Director of Tam Tam Mandingue in Chicago. At the time, several folks had earned a Tam Tam Mandingue Teaching Certificate. After Mamady started TTM in Brussels, Belgium in 1992, he had more than 300 students a week for about fifteen years. He realized some folks from different places in the world could represent him and his school because of the time they spent learning from him. No set list of criteria was required to earn those early certificates. You'd hang with Mamady over years, sometimes for months at a time, and then he granted it to you when he felt you were ready, based on what he saw in class with you as a student as well as your comportment. A very important component was the type of person you were; he was trusting you to be a "messenger of tradition" and to represent him as well.

When I originally approached Mamady about receiving certification, my first question was "What do I do?" He really didn't have an answer; criteria had never been scripted; a specific test had never existed. He moved from Brussels to the United States in 2003. As time passed, I kept asking. Then one day in early 2004, I brought Mamady and Monette Marino to Chicago for workshops. They asked me to come to their hotel to talk about test criteria. When I arrived, they showed me the rough draft of what is now the criteria for the Tam Tam Mandingue Djembe Academy Instructor

Certificate. They asked me what I thought. Was it too much? Not enough? Any suggestions? I was very happy to be involved in the proofing of this template for certification in Mamady's international school of djembe.

On the first day of the camp in Conakry, Mamady announced he would be testing all potential TTM professors for the first time. He would also have these folks do the setups and warmups for daily classes, plus other duties. The phrase "be careful what you ask for" resonated with me. Clearly, this camp would be like no other. I recall the names he called out were Darryl "Sékou Soumah" Walker (Portland, Oregon), Menes Yehouda (Baltimore, Maryland), Bill Scheidt (Winston-Salem, North Carolina), Martin Klabunde (Tucson, Arizona), and me. I didn't know it would go down this way, but I did know about the criteria and I'd had a feeling he would start the testing at this camp. I got together with the other five and brought out a tattered, yellowed draft copy of the list of criteria that had not left my side since receiving it from Mamady the previous year. Everyone looked at the list, wide-eyed. Bill and Martin said they weren't ready at that moment. Menes, Sékou, and I gave it a shot.

I had no clock or watch this time; time was told by classes, meals, and malaria medication. This year I was pushed far beyond my physical, psychological, and spiritual limits. I wish my fleshy confines didn't need rest, but alas, they always do. So I tried sleeping in this place where I simply wanted to *be* fully.

I spent a lovely night on Roume. I had once held it sacred, and it had been so pristine that the sand would squeak under your feet, but now little businesses were on the far side of the island in a place named Konkoba; it seems modernization knows no boundary.

After spending a day on the beach at Roume with Mamady and everyone else, a bunch of us hung out on the rocks on the other side and chilled. We talked, played flute, and sang in anticipation of the dununba taking place that evening. Well, the dununba was no dununba—it was a wanky party with drummers that, suffice it to say, "'twasn't right." The ensemble was mediocre; the lead players were good, but they were not representing well, and therefore, misrepresenting. At one point, one drummer I knew asked me to play accompaniment. Why I agreed is another subject, but now I was part of the misrepresentation. I was in djembe jail! Goddammit, what a situation. After the rhythm ended, I left the stage abruptly and stood away from everyone. Eventually, I found my way to the water's edge where I had looked for crabs in years past. No crabs were anywhere. It began to sink in that the sacred experiences I'd had on Roume were a thing of the past. No crabs, no real dununba, no solitude—nothing that had made Roume a mystical experience for me existed anymore. Modernization, capitalization, etc. knows no limit. Roume had left the building.

This camp was the most intense I'd ever experienced. It was a rare thing to be there doing what we were doing. I didn't miss home much; I really enjoyed these study trips—drumming six hours a day, being pushed to my physical and skill limits. I was thankful to have my *I Ching* as my travel partner to consult for larger perspectives on things. Those of us being tested for the TTM professorship didn't know how it was going to look, but we suspected some measure of the test was happening every day for us.

It's hard to say whether or not I missed the Lariam-induced lucid dreams. It's a humbling thing when you can't tell the difference between dream and non-dream states. Every time I've been to Guinea, I get sick for a while; sometimes I know what made me sick, sometimes not. This year, I got something that had me on my back for twelve hours. It gave me an opportunity to tear through *Siddhartha*—an incredible book in language I could really dig. It didn't matter to me at all that I would nod off to sleep and wake up to begin at the same place over and over. The writing echoed that of J. Krishnamurti for me. Once this sickness was over, an old friend returned—a hemorrhoid that rarely flared up. So rarely that, in the very limited number of times it has expressed itself, I know why each and every time. It was always associated with very infrequent moments of life imbalance involving alcohol, dehydration, stress, a crappy diet, etc. If I kept those things in balance, this teacher would not show up—a very good motivation to keep things in balance. Perhaps I should give it a name? I thank my hemorrhoid for helping to keep me on the straight and narrow!

In this time and place, flow, and health (sprinkled with enough pain to keep me humble), I consulted my seeing-eye-higher-self, the Oracle, about my general state, seeking advice/guidance. In an I Ching (pronounced ee-jing) reading, one way to do it is to throw coins. Heads has a value of 3 and tails a value of 2. You throw six coins six times (double this if you get a value of 6 or 9) and the result gives you a hexagram that you reference on a table of hexagrams. Each hexagram has a number that gives advice/guidance in the form of a brief explanation followed by a more in-depth explanation. The translation of the I Ching that I use is the one by Brian Browne Walker. So this time my reading was (I included only the brief explanations):

Hexagram 57 - Sun - The Gentle (The Penetrating Wind)

"Consistent correctness turns every situation to your advantage."

Hexagram 52 - Kên - Keeping Still, Mountain

"Still your emotions through meditation."

Thank you.

I got sucked into *Journey to Ixtlan*. A passage about the eyes of a white falcon jogged my memory of a dream I'd had the night before about eyes. The dream was, at times, creepy, involving bloody eyeballs and very large tear ducts—remembering it still gives me chills. Castaneda's book turned into my other world in Guinea.

We were at Mamady's compound in Matoto when Conakry celebrated Tabaski, a major Islamic holiday. It celebrates the Prophet Abraham's willingness to sacrifice his son Ishmael at God's command, but then God provided a ram for the sacrifice instead. (In Christian and Jewish tradition, Isaac was the sacrificial victim; in Islamic tradition, it was Ishmael.) The celebration was marked by drums being played at full volume beginning around 4 a.m. The drummers paraded around the compound until we were all up, relatively speaking; then they gave us a short performance and left for the next house.

A few days later, I tested to be a Tam Tam Mandingue professor—something I'd been looking forward to for a very long time. The test was conducted thusly: In Mamady's presence, with Monette playing songban only, I performed all the "original solo" phrases for the twelve rhythms Mamady teaches that have said solos. Each rhythm has three to twelve technically challenging solo phrases. Additionally, you are required to know at least sixty rhythms from Mamady's repertoire, with full oral history. (If you knew a rhythm from another reputable master, you couldn't use it for the test. After receiving a TTMDA certification, you can teach rhythms from reputable masters/sources other than Mamady as a representative of TT-

MDA). Then, Mamady picks five random rhythms you must demonstrate fully—ethnic group, purpose, geography, all djembe and dunun parts. Well, the test was grueling—it probably took more than two hours. I performed almost every solo technique two or three times, with Mamady giving an excruciatingly detailed critique, which would have to be implemented on the fly. Eventually, I got through with demonstrating the twelve solo techniques. The five random rhythms out of the sixty you're required to know worried me because of the statistical probability that he would choose rhythms I was unfamiliar with. He is said to know more than 300 rhythms. If this happened, however, he would ask you to perform other rhythms until you demonstrated five. After I got three good ones, I had a stretch of almost ten rhythms I simply did not know—my fear realized. Eventually, I got the last two, but all the ones I did not know did not, by any means, go unnoticed. Mamady said he would consider all he saw and make a decision. So I sat, not knowing if I had passed or not. I was really crushed about how the test went, even offering to redo the second part.

Eventually, Mamady agreed to let me redo the second part on the last Saturday in camp, after our final recital. This meant I had a couple of weeks to prepare, so I did just that, tirelessly. I had a list of sixty-three rhythms I had prepared for the test; I had been living with this tattered and worn single page list, taking it wherever I'd go to study in moments between moments. Several times a day, every day, I would give it to my peers so they could quiz me. By the time test day arrived, I was prepared to the hilt. I wasn't interested in the statistical probability that Mamady would choose rhythms I didn't know like last time, and since the requirement was sixty rhythms, I went into the test with a proposition. I gave him my tattered list of rhythms, saying they were the sixty-plus rhythms I knew from his repertoire. I said if he chose a rhythm not on my list, I would definitely not be able to demonstrate it. It was a bold and reasonable request that he allowed. I executed each rhythm he asked with precision and confidence and passed the test. Three of us, Menes Yahudah, Derrell "Sékou Soumah" Walker, and I took the test. It was the first time this test had been given, and all of us passed (even though two of us had to take parts of it twice), all certified by none other than Grand Master Mamady Keïta himself. This test pushed me to a point of growth and clarity I had never felt before; it was as if I were seeing the matrix, able to see the music in a multidimensional way. I may be among the least qualified to make such an assessment, but I think it was the most I've ever grown in one circumstance as a musician—perhaps as a person. It was one of the greatest moments of my life.

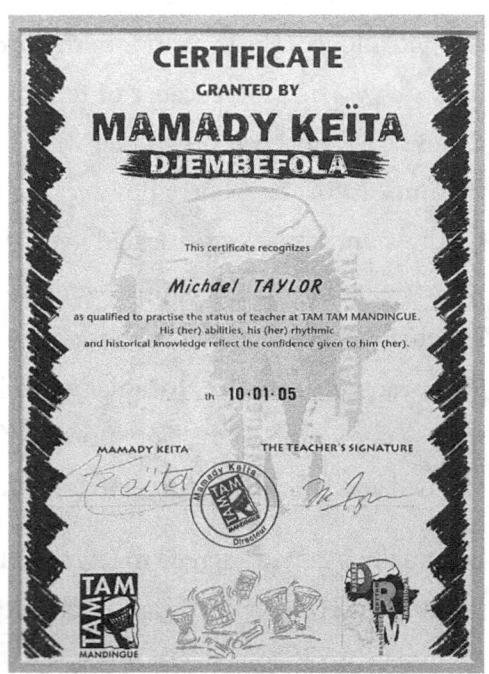

My Tam Tam Mandingue Certificate, 2005, granted by none other that Grand Master Mamady Keita himself.

As with so many books I have read on my various pilgrimages to Guinea, *Journey to Ixtlan* hugely illuminated my own journey of never returning as the same person and, therefore, never returning to the same place. I love and hate my trips to Guinea, partly because a part of me always dies there, but also because it is an unwavering source of rebirth.

I couldn't tell whether I was reconstituting or de-constituting on the plane ride home. Thankfully, I had enough hours to get deep into whatever it was. I took time to ponder the nothingness, the silence, for a while, and to reacquaint myself with myself. At times, I felt like my head was made of clay.

Getting back to the United States was quite a ride. The first week I was back, I would wake up spontaneously at 4:30, 5:30, or 6:30 a.m. Then, on my birthday, I got what I believed to be a new strain of flu. My party the next day was fab-o! An interesting marriage of old and new friends and family.

Once home, I began my nurturing rituals again—I had fallen off almost all of them. I also shot another DVD—this one with Mahiri and Menes. We told Mamady about the project to get his blessing and asked him to name it. He suggested a name based on what they would say during rehearsals when he was with the Ballet Djoliba *"Akaran Iko Iko (Learn Again, Again)."*

Akaran Iko Iko (Learn Again, Again), my second DVD project, this time conceived by me and Mahiri Fadjimba Keita-Edwards

> "Akaran Iko Iko is very good, very easy to understand, the pedagogy is very good and at the same time will make you laugh. My advice is that every student should have this video in their library."
>
> — Grand Master Drummer Mamady Keïta

The 12th Annual Midwest Drum and Dance Fest happened. I met with Mamady and the crew two more times for workshops on the East and West Coast, and I finished reading the DT Niane translation of the book *Sundjata, an Epic of Old Mali* (adding yet another dimension of depth to the djembe experience).

Feelings of strength and change were all about—full moons, Mars was visible. Feelings of weakness, honesty, and dishonesty filled me. I practiced patience and non-reaction. I was at war with myself: Sméagol has consistently outsmarted Gollum—perhaps my path was fulfilling its destiny; my destiny. Fairness is crucial, but you must be the guide to the balance.

Chronologically, 2005 was a long year, but it was much longer in the non-chronological realm. Many lessons were learned. "What is good for me?" I keep asking. Each asking adds greater clarity.

CHAPTER 9
THE INCLUSIVE "OR"

"Be impeccable with your word; Don't make assumptions;
Don't take anything personally; Always do your best."

— Don Miguel Ruiz' Four Agreements

 find myself more concerned with truths than facts. Many things are mutually *in*clusive. Are you seeing when you look; hearing when you listen? Would you know if you weren't? Are you sure?

Part of the practice of greater awareness is having to choose your battles far more carefully because you realize there are far too many to fight at once or in a lifetime. A lesson I learned from studying djembe with Africans (from Senegal, Guinea, Mali, and Cote d'Ivoire) is their use of the word "or." In English, "or" is usually used exclusively. For example, "this or that" means "this to the exclusion of that." In learning djembe with Africans, I had to get used to not mutual exclusivity, but mutual *in*clusivity. For example, if it was this way, it was also two other ways, and all of them were correct. It took me a while even to realize it was happening, let alone to get used to redrawing the line of what anything actually is. At what point does a traditional rhythm named Kassa, played by the Malinké ethnic group in Upper Guinea, West Africa, for agriculture, cease being Kassa? I would learn that what would appear to my ear and eye as two different rhythms were the same. It made me quiet because I realized I was missing some key element that would bridge the gap between my massive ignorance and blissful knowing. How could these things that seemed different to me be the same? What was their sameness? Sometimes, I would eventually find out they were talking about meter; sometimes, they were the same if they were played for the same reason or in the same place—sameness. I started using the idea of the "list of truths" when teaching, since one could make many truthful observations about a thing. If you could make a list of ten truths about two things, how many of those truths would be the same between two apparently different things? And how much does semantics have to do with all this? Are we just redefining terminology? I was left sometimes thinking this whole thing was more about communication than language. To understand some things more fully is to understand them in a broader, less specific way.

In regards to djembe music, what makes a particular rhythm *that* rhythm? What are its essential elements that uniquely define it? What is its sine qua non? That answer lies in the single thing that is the combination of all the parts to the rhythm, as well as the oral history. I regularly ask my students to hum the rhythm, harmony, and melody of Kuku, Senefoli, or any rhythm. Hum the *music* of the rhythm—the one thing that is the combination of all its constituent parts. An easy way to see this is to close your eyes and listen to the rhythm without listening to any particular thing. Hear the one thing.

The Wisdom of the Six Taylors: On my first DVD are two ensemble sections that use the practice rhythms in a rhythmic context, combined with improvisation. It's a six-person ensemble of three djembes and three dununs. My idea was to isolate different combinations of the instruments. For example, one of the djembe parts with one of the dunun parts; the two djembe parts combined only with one of the dununs, etc. I believe if you understand all of the music's interactions it means really understanding the music—getting very inside the music. I asked Jeremy if it could be done. He said, "No, but give me till tomorrow." The next day, he said, "We can do it, but we're limited to the eight audio tracks we have." So, eight different combinations of instruments—less than I wanted, but I could live with that. It would be done with six versions of myself. Many people ask me how I did the ensemble sections on *Remembering*. If you reach out to me, I will tell you. You can hear only the dununs, or only the accompaniment, or only the solo while viewing; eight different scenarios uninterrupted. Suffice it to say, the Wisdom of the Six Taylors is that I asked for something without knowledge of technical limitations; my not-knowing, my ignorance was the creator, facilitator of my idea. I began with the end in mind. I ended up creating a way of doing something that no one in the world had done (as of 2003) and no one would do until smartphone apps and a few YouTube videos were created many years later. The Wisdom of the Six Taylors is: Don't let what you don't know hold you back; let your intuition, your wisdom, breathe.

Journal Entries: 2007—Yo-Yo Ma and Performance Tour in the Birthplace of Mamady Keïta

I have so many things to be thankful for in life; many of them have manifested as a result of my drummer's path. In 2007, my friend John Knecht approached me because a bunch of teaching artists were needed for a big, upcoming project that would combine Yo-Yo Ma's Silk Road Ensemble, the Chicago Symphony Orchestra, a storyteller, and 500 Chicago Public School youth (directed by eight teaching artists), all performing together to tell a story called *The Stone Horse*. It was an amazing thing to see it all come together at Millennium Park, Chicago. Yo-Yo Ma was an amazingly sweet and approachable man. We talked at length about the impact of arts on youth and how important it is to set good precedents for artists' compensation. I befriended his main percussionist Shane Shanahan; we'd later meet up at the Percussive Arts Society International Convention in Indianapolis and in St. Louis, where we were both doing performances and/or workshops. I'm so blessed to know such folks.

The incredible Yoyo Ma with me and Master percussionist with the Silk Road Ensemble Shane Shanahan c. 2015.

"If you like the snake, then you have to like slithering."

— Mamady Keïta, 2007,
(in a speech about how rough Guinea is,
in preparation for our performances tour to Upper Guinea)

This year was also a historic, once-in-a-lifetime trip to Guinea with Mamady Keïta and a contingent of many of my djembe peers. Since he had left in 1964, Mamady had been back to his village of birth, Balandugu Djomawagna, in 1991 and 1999. He told us he was bringing us to Balandugu to wake up his village to their mostly lost drumming traditions. The historical momentousness of this trip inspired a film crew to accompany us and document the occasion. The performing ensemble was fourteen strong and included men and women representing Belgium, The Congo, Japan, Canada, Morocco, Guinea, and the United States. Many of us were or later became Tam Tam Mandingue school directors, TTM Certificate holders, or otherwise some of Mamady's top and most seasoned students. At the time, I was one of two on the trip and in the world who had passed the TTM Diploma exam. (I was the first.)

My TTMDA Diploma (now called the Senior Certificate), 2006.

I love and hate Guinea. Is it part of the essential rites of passage that it should require so much effort and suffering to experience? Indeed, I think so.

This trip's read was *Divide and Rule: The Partition of Africa 1888-1914* by H. L. Messeling. The exchange rate this year for a good condition $100 bill was 700,000FG; my first year in Guinea, 1997, it was $100/120,000FG. It rained (poured, actually) for the first couple of days after our arrival; my previous trips we'd had little to no rain during the non-rainy season in Guinea. Ever since a high-level government official moved into the neighborhood, a paved road has been built outside of Mamady's compound—it's dangerous because folks drive too fast and there are no streetlights; I prefer the rough, pothole-pocked old road where slowness was a requirement.

The mosquitoes again reminded me of how bad they could get. I also got sick from some fried eggs—a seasoned veteran like me should have known better! Thankfully, a couple of folks on the trip had some neem from India that enormously helped my constipation. Thank goodness for my battery-powered fan. With the other incredibly healing medicine and rest, I was back in the game the next day.

While in Guinea, I was frequently homesick. The importance of suffering for your art is paramount. "What you survive makes you stronger." Another They-ism. I found a working phone and called my mother. She was doggie-sitting my animal children, Yoda and Leia. She had taken Yoda to the vet because he was having trouble walking and found out he had arthritis. I will dedicate my time in Guinea to little Master Yoda, so full of love and happiness. I missed Yoda, Leia, and my two cats, Shishi and Legolas, more than any human.

Random side note regarding my animal-children: Just before I left, I was in my house and could not place where a questionable odor was originating. This is not totally foreign territory with four animals in the house, but this was really something. So I looked around and moved a blanket to find the result of what happens when cute little doggies eat cat poop out of the litter box—poo vomit. I almost hurled. The blanket was removed from the house in its entirety. And I now know how to create a cat box dogs can't get to. That is all.

> "We are going to the village to show them how important their tradition is to us."
>
> — Mamady Keïta

The room I am staying in is called N'zerekore. (All the rooms in Mamady's compound are named after different regions around Guinea.) It was where I had also stayed in 2005. The days were remarkably hot, even for coastal Guinea. We learned what a "pyramid," as Mamady calls it, was. It's a big performance piece composed of numerous djembe rhythms strung together with fancy unison transitions. The show lasts about one hour with solos. It took us two-and-a-half days, six hours per day, to learn the entire thing.

I learned some interesting stuff about djembe woods in Guinea. Hardwoods (doukie, jalla, m'beng, lenge) are acquired by "extraction," meaning taking one at a time. You could not use power tools of any kind, including trucks in the forest, per the rules established by the forest's guardians. You paid the guardians a small penance to harvest a tree. Melina wood is quick-growing and lighter. There are Melina farms. Wula, the drum company in Guinea founded by my first djembe teacher Michael Markus and his partner on the ground in Guinea, Tom Kondas, is making djembes out of Melina, and they are remarkable. When stained, they are indistinguishable from hardwoods—the ones I saw, at least. A 2006 law made it illegal to export wood from Guinea for production; all furniture using Guinean woods needed to be made in Guinea.

I again had nightmares during this trip. They were so intense that I am surprised I didn't wake up screaming. One was about fear of loss. I didn't take Lariam this year since too many strains of malaria were resistant to it, so that wasn't the cause of my nightmares. My theories for why I had them were:

- A conditioned mind from my last five times in Guinea when I took Lariam.
- Bad grigri (the energy in objects associated with spells, charms, and incantations) in my room.
- The earth being stained with the blood of so many murdered by former president Sékou Touré.
- Psychic echoes of intergenerational trauma inflicted by French colonization.

As I contemplated these things, a feeling of calm came over me. Perhaps to feel terror is part of a greater effort to understand real inner peace. How could it not help to experience the far reaches of the spectrum?

While preparing to leave for Balandugu, I learned something interesting in *Sundiata: an Epic of Old Mali*. Sékou Touré, the dictator who took over rulership of Guinea after the French left in 1958, was a descendant of the evil Susu Sorcerer-King Soumaoro Kante. Touré was a great patron of the arts, but nonetheless, a paranoid murderer. Kante was supposedly buried in Gabon and moved to Guinea under orders of Sékou Touré.

As we left the compound in Conakry, we had to push-start one of the vehicles; we chose not to see this as an omen. Not long after getting on the road, our vehicle trouble started. The gasoline container inside our magbana was leaking. It is not uncommon to have gasoline and/or exhaust fumes inside a magbana or taxi in Guinea, but this was far worse. We pulled the entourage over to get some fruit—we had been driving with the gas issue for a while and decided to address the situation. We found the bottom of the magbana was, indeed, soaked with gasoline. Luckily, no baggage was affected. And we did not suffer a horrible death.

The next time we stopped was to wait for the rest of the convoy—one of the numerous times that, for no reason known to me or anyone I spoke to, the convoy of four vehicles got completely separated on one road. We waited for forty-five minutes outside a small mosque. Not knowing if they were ahead of or behind us, the driver left and eventually found them a bit up the road by some fruit stands and a small village. One of the magbanas was pissing out water from underneath. Eventually, we learned that not only did the drivers forget to add water to the radiator, but the radiator was probably from a small two-door taxi. To be sure, it was way too small for a vehicle hauling a dozen people and luggage.

Then one of our magbanas died. Several of the group waited in Tamakali while the rest went on to Mamou. Mamady advised us that Mamou was full of thieves. "The heart of crime in Guinea" or something like that. After numerous stops, we changed plans; instead of spending the night in Kankan, we hoped to find a hotel in Dabola. It's good to embrace the chaos! One of our guides was songbanfola (someone who plays the songban drum) Sékou Konate—a military man sporting an AK47 with a loaded clip. (He was in Mamady's group and on the *Mogobalu* and *Hamanah* albums.)

Mamady conceived a plan for two taxis to go back to Tamakali to get the other folks and luggage from the dead magbana, pile everyone and everything into the two taxis, and meet us, hopefully, in Dabola.

On our way out of Mamou, we got gas. There was an argument over the price of our gas, but then we were on our way. We had only filled up with

5.7 liters for reasons unknown/undisclosed to us. We would later run out of gas two times. On our way to Dabola, we prayed to find a hotel. With all the delays, Kankan was still too many hours away.

The roads were in bad condition. Potholes were everywhere. One of my fellow travelers, Bruce, said of my journal, "There are 200 potholes for every period in this writing." Sometimes, we contemplated whether walking next to the magbana would be a more efficient mode of travel. The magbana's inside had many unkind welds and sharp metal corners. The roll bars were made of square bars; one was in a corner behind my right shoulder, so I developed a very specific relationship with this metal bar. Suffering is a good teacher. Jan had Belgian chocolate treats to distract us—yummy and timely!

Goats, cows, potholes…. We finally arrived in Dabola; there were no rooms available at Hotel Tinkisso, but we were able to eat there. This meant that we would go on to Kourussa, where we heard there might be two hotels. We got our drivers some cola nuts (a highly caffeinated African nut originally used in Coca-Cola when it was invented in the nineteenth century) and hit the road again. After a long while we realized, like so many times before this moment, that part of the convoy was missing. We urged the driver to pull over so we could wait for them. That evening, I would see about twelve shooting stars and more stars overall than I could count.

More stars…so beautiful….

Eventually, our friends arrived. They said they'd had a flat tire. We continued on….

As a group, we made a more concentrated effort to take responsibility for not losing track of vehicles in the convoy; we had already lost so many hours on this.

I was asleep when we arrived in Kouroussa. Someone arrived with some bottles of fuel. I then became aware of why we were being towed—we had run out of gas again. Yes, it's true.

A decision was made, with only seventy-two kilometers to Kankan, to go the distance.

The road between Kouroussa and Kankan was paved and perfect—no potholes, nothing. We flew. It was a double-edged sword. We *did* fly, but the temperature fell to an unprecedented low. The nighttime temperature in Upper Guinea is very much like that in the desert. Frozen in Africa—go figure. In this frozen reality, traveling at the speed of a magbana bullet, we saw the sun rise—no words. It's beauty, majesty, and promise of heat was everything. We had planned to arrive in Kankan at 8 p.m., twelve hours after leaving Conakry. Eventually, we arrived at the Bate Hotel in Kankan some twenty-five hours after departing Conakry; its similarity to Hitchcock's Bates Motel was not lost on me, but I was too delirious to worry about being murdered in the shower. The sound of the Quran being sung over a PA system somewhere in Kankan filled the night air.

In the morning, our next leg was estimated to be four hours from Kankan to Balandugu, but it took nine. We literally left the pavement at Kankan; it was red-dirt roads from there, and the bongbong, the omnipresent reddish dust, was our enemy (or another teacher?). Thank you to my compatriot from Japan, Ken Tokuda, for the dust mask. It seemed like all the potholes we missed between Kouroussa and Kankan were waiting for us in this last stretch. Some earthen potholes were larger than our magbanas, forcing us to drive into the bush to avoid them. One last time, somehow we lost the caravan in the middle of nowhere, on one road. At this point, there was no getting upset; it was par for the course. When we asked someone walking along the road where Balandugu was, they replied, "Which Balandugu?" Our hearts sank. "Which Balandugu?" was a question no one was prepared to hear at this point. One thing I've learned in all my trips to Guinea is that time is a game-changer. When a situation you don't want is upon you in this place, all you need to do is sit tight and the chaos will carry you. Usually, something totally unforeseen and/or unrelated will intervene—a deus ex machina—that redefines the entire context. Then your problem is gone. So we waited, then drove.

What saved us was us—we began demanding that our driver ask people where Balandugu was. We saw a hunter, adorned with many talismans and many fetish objects—the real shite. We pulled over and asked him, adding the name Mamady Keïta to Balandugu. The response was "Oh, *djembefola* balandugu, that way!" We would later learn the Balandugu that Mamady is from is officially called Balandugu Djomawagna. Founded in the twelfth century by Nankababa Keïta, it is one of the oldest villages in the area. Mamady's eldest brother, Nankaba, was named after the village founder. Balandugu means "the place where we have lasted well."

The hunter put us back on the right path, which headed us back to where we should have turned ninety minutes earlier. When we saw Moussa Keïta (asunam) on the road, we thought we'd arrived. He was waiting for us so we could be part of the big entrance to Balandugu.

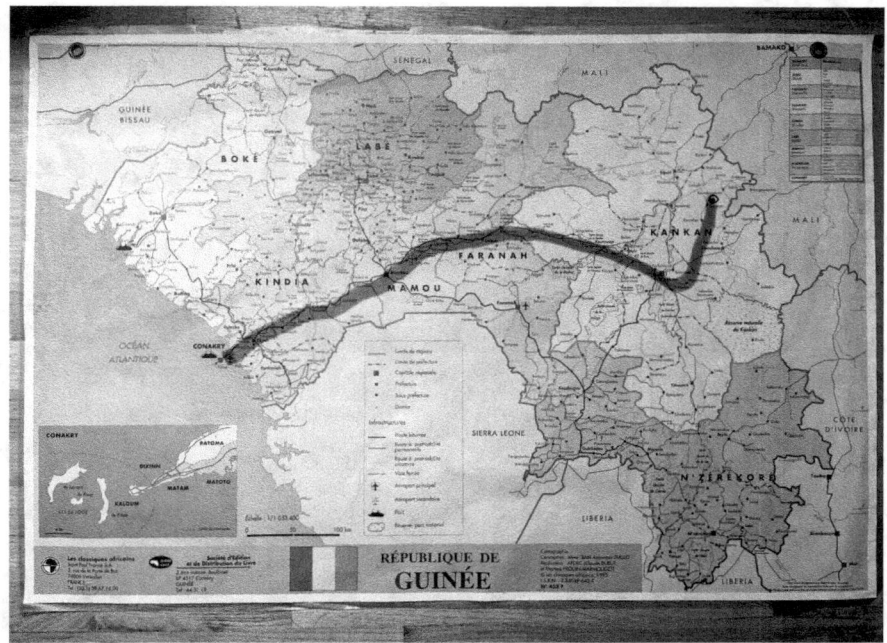

Our route to Balandugu Djomawagna, Guinea West Africa.

Eventually, we found our way, in the dark, to Mamady's place of birth. My mate, Quinn Reisor, and I decided to stay outdoors in tents instead of an indoor structure; we wanted to be as close to nature as possible; love my headlamp! We were placed in Toumani's part of the compound. Each of Mamady's brothers had an area of the compound, Toumani, Fadjimba, and Nankaba. After setting our tents up in the dark, to our surprise, hot water was prepared for us over a wood fire in a cauldron. The bathing areas were like little lidless silos, just about shoulder height, with an arched entrance you'd stoop down to pass through. I was a full head above the top of the walls. That water felt amazing, cleansing, as if the experience were pouring itself over me. It took going to this place in Guinea to get a hot bath in Guinea.

I heard cocks crowing in the night. I awoke to the tubaninlu könölu [bird] cuckooing and the rhythm of the kolon-kalan (large mortar and pestle for preparing foodstuffs) coloring the morning air. Nature was very present in this village.

I put my hand on a piece of a wall that surrounded the original incarnation of this village in the twelfth century. I wondered if the great King Sundjata Keïta had laid eyes on this very wall.

Some of the village members I met included a tiny praying mantis, donkeys, chickens, a toad, goats, cows, sheep, guinea-fowl, a cat (rarely seen in Guinea), and dogs. I've only ever seen one type of dog in Guinea, and only occasionally was one a different color than deer-brown. They are like dingos, primordial, un-inbred, undifferentiated dogs. In Conakry, I could only tell the dogs apart by their different oozing, open wounds with matted hair; from what I could see, they were all feral and they were treated more like rats. In Mamady's village the doggies are clean and happy. All these animals were just in the mix of the village like everyone else. I was impressed by the lack of animal poop all around. I think it made sense to them not to arbitrarily crap just any old place. I wondered if they spoke animal-Malinké?

The first time we played in Balandugu was when we practiced for our first of several gigs, which would be in the nearby village of Kinieran. It was late morning and definitely over 100F in the shade. It was great playing again. Mamady told us we would be a gigantic curiosity to the folks in his village, which was hilariously true. Many of them had never seen a non-Malinké person, let alone a non-black man or woman playing a djembe! The rehearsal went well.

Then we suited up and prepared to drive to Kinieran. It was a few hours on red dirt roads with my old friend the red dust, the bongbong. We had to play in the sunlight because the moon was the only light after the sun went down. We were far, far off the grid. Before we started playing, Mamady gave a long talk in Malinké about how traditions are being lost and the world loves djembe music, so we should not let this artform, in its place of origin, die off. His remarks were punctuated by a djeli periodically shouting, "Namu!" as if to say, "Amen!" or "Can I get a witness?" "Namu" means "yes" in Malinké, but an uplifted kind of yes. The crowd was several hundred at least. Rows and rows of Guineans surrounded us in concentric circles on all sides. When we started playing, it was eerily calm. I remember wondering whether they hated or loved us. Then, at one point, when our choreography started with Mamady's gesture, the crowd erupted in cheers. The gig went great.

Me at our first gig, Kineran, Upper Guinea, West Africa. Photo courtesy of Scott Griffiths and Kellie Pederson.

After the gig, we were so thirsty that our bottled water, now about the temperature of hot tea water, was an amazing relief. So much about this trip put so much in perspective. We left in the late afternoon, arriving back at our home base in Balandugu in the dark night. Soon, hot water was prepared for our bathing. This time, I saw how they filled a cauldron with water from the pump and heated it over burning wood. Old school, baby, old school. (The only modern things in Balandugu were the mechanized deep-well hand pumps to get water; the government installed them in the late 1990s.)

After I bathed, I took a walk across the compound. I hadn't met the huge bull until this moment. Outside it was cave-dark—not a sliver of light. So dark I could tell no difference between open and closed eyes. So dark I could not see my hand one inch in front of my face. So dark that by the time I realized a huge bull was in front of me, it was too late to avoid some kind of interaction. We almost did a nose-to-nose kiss, but I stopped just before. He was chill. I was chill. We took a nice long moment to be chill. I

Me at Balandugu Djomawagna's water pump 2007. Photo credit Ali Thomas.

slowly added space between me and the huge bull in cave-dark Balandugu, and we were all chill. Whew.

Mornings began with pumping, then filtering your water for the day. The tubaninlu könölu kukooing and the rhythm of the kolon-kalan were the opening act for each day. This area was so rich with gold deposits that Mamady said when he was young, after a hard rain, the ground would glisten with gold. The hills surrounding Balandugu are pocked with small gold mines. These mines are vertical holes hand-dug into the earth, about a meter wide. I was told some folks died in some of these very unstable holes, looking for gold. Well, today, I needed a place to move some of myself out, so I went up one of the hills and found a good hole to squat over. My view of the village was beautiful. The sound and presence of children and animals was omnipresent. It was truly a beautiful moment.

Our next gig was in Koundian. When we arrived, after battling two hours of dirt, potholed roads, and bongbong, we were very tired. We were informed that there had just been three deaths in Koundian, including that of the president of the village's mother. The gig was canceled. Then there was a lengthy conversation that resulted in us actually doing the gig. We performed on a soccer field. Many villagers were not present, but many were. The village president was there, and they loved us! There was an enormous Baobab tree. Methinks it was the Tree of Life, or at least *a* tree of life—there were so many there!

One remarkable day, Mamady took us to several significant places for him in Balandugu. They included where he was born, where he was when he was taken by the ballet, the Moribayassa tree, a kassa (a granary as well as a family of rhythms about agriculture), his mother's family's house, the site of the tree where he used to play when he was a child, "toda" where they got the dirt to build the old homes, the djin (the wall built around Balandugu around the twelfth century), and Da Kurunin (the mouth of Kurunin, a small hill where three spirits live who protect the village and are the source of Mamady's spiritual power). To say that this was a deep experience does not do it justice; it was unbelievably profound.

In Mamady Keïta's definition, Moribayassa is: a rhythm/dance/song by the Malinké ethnic group played in Upper Guinea. Moribayassa is special in the lives of women. If a woman has a serious problem in her life, such as childlessness, an illness in her family, missing someone terribly, etc., she may make a wish for resolution. She may then take the vow to dance Moribayassa when her wish is granted. In the old days, the vow was so significant that a woman could take it only once in her life. As part of the vow, the woman promises that if her wish is granted, she will dance Moribayassa. When/if her prayer is answered, she organizes the Moribayssa dance in the village to celebrate her joy. As she circles the village, wearing old and torn clothes, three to seven times singing and dancing, she is accompanied by one or more musicians. Most of the dance styles you see in this area of Africa are very fluid and in time with the music, but not this dance. Moribayassa's improvised movements are chaotic, often knocking things down during the dance. The other women of the village follow her, pick up after her, and sing as well. After the dance, the woman changes back into her normal clothes, then buries the old and torn clothes she wore for the dance under a mango tree. In Mamady's village, this mango tree is called Moribayassa. Once when I shared this oral history in a class, someone shared with me that there is a Native American nation that has a ceremony where, if someone has a bad spirit on them, they dress and dance unlike their normal selves. Afterward, they bury the clothes to trick the spirit away from them. It made me think of *The Hero With a Thousand*

Faces, where Joseph Campbell showed numerous disparate indigenous cultures having the same mythological archetypes and stories. We are far more similar than different as a global village.

What Mamady shared with us was so pure, so transformative, and something never to be underestimated or forgotten. I could tell at the time that I was shifting as a person. Only a return to my previous context would tell where I really was.

We didn't do one of our gigs because someone died in their village as they were rehearsing for our arrival. Combine this with what happened recently with other deaths in another village we visited and death seemed to be following some peripheral, parallel course. Bizarre, yes. Meaningful? We certainly didn't think so and hoped not!

On one of our days off from performing, we organized a jam. I played dununba on the rhythm mendiani, then songban on bolokonundo, konuwulen (Hamana version), and soko, and we rocked out for/in/with Balandugu. We got to blow, and we all needed it and loved

Cover of Messengers of Tradition documentary, c. 2008. On cover is Mamady and Nasira.

it! Afterwards, Bruce ("Brucestapha" was a member of the ensemble and led the film crew) interviewed me for the *Messengers of Tradition* documentary about this tour, which was very exciting!

I went to Da Kurunin (with at least one other person on Mamady's advice). Mamady told us that we could go there to seek advice or request wishes be granted from the three spirits who live there. I didn't know what to wish for since I felt my life was so full. Mamady's grandmother was Kurunin's keeper; the task was eventually given to Mamady. At the spot, I had a conversation with the three spirits who live there—very, very profound to be in the presence of such significant non-manifest entities; significant to me because of my deep connection to Mamady.

Afterwards, more star gazing as the sounds of nocturnal nature lulled me asleep.

For this year's Tabaski, we planned to be the drummers who would drum for the village before sunrise. I was the songbanfola, backing the leader, Sékou Balandugu. We played in the dark morning air, eventually encircling the entire village of Balandugu, all before sunrise. The shoulder strap for my drum was a thin piece of rope—it required a deep amount of detachment to manage the pain this caused in my shoulder as we played while walking for a very, very long time. The group of us played a rhythm that is traditionally played for Tabaski, called Djagbe. At one point, the oldest person in the village came out of his teebo (the thatch-roofed, mud-bricked small homes), so moved by a bunch of non-Guineans drumming for this holiday that he gave my little drum brother, Bill Scheidt, a live chicken that he proudly continued walking with as it thrashed about in a strange, inverted dance. After the Tabaski drumming festivities, I went to the hills to an abandoned gold mine to move some of my bowels. I'm noting it because good bowel-balance in Guinea is a rare, beautiful, and very noteworthy thing. Then I went to the Moribayassa tree to get some soil and leaves to bring home as a keepsake from this incredible adventure.

When Tabaski was celebrated, I witnessed about one-thousand folks do a group prayer. The contrast of the amazing array of colors from their clothing on the backdrop of reddish earth was incredible.

Since Tabaski involves the sacrifice of an animal (traditionally a ram), walking back across the village, I saw numerous slaughtered sheep and cows. I saw two men carrying a cow stomach that was very, very large. Around almost every corner was some scene of carnage. Some of the vegetarians on the trip needed to carefully consider their walks that day. It was gruesome to my eye. Do the cows know they are standing only a few feet away from organs piled on the freshly liberated skin of their own kind? Probably not.

During this walk, I ran into Doug Kane and Beth Dyer. I asked them to accompany me to the spot that protects Balandugu—the spot from which Mamady draws his power, the spot he told us not to go to alone—Da Kurunin, the mouth of Kurunin, the great trio of spirits and protectors of the village.

Each day in the village seemed like a week's time.

We did our next two gigs in one day. One at Bankoumouna and another at Kunjana Koro (where circa 1963, Mamady was "discovered," leading to him being recruited into the National Ballet of Guinea, The Ballet Djoliba, and being introduced to the world.)

The first gig was near the hottest time of the day, so many in the ensemble were on the verge of passing out. I learned something more about how a fish feels frying in a pan. It was a remarkable and amazing show. The second felt like the best energy show yet.

We—Sékou Balandugu, Rich (from Vancouver), and I—made a beer run to Kinieran—a beer run in Upper Guinea! A warm beer run in Upper Guinea! It was an adventure, of course, and we arose, went forth, and conquered. We collected enough Guinea-Francs for seventy-eight beers at 5,000FG each—Skol and Guiluxe, the two main beers you could find in Guinea at the time.

The next day's performance was for Balandugu Djomawagna, the village that created Mamady. It went swimmingly! After this, just after sunset, we had our beers—I was butt-drunk on one-and-a-half warm beers, so when I reached three, I was feelin' no pain. I sat in my tent, incense and candle burning, hearing the sounds of a village, still very awake, as I prepared for sleep. Our gig ended as the sun came down; we began before the sun rose—sleep came deep.

A dream came to me. Five tornadoes were approaching. I eliminated three of them. I took on tornadoes and dispatched them as if I were omnipotent.

One of the last things we did in Balandugu was the naming ceremony for Nasira, Mamady and Monette's young daughter. During the ceremony, lots of very old men gave old-man-length speeches in Malinké. The goat sacrifice was intense; I had never actually been at an animal sacrifice before. A goat can live with its throat cut, gushing blood, for a surprisingly long time. And the sound. Thankfully, I don't remember the sound of the dying goat's bleat bubbling through blood. Or perhaps I've buried it deep in my subconscious, in hopes of never hearing anything like it again. I asked why it was necessary to sacrifice an animal. I was told the animal's sacrifice would take the ceremony's message to the other side; glad I asked the question since it was an answer I wasn't expecting. Afterward, everyone drummed and danced in celebration.

After the naming ceremony, the villagers asked—Mamady said they begged at his feet—for the group to play one more time. Many surrounding villages had come, and it was time to rev it up again! I personally would not have chosen this, but the mission was larger than my petty personal discomforts and extreme fatigue.

Did I mention that even at a sliver, the moon in this cloudless sky provided so much light that we didn't need our headlamps? Did I also mention the 100F-plus days that felt like we were in an oven?

After our last show, Quinn and I visited Da Kurunin; 'twas deep—very good shit. The three spirits at Kurunin will be with me from now on—we know each other now; that is forever.

In the dark of the early morning, we began the journey back to our home villages. We began hoping the outbound leg of the journey would be eventful in more positive ways than the ones on the inbound leg. Although, I must admit, for an initiation (and I most definitely believe this entire experience was an initiation for me), it was perfectly what it needed to be, as things in flow always are.

About seven hours after we left, we arrived on Kankan's outskirts relatively on schedule. We spent the night in hotel Tinkisso in Dabola; it was very nice by Guinean standards. Quinn and I went to a nightclub close to our hotel; it was like a steam room. We had one beer, saw a dude get tossed out, and called it a night. The next morning, we hit pavement for the first time since we had left Kankan on the way to Balandugu ten days earlier.

As on the inbound trip, I lost count of how many times we lost one of the vehicles in our four-car caravan. I don't know how this was possible when we were always on one road with no turns. The waiting ate up numerous hours. Frustration was mixed with relief and happiness when we were all together again.

On our way again, one of the magbanas got a flat. The catch was the spare tire required a different number of lug nuts than any of the vehicles we had. At that point, with all that had happened, none of us was even mad. For my part, I found it amazing. "So it's gonna be like that, huh?"

While waiting for the aforementioned magbana at a gas station in 100F heat, we learned the gas station had no gas. Why did it have no gas? When gas is delivered, the black market folks (I call them "gas bandits") show up first thing with their five-gallon yellow containers, some rolling with four at a time on a cart that has as its axle/wheels part of an old taxi. They buy up all the gas so the black market will have a monopoly and can charge whatever it wants in that area, which was about $10/gallon (that's US dollars) that day in Kouroussa. The surprises never ceased! We had to deal with gas bandits again the next day. Luckily, we all had enough extra cash.

On December 23, we pulled in about 9 p.m., after getting on the road at 8 a.m., another twelve-plus hours of road time. The tailpipe was welded on in Dabola, which made a big difference in the carbon monoxide levels inside the vehicle. The absence of bongbong from leaving the dirt roads behind made all the difference in the world. An early Christmas gift was that the power went off, then came back on that morning—it was very unusual for it to actually go back on at the same time of the day in Conakry.

I would absolutely love to go to Balandugu Djomawagna again. The trip had largely been planned to learn how to do a trip like this efficiently. We were Mamady's "Guinea" (pun intended) pigs for trying to do the best he could with numerous details beyond his control and, with his calm leadership, we made it.

This experience gave a window into the possibilities of human endurance—physical, mental, and spiritual. We all held together knowing, no matter what, we were with Mamady Fucking Keïta—no one ever doubted him or his/our mission. We kicked major ass in our performances, always rising to the occasion. We reveled in tapping the root of the djembe.

A layer of humidity and pollution is omnipresent in Conakry; it will not be a major part of my next trip. It would be minimal time in the capital city, then off to the bush again, hopefully with fewer travel debacles and harrowing vehicle experiences.

On the plane before takeoff, we took on numerous mosquito stowaways; I would not miss them. Otherwise, the plane was almost empty—no one was in the seat next to me. I wondered how things would be different upon my return to the place where I live, and how would they be the same.

I flew out of Conakry, ate, and woke up about six hours later when we got to Paris. I had about a five-hour layover at Charles-De-Gaulle Airport and got to check email; otherwise uneventful. I'm feeling a bit strange about calling the Chicago area "home." Balandugu seems to be a place I should call home.

Slept a lot on the last leg. Seems we were over Canada a looooooong time.

Speed: 510 mph

Altitude: 38,000 feet

Outside Air Temp: -54F

I had interesting bits of communication with an elderly woman next to me. With absolutely no words, I showed her how to operate her video, remote, etc. How often words are unnecessary; how often words are the default.

To recap the order and days/dates of our gigs in Upper Guinea:

12/16/07 - Sunday - Kinieran

12/17/07 - Monday - Koundian

12/18/07 - Tues - Bankoumana

12/18/07 - Tues - Kondiana Koro

12/19/07 - Weds - Balandugu - Tabaski

12/20/07 - Thurs - Unscheduled command performance at Balandugu for about fifteen surrounding villages.

A performance tour with Mamady Keïta in the Wassolon in Upper Guinea, West Africa—that is core-of-the-earth deep! Feeling thankful.

CHAPTER 10
SILENCE, MY FAVORITE NOTE

"The music is not in the notes,
but in the silence between."

— Wolfgang Amadeus Mozart

Around 2000, my friend Chris Pawola and I financed the step up into the digital 8-track world in this way: one third from sales of our first record, *A Touch of Chaos in the Rhythmic Soup*, one third from him, and one third from me. *Silence* would be the first CD I would compose, play, and produce myself, with my good friend Pawo-

Silence CD, cover art by Elizabeth Nuti. Cover art manipulation by P. Vojtik.

la at the engineer's helm. It would be a version of a creation story in rhythm. In "Stalker," the first tune, I played every instrument. The Stalker is one's higher self, waiting in the shadows, benevolently stalking the lower self.

Next, in "Come to Become" (me playing with Gabriel Shaffer on words/chant), we have the higher-self finally coming through, being born via the lower-self. As with any birthing process, this tune feels uncomfortable. I would learn, years after the recording took place, why this track feels so unsettling. A smart friend of mine heard that the track contained several time signatures—3, 4, 5, 7—which have a least common multiple of 420. This means all parts of the track only came together every 420 beats; I have no idea how often this happens in the track. The bass drum tracks were based on the heartbeats of three different-sized animals. To give an example of the heartbeats of different-sized animals, hummingbird's heartbeat can exceed 1000 beats per minute; a goat's is 70 to 95; and a blue whale's about eight to ten beats per minute. I combined those voices with a djembe part that had come to me on the lakefront. The last voice would come together in-studio, when I asked Gabriel Schaffer, a friend of Amon's who was staying at my house for a while, to compose a spoken word flow to go with the music. "Come to Become" has become and is unapologetic in its ordered chaos.

Track 3 is "Entre Nous." The title means "between us" in French to represent the relationship between self and other. It was improvised in-studio with me and Master Drummer Madou Dembele. He asked me, "Do you want a Mendiani feel or a Kuku feel?" I replied, "Mendiani." Then we began.

"The Jungle" is next, exploring the relationship of self to plurality. Elizabeth Nuti is on Native American flute and didgeridoo. There are twenty-five tracks of me on wassamba, various shakers, jaw harp, kenkeni, songban, dununba, dununbaba, dununbababa (in Malinké, "ba" is a suffix meaning "great" or "big"), djembe, conga, clave, and various bells.

There is one extra track, where I accompany Dave Cherniac as he plays Afro-Cuban Lullaby during a live performance of "The Jungle" in 1999 at the Old Town School of Folks Music, Chicago.

There is a surprise hidden track created by Pawola. He had taken numerous answering machine messages I had left for him over time and combined them into a trippy song. Brilliant!

Journal Entries: 2008-2009—Vinx and Japan

In 2008, I had the pleasure and honor to do a couple of gigs with the amazing artist Vinx. The first night was kind of an audition; then he asked me to join him the second night. He's an amazing talent. I'm thankful that because of my years of effort playing djembe, I can hang with him on the drum. A friend who knew I was into Vinx mentioned that he was usually open to playing with local artists who can hang. So I contacted him and sent him some videos. He asked me to meet him at his show at Elbow Room, Chicago. He was one of my earliest influences as a musician, so it was amazing to run the rhythmic realms with him. I was made aware of him and his first album *Rooms in My Fatha's House* in 1994 by my lifelong friend Michael Criddell, who characterized him as Bobby McFerrin meets drumming. His drum—he calls it a "Vinx drum"—is a lovechild of a djembe and a talking drum, which is part of the essence of his sound as a performer. And that voice—amazing.

In 2009, I was invited to go on a performance tour with Mamady Keïta and eleven other TTMDA school directors in Japan—a huge honor. This was my first time in Japan; I experienced my first earthquake in my hotel (scary!) and my first bidet!

The folks in the ensemble were really amazing—rich in personality, worldly experience, intelligence, and talent. Four Americans were on

Me and Mamady at Tam Tam Mandingue Japan on the island of Ioujima 2009.

the tour, and three spoke only one language; everyone else on the tour spoke two to four. It made me feel like a dumb American...again.... Representatives from Israel, France, Germany, the United States, Australia, Belgium, Korea, Malaysia, Taiwan, China, Singapore, and Japan were at the camp where we learned and rehearsed the show. Tara Tucker, the one Australian, was by far the most interesting person I met on this tour; one of the most amazing, talented, and intelligent people I've ever met, she is fluent in French, Japanese, and English and is an incredible human and musician.

From mainland Japan, it was a four-hour ferry ride to our main destination. I took Dramamine for the first time in my life after hearing several warnings about seasickness on the enormous ferry. After finally arriving on Iōjima (one of the Mishima Islands in the Kagoshima prefecture), where the only standalone Tam Tam Mandingue structure exists in the world, we finally started drumming. We learned a 45-60-minute performance piece that we staged four times in two weeks. During rehearsals, Mamady raised the bar incredibly—so much so that some of the school directors couldn't hang.

One evening, the men of the village did the Sorota ceremony. The ceremony dates back more than 800 years, originating with two warring families. One family won the fight and the other lost; the loser ran away to very southern Japan, where, eventually they were laid to rest. All but

Mahiri, Monette, and me in our Sorota gear, 2009, Ioujima, Japan.

one was exhumed and taken back to the north. The one spirit left behind was restless, so this ceremony was held to calm the restless spirit. It is held on August 15 each year.

In the ceremony, two towers made of straw material are used. They are maybe six meters tall and a meter wide. In our kimonos, we had bunches of wood that were on fire. The objective was to toss your fire (read "flaming pieces of wood") onto the top of one of the six-meter-tall towers; then, after the first was lit, the second. This proved difficult. Mamady mentioned that in fifteen years of trying, he had not been able to do it. It was tiring and, at times, dangerous because bunches of flaming wood were being cast to the sky from all directions around the towers—dangerous and exhilarating! Afterward, we did a dance with two drummers, all in a circle. We took a break, drank beer, and danced again, attempting ridiculously to sing the Japanese song none of us knew.

After the Sorota, we went to the hot springs on the volcano's other side. Some cool cats—Fred and Arnaud (France), Jeremy (Belgium), Pierre (Tel Aviv), Mahiri (USA), and I marinated in sulfur-infused hot water, beer, and saké. An *I Ching* reading was my last activity before a profoundly deep sleep.

The next day, after a few hours of class, we went to the lagoon to swim in the ocean water. It was incredible. I snorkeled for the first time in my life. A deadly sea snake was in the water, plus some squid and numerous fish. I found I could tread water for an unusually long time (thank you, yoga), and I swam like I do it all the time. The mayor of Kagoshima took a few of us out deep-sea fishing, another first for me. We saw flying fish, a sea snake, and sea turtles, and a few of us caught fish that were part of the sushi we had for dinner that night.

On our last day on Iōjima, we rehearsed longer than any other day—more than seven hours in wicked, African-type heat. The callus on my middle finger, born from the cow skin on my djembe (this djembe I named Oshun), became very, very problematic; first, it was incredibly painful, then quickly turned into a blood blister. It was suggested I play another drum because I couldn't be heard; the pain was making me pull back from fully playing. So the fight with the cow skin ended and I began playing Tara's drum that she had recently bought from Jeremy—it was a welcome change and clearly another lesson in honoring resistance; if it comes with "too much problem," let it go. The next day, we found the djembe skin had busted! This led to Mamady offering one of his drums for me to play—sweeeet! Reward for embracing the wisdom of a lesson, methinks!

The next day, we headed back to the mainland and had our first show on August 20 in Kagoshima—an unbelievable, sold-out, standing-room-only event. The energy from the stage was off the hook; from the audience, off the hook! I felt very good about my solo and felt honored to share the stage in the front line of TTM directors. The after party was almost as incredible as the show! All paid for by the mayor of Kagoshima with the help of Katsuo Nonue, our incredible host. So much shōchū (Japan's traditional alcoholic beverage), beer, and saké, and we lived to tell the tale. The next

Me beaming with Mamady's djembe after Kagoshima performance, Japan 2009.

day, we were on a flight to Tokyo where we stayed in a five-star hotel for the next two days.

As soon as the tour was over, the group headed back to the mainland, and I spent a day with one of my tourmates, Bruce Rudolph. We rented bikes and rode around visiting temples. As it turns out, Japan has a lot of temples. The ride gave us a great perspective on Japan. Later, I went out on the town with some of my drum brethren in inner-city Tokyo, an area called Roppongi. I had never really known the club scene back home. We went to a place with numerous temptations—fishing in a bucket basically. Perhaps it is age (read "seasoning"), but I had largely lost my desire to "pick up" women. We had a great time just being with each other. When someone accidentally bumped my beer-holding hand, I accidentally spilled beer on Arnaud's lower back, and I knew it totally went down his butt crack, which he quickly confirmed. Oops! We stayed out until 4 a.m., arriving back at the hotel about 5 a.m., literally running from the rising sun like vampires.

The next day was my first time traveling in a foreign (non-English-speaking) country by myself. I was nervous. Katsuo Nonue was great at educating me about the trains; my execution or lack thereof of said brief education was my test. My first Shinkansen (bullet-train) ride was incredible. No one mentioned it feels no different from an airplane, except that you always stay at cruising altitude. I watched the outside world at ground level go past as if reality had been sped up. I had saké, some squid, and two other things I didn't recognize at a restaurant called Kan Teki Ya in Hakata, far west in southern Japan. It seemed like an upstanding place. The other two items turned out to be white pizza with an unknown (to me) meat and what appeared to be pot stickers. Should pizza be eaten with chopsticks? Well, I did it, dammit!

I called my drum brother in Tam Tam Mandingue, Hiroki Murai, because I would be staying at his place sometime in the next few days. On the suggestion of an employee at the Starbucks by the train station, I went to an area called Tenjin. This place had lively nightlife—lots of shiny lights. I felt a bit like a moth watching out for bug zappers! Drinking alcohol on an empty stomach is highly efficient. Then I got some sleep and was feeling fine with all my supplies for the next five or so days on my shoulder.

The next day, I went to Miyajima, the "God Island," which was an amazing and mystical place. After the island, when I was attempting to order food at a place with no pictures on the menu, I got the same feeling I got on the first day of first grade and when I first went away to college—yes, I was homesick. Very quickly, an English-speaking Japanese woman appeared. Her boyfriend had sensed my anxiety over ordering shōchū after the waitress and staff began asking me questions I could not understand.

The Hiroshima memorial was astonishing. I spent hours in Hiroshima Park and at the museum. I learned a lot about an event I had never known much detail about. Then I got a Shinkansen (bullet train) to Himeji. After I got to the hotel and did laundry (in the sink, per normal), I headed out to see what awaited me on my path.

After walking a mile or so (I liked to get out of the immediate vicinity of the Japan Rail station), I happened upon an open-air restaurant. It was very small and loud with a few folks there. I had a glass of shōchū and "talked" with the owner and three regulars for an hour or so. Then I headed off in another direction, mindful to remember the approximate direction my hotel was in. Seeing bright, shiny lights, I went toward them. A middle-aged woman was asking for something I didn't understand. Then she gestured toward my cock and made a blow job gesture. I laughed and politely escaped. I saw many women and pimpy-looking young men and really didn't understand what was going on.

After a while, I saw someone who looked American and talked to him. Nadef, who turned out to be Israeli, spoke perfect, articulate English, and was waiting to set up his sales tables. (He sold high-grade replica watches, designer jewelry, etc.) He worked for someone in the Israeli mafia and told me it had taken him about two months living in Japan before he knew what he was doing.

All the "clubs" up and down the street(s) lined with pretty women and young men in suits with David-Bowie-from-the-'80s haircuts all seemed to be trying to get folks to come into their "clubs," where you pay for an hour to drink with a pretty girl who laughs at all of your jokes and makes you feel important. That was the gig—there was lots and lots of that. Very strange. Since that was something I was definitely not interested in, I hung out with Natef all night, talking about philosophy, music, religion, politics, etc. A really great time had by all.

The next day, I visited Himeji Castle, a hilltop Japanese castle complex situated in the city of Himeji, which is located in Japan's Hyōgo Prefecture. The castle is considered the finest surviving example of prototypical Japanese castle architecture, comprising a network of eighty-three rooms with advanced defensive systems from the fourteenth century feudal period.

After Himeji, I got on the train to Osaka and met up with Mark McCracken, a friendly acquaintance from junior high and high school. His father had been a teacher at O'Neill, my junior high school when we were there circa 1980. Mark told me Doc Freidl, one of our teachers at O'Neill, was still there! Wow! I was in speech team and theater with Mark, and while we never really hung out, we were friendly, cool cats. He came to Japan to teach English years back and never left. He gave me an incredible tour of Osaka and we shared our life stories since high school. I ate Ebi-Hirekatsu Tonkatsu (Japanese pork cutlets) for dinner. We walked along Dotonbori and saw the neon Glick sign. Then we walked up the Shoutengai toward Shinsaibashi. We visited Big Step. We had a couple of Chimay Belgian ales (yes, Chimay) and shot pool at Balabushka. Got some takoyaki (octopus balls, a traditional Japanese snack) from an outdoor stand and sat along the sidewalk of midosuji-dori to eat it. (Thank you, Mark, for the evening itinerary!)

In Japan, many relationships from all over the world were forged and deepened again via the grace of Mamady Keïta. On the flight home, I finished another reading of *Sundjata: An Epic of Old Mali*. I can say I am the same and changed forever.

CHAPTER 11

ZEN AND THE ART OF DJEMBE MAINTENANCE, STARRING MY TEACHER AND NEMESIS, ROPE

"Nyininkalila Te Filila."

"If you ask questions, you're never wrong."

— Malinké Proverb

Rope is one of my greatest teachers. A piece of rope is a magician that can tell the truth in the same moment as a lie and challenge you to figure out which is which. Rope can make a thinking person look like a fool, mocking you as it hides in its own twists and length. If you've ever run a long length of rope in your hands and had it create a knot out of thin air, you may be able to relate to this. Everything about djembe construction is right there for the eye to see; it is amazingly simple and, simultaneously, amazingly complex. The teachings of djembe do not end with the playing of the instrument. If you choose to delve into the world of djembe repair/restoration, that is a whole 'nother animal. The softness, hardness, tension, power, perfection, and sometimes perfect imperfection of how this instrument is constructed carries with it so many lessons. I believe that after my fifteenth year playing djembe, I had made all the mistakes you could make in the process of fixing one. Every possible thing that could break had broken and every logical test had been given. I am proud and somewhat embarrassed to say that the only mistakes I now make in djembe repair are mistakes I've already made!

When I purchase rope to use for drum repair, it is usually by the thousand-foot spool. Well, one fateful day, I saw in the bottom of an empty rope-spool box a small pamphlet titled *Rope Instructions*. I thought, *Rope instructions—really? What on earth could this say?* Curious, I read the pamphlet. One thing I learned was this type of rope loses 50 percent of its tensile strength at the site of a knot. This information made me realize I needed to think about how I worked with it, and it gave rise to many new ideas about systems of tension at the start and end of a rope. I had learned something from rope instructions. My assumption that I couldn't learn something from a thing so apparently simple had vanished, and it set a precedent for how I began to approach any simple thing.

At some later point, I got a new yoga mat that came with *Yoga Mat Instructions*. Since I had learned something from *Rope Instructions*, I couldn't resist seeing what these instructions said. Well, that day, I learned how to roll my mat in such a way that it didn't curl up at its ends. I had been doing yoga for about ten years at that point, but I had never realized this beautifully simple process existed that would allow my mat to lie flat. Sometimes, my profound unawareness makes me grin.

I hated green tea for many years—thought it tasted like fish ass. One day, after reading *Rope Instructions*, I saw directions on one of the tea boxes. I learned the heating temperature and steep-time to make green tea: 175F and 2-3 minutes. I had been boiling the water (212F) and steeping indefinitely and indiscriminately, which can actually make this antioxidant tea toxic. I started reading other tea boxes and found specific directions on almost all of them. That was the way to get the best cup of tea, and each had its own way—of course. My first cup of green tea done to specification was a new world of appreciating green tea; now I love it. Almost all the teas I was consuming at home were not prepared in the best way for that particular leaf. Until then, I didn't really know how tea should and could taste; it took until I was forty to learn. So very simple and always right there in front of my face.

My early mentors for djembe repair included Whitfield Holmes, a very talented drummer and entrepreneur who became my friend. We met at Weed Fest in Chicago in the summer of 1994, where we connected via a drum circle. He said something on his drum; I replied. He spoke; I replied. I spoke; he replied, and so on. So we talked after, with voices that spoke in English. I believe he was the first person who helped me understand djembes can be tuned and what that means. After we drummed together in the circle, he asked me to sit in with him and his act. He had two background singers and a backing-recording and, now, me. I think this was my first gig on djembe!

Afterwards, a tense moment was brewing backstage that had to do with the next act not being there. I had been listening to Vinx, one of my earliest musical influences, nonstop for months and could perform some of his tunes. (For the record, Vinx has an incredible voice and is an incredible percussionist; I have had the great honor of playing with him and can hang with him on drumming, but that voice—I'm not anywhere near his league. So I told the person in charge I could do a few tunes. He replied, "You'd do a few tunes?" I replied, "I'll do a few tunes." So I stepped in front of maybe one thousand folks at Peace Hill near Montrose Beach in Chicago and did my best, and they loved it.

At the same festival, I met fourteen-year-old Jeremiah Glauser. We drummed together under a tent—me on djembe, him on his turtle shell with mallets. He and Whitfield are two of the most gifted people I have ever met. Already this early on, djembe seemed to be creating for me a path adorned with characters with rare gifts. My tribe would transform, and the gravity of passion would bring all manner of goodness. Anyway, now you know about Whit and his connection to djembe repair.

Jeremiah Glauser, me, and Yaya c. 1996

Journal Entries: 2010-2011—China

In the spring of 2010, Tony Webb from Toning Beijing Culture and Development Co. Ltd., emailed me. He said he had wanted Mamady Keïta to come to China for a few months to introduce traditional djembe to China, especially the state schools. Since Mamady was not available, he was searching for someone else. He had seen me in an online interview on djembefola.com, a website for djembe enthusiasts created by James Farrell. The first interview James did for his website was with Mamady Keïta, and in March 2010, he chose me for the second one; I was very honored. James and I discussed many things, but mainly focused on my experiences and advice regarding getting certification in Mamady Keïta's Tam Tam Mandingue Djembe Academy. After Tony saw this interview, he approached me. After a fair amount of back and forth, much of it because

In Tianjin, China 2011: left to right, me, Tony Webb (my organizer), Mr Li (director of The Nine Beats Music Education Institute in Tianjin, China), Aldo Mazza, unknown.

I didn't really believe it was for real, we struck a deal and in August of 2010 (and 2011), I was on a plane to Beijing, China.

From Chicago, the flight took me north over Canada's northern territories and the North Pole. After a thirteen-plus-hour flight, Tony picked me out of the crowd coming off the plane in the Beijing airport. I was set up in a single room in a hostel in the Sanlitun district of Beijing. It was very basic, but it had all the things I needed—electricity, internet, bed, and shower. After spending a couple of days getting acclimated, we began work. From the largest building (by area) in the world, Terminal 3 of the Beijing Airport, we embarked on a twenty-day tour. Tony is a white-haired Brit in his sixties who had owned many businesses in his life. He described himself as an entrepreneur, author, creator, storyteller, father, and grandfather. I'm especially thankful that Tony made it a point to make sure I saw China between teaching classes. Ning, Tony's Chinese life-partner, had a history playing symphony-level traditional Chinese Guqin, a plucked instrument of the zither family. Sam was my translator and sidekick, playing in all my classes. He was a thirty-something Brit who spoke Mandarin better than many native speakers. He was also a very good percussionist, who spent several months in Cuba studying congas. He was a great friend to have by my side and was always smiling! Tony, Ning, and Sam would attend all my classes.

China is the most high-tech and low-tech country conceivable. I'd see an ox-drawn cart that looked like it was from the twelfth-century one day and a high-definition screen that was the entire side of a skyscraper the next. I can say I experienced the absolutely worst-smelling bathrooms in many places on my tours; my ability to hold my breath increased dramatically; Wim Hof would have been proud.

While in China, I ate fish brain and eye, tried chicken feet, and saw a whole fried chicken head staring back at me from a plate. I didn't try pigs feet, cow penis, live octopus, fried scorpion-on-a-stick, or pig brain. I almost ate dog, but I made a lucky choice to pass it by at a buffet before I knew what everything actually was. I ate fish in Sichuan, a name famously synonymous with hot food. I learned a new definition of just how hot *hot* could be when you're actually in Sichuan! That shite was HOT! They certainly like their chilies in China! I tried drunken shrimp in Dōngběi (very northeast China, near North Korea) where the live shrimp swim in rice wine. I did as they do, as I grabbed the live, slow-moving (literally drunk) shrimp, crunched the whole thing in my mouth, and swallowed. I paid the high price of a gastrointestinal firestorm for the whole next day; lesson learned?

Too many meals had unknowns all the time. I had heard tell that in the Canton, in the south of China, they will eat *anything*. I heard about a dish called "three squeals" or "three squeaks." Trigger warning for the faint-of-gut: The first squeal is when you grab the live rat fetus with your chopsticks. The second squeal is when you dip the live rat fetus in soy sauce. The third squeal comes when you eat the live rat fetus.

You may need to take a moment.

Since I was in the very part of southern China where this dish is said to have originated, I had to ask my peeps there if the "three squeals" was urban legend. They spoke among themselves for a good while. The response I got was "Oh, they haven't done that here in years." Wow. Just wow.

I got a massage for 68 yuan (about $10 USD) for forty-five minutes on my back, focusing on my left scapula. Add 28 yuan for a cupping ($4 USD).

2010 China Tour synopsis (2011 was very similar):

Date	Province	City	Notes
8/18-21	Shanxi	Jincheng	KungFu Kids
8/26		Beijing	
8/27-8/30	Shandong	Qingdao	As in the beer
8/30-9/4	Henan	Pingdingshan	Private percussion school
9/4-9/7	Guangdong	Guangzhou	Private music school
9/8-10	Liaoning	Shenyang	Shenyang Conservatory of Music
9/11-13		Shanghai	Shanghai Conservatory of Music
9/13-9/15	Sichuan	Chengdu	Rehearse 14th, gig 15th
9/15-9/17	Shandong	Zaozhuang	Rehearse 16th, gig 17th
9/17-9/20		Beijing	The Central Conservatory of Music

At the Kung Fu school in Shanxi province, central China, our first stop, there were 100 drummers between the ages of six and ten. I loved teaching them because, being kung fu students, their discipline with repeating what I was doing was really impressive. In no time, we were playing a grooving rhythm! I'll add that kids are universally kids, no matter where they are from; I love some of the universalities between humans around the world. In a demonstration the school did after we drummed, I saw that these kids could do some mad acrobatics and kung fu!

In Qingdao, the daughter of our organizer was an absolutely phenomenal player; she was very much an exception to the norm in this place. At dinner, the organizer took us to a place far away from our hotel, and after a few hours of Qingdao beer and food, we told him we wanted to go back to the hotel to get a good night's rest. His reaction was to puff his chest out and declare we would leave only when *he* said we'd leave. I can say without judgment that he was an absolute idiot who was obviously using this moment to assert his power. At one point, a live octopus was brought out in a lidded glass container. He thought it would be funny to pour some hot tea in with the octopus, at which point the octopus got out of the container and, with amazing speed, "ran" across the table until it was caught by waitstaff. I felt horrified and sad. When it returned to us, it was part of a cooked meal.

In between Sam and I challenging each other with how much scorching hot wasabi we could eat at once; some new wasabi-dances came through us. We increased our orders of pitchers of beer in an effort to get our organizer drunk enough that he would have his driver take us home. This took an amazing amount of beer. I learned that many Asians have a low tolerance for alcohol and get something called "Asian flush." This blushing reaction occurs because of a genetic variant that impairs production of an enzyme that helps metabolize alcohol in the liver. For my part, I was bloated, tired, and really wanted to go home. We were captive to this idiot in Qingdao.

In Henan, in three solid days, we covered the traditional rhythms Moribayassa, Kuku, Djole, and Soli(rapide); they couldn't get Soli(rapide). Soli(rapide) hit at the heart of what the Chinese didn't get—swing, or whatever term you put to those rhythms that have such an elusive feel; I saw this in all but one place I taught in both tours (2010 and 2011).

In Guangzhou, my students (who were private percussion teachers at a percussion school) asked, "When's the test?" I replied, "I don't know. When is the test?" It felt a bit like Abbott and Costello for a moment. I had no idea what they were talking about. After a bit of back and forth translating, I was told I was being asked to create tests for folks—single rhythm tests. So I created the first-ever djembe rhythm test in China. The test included demonstrating all parts individually, in an ensemble, and with signals; it included oral histories that were written down. About half of those testing passed; it was sobering for them because, as private percussion teachers, their perception of their own ability was overblown.

The Shenyang Conservatory was a great group, mainly composed of percussion students of high school age. They were quick on the uptake, but they had problems getting beyond repeating and really feeling the groove. It was really hard to explain groove/feel beyond demonstrating.

In Changsha in 2011, our organizer was a professional jazz drummer named Funky. After a day of great classes for the public in his club, he and I jammed for a long time. It was the first time in China that I was really able to flow in the music and not only play, but play with the music, navigating to places only a seasoned improvisational musical artist can go and with someone who possessed mastery of their instrument. Thank you, Funky!

In Zaozhuang, we did two "team-building" drum circles—the kind I had escaped from more than ten years before. I don't love doing drum circles. I'm thankful that other folks like doing drum circles so I don't have to do them as often as when I first started my drum life. We also did a gig that lasted six minutes—perhaps my shortest gig ever!

After teaching for a few weeks, I started to see some commonalities in the places I'd taught. I didn't see concern with quality or process here, only advancement at any cost, regardless of shortcuts or misrepresentations. Seems like this stereotype about the Chinese was true when it came to learning djembe as well. In fact, when I returned in 2011, I saw many performances of things I had taught in 2010 being done in a way that did not indicate a focus on representing quality djembe music or the djembe itself; it was quite upsetting, quite pervasive, and made me sad that I was connected to it.

Sam and I went to a couple of bars in Chengdu. One was a djembe bar, which, contrary to cynical expectation, was very cool. They had a set of dununs and some decent djembes. Sam and I jammed freely. One of the folks at the bar said he had seen me on YouTube! The other place was the "Hemp Bar"—how could we resist? It was good to chill and play for a while.

The first time I was on a bullet train in China was on the way back to Beijing for our last date at the Central Conservatory of Music. The cars on the bullet trains were non-smoking (the windows are sealed like on an airplane), but in typical Chinese fashion, some passengers ignored this and no one enforced the rule. But I'd had it with smokers in China and took to vanquishing them from their ill habit each time they offended. The beast will come out if you put me in a sealed container with cigarette smokers; the dude will not abide. After detecting the smell of cigarettes, I would walk the car until I found the offender and, while staring them straight in the eyes, would point to the no-smoking sign. Each time (three different times), they would shrink away in shame. This method was very effective because of this culture's desire never to lose face; use your opponent's strengths against them.

The Central Conservatory of Music is the most elite music conservatory in all of China, so it has the very best and brightest music students. These young folks were right on time in more than a few ways. Unlike almost everyone else on the tour, these folks could really listen, remember, and play with feeling—they were amazing! We did Moribayassa (with arrangement), Djansa (with arrangement), Soli, Mendiani, Soko, and Yankadi/Makru (with arrangement) in nine hours of classes over two days. That was the most I was able to do with any group on this tour, and it was with the highest quality of musicianship and representation of the djembe and djembe music.

CHAPTER 12
DRUM CIRCLES

"True wisdom comes to each of us when we realize how little we understand about life, ourselves, and the world around us."

— Socrates

In case you don't know, a drum circle is an improvised drumming session, usually in public where anyone can participate—usually no rules, sometimes someone helps guide (facilitate). It's important to understand there is a difference between a drum circle and drummers sitting in a circle. I often teach traditional djembe rhythms with the class in a circle; this is not a drum circle. While I'm at it, over my long years of study, I learned that even the term "traditional djembe rhythm" can be misleading, since not all valid djembe traditions are the same (needless to say, not all places have a valid—meaning a historical—link to djembe). "Djembe orchestra" is a term that has been coined to represent the standardization of djembe music being presented with two or three djembe accompaniment parts and one part on each of the three bass drums (songban, kenkeni, dununba). I can speak mainly to Guinean djembe music saying that not all areas in Guinea, for example, have a dununba drum; some areas don't use dununs at all. Well, drum circles are the Wild West of the hand drum experience. You see many types of drums in a drum circle—congas, bongos, ashikos, djembes, drums with no name. Usually there is a disproportionate number of djembes in your average drum circle.

Me in 1994 at a small drum circle in parking lot of Soldier Field, Chicago at Grateful Dead Show.

Since the drum is often an instrument that expresses one's personality loudly (for better or worse), drum circles can really be hit or miss. Some of my best and worst drumming experiences have happened in drum circles. I guess I'm mostly thankful for the natural potential of drumming since most folks in a drum circle are non-musicians by Western music standards. Drum circles are where I got a lot of my playing done with other folks in my first few years with djembe. And, like with many things, sometimes it was incredible and sometimes it was very much the opposite. I started paying close attention to when it was either because I wanted to understand why drum circles would sometimes suck. It boiled down to listening and awareness. So many folks were not listening; some were. Some lacked the awareness to realize they were doing something together in a group, like it or not.

> "You can drum by yourself. You can drum in a group.
> But don't drum by yourself in a group."
>
> — Taylor

Then I realized the drum circle experience is the experience of communication in a different context. It's how people speak to or at one another. It's how they listen, don't listen, or simply wait to speak. It's how they know how to do what they know how to do; it's where they don't know how to do what they think they know how to do. It's where they know more about what to do than they are allowing themselves to contribute. It's where the egoic can find nourishment and so much more. I began to see an amazing array of things at work that would collectively show me how drum circles are a microcosm of the world. My greatest wish regarding drum circles is that individuals allow themselves to contribute at their own level and that folks consider that listening may involve *not* speaking/playing sometimes. You don't need to be a drummer to effectively participate in a drum circle just like you don't have to be a professional speaker to have a conversation. Noticing the difference between noise and music is key; noise is sound without organization; music is organized sound. Creating music together is a listening skill, not an instrumental skill.

> "I am a musician, not a noisician!"
>
> — Taylor, inspired by his younger students

CHAPTER 13

PAUL CALDWELL, TULUM, AND MALIDOMA SOMÉ

"We ought to live sacrificing, and singing, and dancing."

— Plato

Paul Caldwell, director of the famous Jubilate Children's Choir of Chicago's northern suburbs, was looking for a djembe teacher for himself and this person would also be the djembe player for the choir. I was the second person he contacted after he saw my name in *World Percussion and Rhythm Magazine* and checked out some stuff I had online. We spoke on the phone, and he dropped off a folder of the music for the show. About a week later, we met when I walked down the aisle of a huge church in Evanston, Illinois, at our first gig. We did not meet until I showed up at that first gig. We hit it off swimmingly, and I became an integral part of the choir.

Paul has a genius and eccentric charisma with the kids that is magical. One highlight of our time together was when the choir toured Ireland with *Adiemus—Songs of Sanctuary*, an absolutely gorgeous album that is only percussion and voice. The band that toured with the choir consisted of me and a brilliant pianist named Mark Thomas. I had to do the entire percussion score. I did as much as I could with four limbs, djembe, and dunun, sometimes playing both at once. I involved cymbals and other hand percussion to flesh things out, all by myself. Paul set up a tour that took us from east to west across the middle of Ireland. We had two tour buses and a very knowledgeable guide to tell us all about the history of the places we'd visit. I can't remember how many castles or monasteries we rehearsed and/or performed in that were built around the same time the djembe was created in the twelfth century in the Malian Empire of West Africa. I have big respect for Paul and his vision, and I have no words for how happy it makes me that we shared such amazing work.

To get his choir exposed to other ways of singing, Paul would do an annual holiday show with Walt Whitman's "Soul Children of Chicago." Playing with and witnessing the Soul Children was amazing. I remember one piece I was watching from back of the house when the wave of music and emotion became so powerful that tears fell from my eyes. It was almost too much to bear and one of the most moving experiences of my life.

Journal Entries: 2013-2014—Malidoma, KoSA

It was predicted that 2012 would be the year the world ended. For me, in some ways, that was true. The anti-anxiety/depression meds I took that year barely lasted six weeks, and several toxic relationships left my life. Burning down the forest of my life was essential for new growth. My wisest friends told me this while it was happening, and I'm thankful that I had faith in their words; it helped me through.

My Africanesque Folktales kept evolving, making me feel they would be a significant part of my future. I loved that my source material was my experiences with my djembe masters, combined with morals essential to stories of old. I believe these stories to be a limitless well that will quench my thirst for creativity in the long haul.

In 2013, I had the honor of being asked to teach at the annual KoSA Drum Camp. This came about as the result of meeting KoSA's creator, Aldo Mazza, while in Tianjin, China, in 2011. Aldo's reputation preceded him so I was very honored to meet him. He had a story about so many of the greatest drummers, especially traps players (Buddy Rich, Neal Peart, Joe Morello, etc.), that I can't stop urging him to put those stories into a book. We were both there presenting and performing at the 9 Beats Drum Camp (China's largest music school). During the week-long camp, I regularly dined with folks like Greg Bissonette (who played for Ringo Starr, Spinal Tap, etc.), Glen Velez (master frame drummer), and Chester Thompson (who played for Genesis, Frank Zappa, etc.). I heard amazing stories from amazing musicians about all manner of everything. Thankfully, many of them sat in on my classes and I sat in on theirs. In my class, I had a young woman who could really play! We did a traditional rhythm or two with full dununs and djembe. After the class, she introduced herself as Jacquelene Acevedo, an amazing Latin percussionist from New York. (She's played with David Byrne's *American Utopia* on Broadway.) Jacquelene is from a family of great percussionists. It was such an honor to meet her.

Each teacher had a slot on the main stage performing a recital-type piece, based on the classes we had taught. We could choose anyone for our ensemble, so teachers had teachers in their groups. My djembe ensemble included Aldo, Ed Uribe (Berkeley College of Music), Marcus Santos (Gypsy Kings, Brand New Heavies), Jacquelene and Jeff Salisbury (Al King, Chuck Berry, Bo Diddley)—a dream team, most definitely. It was really great sitting in on each other's workshops and performing in each other's recitals/performances.

Each teacher also had a separate performance slot on the main stage to do whatever they wanted. After long thought, I decided to perform "Hand of the Master." It was perfect. Not only did I not mess up the performance with any regrettable mistakes, but it was on a great stage with great sound, in front of the staff and participants of KoSA, and it was altogether different. It was also the only percussion and spoken word piece at the show. I can't thank Aldo enough for asking me to teach at KoSA—it was an honor beyond words. Love the global network of good folks!

This year I also started working with long-time friend Rich Logan on his *Akoustikirtan* album and with his band. Work continues with Wood Bone and Steel, a trio with Bill Brickey, guitar, vox, songs; Graham Nelson, vox, harmonicas; me, vox, and djembe rig. (This is what I call playing my djembe with a hand cymbal and two other drums called dununs.)

L to R - Bill Brickey, me, Graham Nelson, aka Wood Bone and Steel c. 2012 at the Old Town School of Folk Music, Chicago. Photo by Miro Ledajaks.

The year 2014 brought some life-altering information and experiences; it was an initiatory year, no doubt. This was my twentieth year with the djembe, and it would take me to the great West African diviner, Master Elder Dr. Malidoma Somé. In the djembe class I teach at the Old Town School of Folk Music in Chicago, I have met many incredible people who were necessary for me to meet to progress on my path. Amy Krutek was a student at OTS who became a friend. When she took a Shamanism workshop on the island of Kauai from Toby Christiansen, she called to tell me how amazing Toby and the workshop were. She felt like Toby and I were cut from the same cloth. She also decided she needed to live on Kauai. Let this be a cautionary tale that if you manifest something while at a Shamanism workshop, the results may be more quick and extreme than planned! Returning from Kauai, Amy arrived home to find an eviction notice on her door—seems the landlord of her apartment building wasn't doing their part to whomever they paid. She took this as a clear sign that her move to Kauai was now beginning. With her life in transition, she stayed at my house until she could leave. During this time, over a few glasses of wine, she asked if there was anyone "famous" I would want to meet. I thought for a while, then said, "Malidoma Somé." Her jaw dropped. Toby was a major disciple of Malidoma. We quickly made a plan for Toby to come to the house, stay for a while, meet and drum with me, do some divinations, and begin the process of getting me to meet Malidoma Somé.

Malidoma was going to be the keynote speaker at the Health and Wellness Expo on Kauai in February 2014, so it was on! This was my first trip to Hawaii. I networked with some folks on Kauai who could put together some djembe classes for me to teach, some gigs I could do, and find a place where I could stay for cheap. On Kauai on my birthday, February 4, I ran the "Sleeping Giant" with Toby, a mountain that looks like a sleeping giant from afar, with a mythical story involving the Menehune, mythical little people in Hawaiian legend. A couple of days after I ran the Giant, Toby brought me and Malidoma together. No matter how deep someone is, we all see each other by way of human eyes and in a human form. We shook hands and hugged as if we were long-lost brothers. Within minutes, we had our first drum session—Toby, Malidoma, and me. This moment began in early 1994 when my friend Todd Tesen gave me a copy of *Of Water and the Spirit*, Malidoma's first book, and now it had come full circle this day. We sipped spirits, smoked cigars, and shared stories from our respective worlds. Such a fascinating and rare experience to commune socially with this dignitary of African shamanism.

I took the opportunity to perform "Hand of the Master," my Africanesque Folktale, for all.

Left to Right: Toby Christensen, Dr. Elder Malidoma Patrice Somé, and me at 2014 Health and Wellness Expo, Kauai. Photo by Amy Krutek.

When I asked what the Dagara word was for "Thank you," Malidoma took a long time to answer. He explained that because of what he called "competitive reciprocity," there is no Dagara word for "Thank you." "If someone does something for you in this culture," he said, "then you must out-do them back." Competitive reciprocity!

In March of 2014, I traveled to beautiful Tulum, Mexico, to be on staff teaching at Mamady Keïta's annual international workshop!

The model for Mamady's international, multi-week workshops had changed. He was in the process of handing over the reins of teaching in TTMDA. Between Jeremy Tomasczk (Brussels), Bill Scheidt (US), Colleen Caffrey (US), Kelvin Kew (Singapore), James Kwan (Hong Kong), and me, we assisted Mamady's classes and took turns teaching djembe, tradition, technique, and solo classes. Each day classes ran from 8:30 a.m. to 9 p.m. More than forty great people from nineteen different countries were in attendance.

I've never been in the ocean so much in my whole life; I felt like I was living on the postcard of an island paradise.

In the final *awesome* performances, there were groups comprised of all of us—a highly rhythmically incestuous situation. Or would that be *poly*-rhythmic? Ha! But seriously, we each played different instruments in so many different pieces—what an amazing gift! I opened the show with a performance of "Hand of the Master." Mamady and everyone loved it! The Tulum workshop with Mamady definitely set a precedent for all his workshops to follow, and it involved his students representing his school, the Tam Tam Mandingue Djembe Academy, doing the majority of teaching with him present. The torch was actively, consciously being passed.

In August of this year, Malidoma and Toby set up workshops about ritual so it was twice to Kauai for me in one year! Damn the debt! I'll live another day to pay it off!

"The journey is the destination."

— Malidoma Somé

At this workshop, for two days a group of about fifteen of us learned how to construct and conduct rituals from Malidoma and Toby. The indoor parts took place in an amazing wood structure affectionately known as the Octagon. Auditory and energetic experiences were magnified in the Octagon. We constructed earth, water, fire, nature, and mineral ritual spaces with natural objects, harvested from nature. Then we did the ritual for each of the five earth elements (fire, water, earth, mineral, nature, per Dagara tradition).

I had a bag of some stuff I had collected for the mineral ceremony. I had left it overnight in the Octagon. When I went to retrieve some items inside the bag, I was greeted by the largest centipede I had ever seen—easily six inches long. Scared the shite out of me.

Drumming for ritual with Malidoma Somé and Toby Christiansen—huge. Toby and I drummed together for several of the rituals, playing rhythms from Toby's *5 Element Drumming* that he had composed. He told me they came to him as an inspiration. He then presented them to the Dagara in Malidoma's village in Burkina Faso to see what they thought about the different rhythmic representations he had created to represent each of the 5 Elements. They loved it—so it was so.

I was asked to drum by myself for the water ritual—what an honor! I did what I did the first time I ever played because I felt the flow of this flow was called by water, specifically Lake Michigan.

> "The Dogon people of Mali say, 'The head of the djembe is the ear of God, so never play it timidly.'"
>
> — Toby Christiansen, *5 Element Drumming* DVD

August 11, 2014 was my first and most significant divination with the most revered African diviner on earth, Malidoma Somé. This reading made (read "*defined*") my experience here (well, it would have been awesome anyway) and crystalized my purpose in life.

Here are some excerpts from my audio tape of the reading:

> "..there still is a lot more to do in order to bring the sacredness of what you are gifted with into the world."

"You are not an entertainer. You are a man of medicine with a tool of the ancestors, called upon to use it for the purpose of contributing change and transformation to people. Your relationship with such a mineral tool is indeed intended to deliver this aspect. Not just to make people elated, happy, very joyful for a limited period of time, but to give them the opportunity to lock on to a path of healing."

"You are yet to take advantage of a quality that you carry inside of you that is meant to create an explosion."

"Because you've got to know and you have to admit, the hand, the gift of the drumming hand that you are equipped with, more than anything else, is, in my eyes, profoundly sacred. It is so much so that every time you touch it (and I'm watching), what I am looking at is not somebody who is skilled. It is somebody who is exhibiting ancient wisdom. It is somebody who is performing a healing rite directed at a collective. It is someone who is tuned in."

"It is like something locks on to you, and at that moment, you're not even…you're not in your head."

"Right, it's like I'm not even there."

"That's right."

"Something has possessed me through."

"It is like at that time you turn on an engine and it's working. Who is the driver? Who is driving? I don't know, but it is really mythical."

"Your life, in light of this, is not designed to be rooted in the same old thing."

"...you were brought on earth to be an agent of the return of authenticity to the earth mother...returning authenticity to the earth mother and through this, forwarding that on to countless souls and hearts, particularly, the younger generation."

"These hands are not your hands. They are the instrument of the ancestors."

"...every time you sit with the sacred drum, just give credit to the ancestors."

"There is something about hooking up with the ancestors in such a conscious way that it translates into a boomland: an explosion…. It will show itself to you at the time when you are willing and able to consciously grant the hand to the ancestors; not just let them take over, just tell them, 'I give it to you; yes, do the job with it.' It has to do with acknowledgment of the ancient source of an energy flow that put you as a conduit, a conduit and, therefore, you are there going with the flow."

"...healing choreography..."

"Surrender.... Get out of your way...."

"There is a connection between you and the Middle Passage.... It has to do with the ancestors who crossed the Atlantic Ocean all the way to this part of the world and the kind of energy they brought with them. It has also to do with those who never made it across or never made it back. I don't want to overwhelm you, but I have to let you know that this is a translation of a healing job that is incumbent upon you that addresses itself to family tree, on both sides of the divide. Oh, boy. This is the reason you are who you are, neither black nor white. It is not just that you are like one of the people they call 'métis,' no, no, no…it has to do with gift and purpose. You are the linking point of a racial divide that puts you in a position of being a powerful reconciling agent; healing agent, we use the word 'healing' because we don't have anything better to call for, and you are being invited to broaden your imagination so it can encompass that. And the tool you are using is not rhetoric full of politics and so forth; it is the tool of the drum that speaks universal language…the people on both sides don't have any way but to understand it—they can understand it. Furthermore, they can't argue with it."

"When the ancestors take your hand and beat on that drum, no one can object…that is why you are presented here as an amphibious entity that can move in and out of situations. Your whole life as you were growing up points to that. You were presented with this issue early on, and later on, presented with a tool to heal it… the issue of this divide; this conflict; this tension."

"So this is why you have to look at this from a highly mythical perspective, making you a healer. I can't emphasize this enough— your capacities are so deep, yet you are skimming the surface. Simply because the surface is fun, but your life is a shitload greater than that. It conveys, it presents matters using a universal discourse that glues people who would not otherwise be glued together. And that's that. And that means that underneath all of that would be the kind of speech that will seal the deal. Making you, therefore, a successful agent of community, planetary harmony, and the keeper of the heartbeat of this planet. The keeper of the heartbeat of this planet."

"You were set in this world to deal with things that are overwhelming—the size of mountains."

<<both laughing>>

"Pretty big responsibility!"

"It is a big responsibility!"

This explains so much and is absolute confirmation for me on my path. (There was so much more in the divination that I am glad I taped it.)

The same day after the divination, I was driving with my wife Asia from Hanalei Bay, after going to Queens Bath. At Hanalei Bay, we swam in the ocean, resting in the late afternoon sun. The rest was meditative and left me feeling very, very good (a baked feeling). After we got on the road again, while the song "Braided Hair" from the *1 Giant Leap* soundtrack played, I felt my hair stand on end. I then had a vision of a multi-toned, gray conical tunnel, a tornado, in my chest, reaching back to the origin of all things. The walls had vague faces in an ebb and flow to the surface composed of ancestors; they were showing themselves to me. The sensation was so intense that I began to cry profusely, as if all the sadness I had ever known was gushing out of me—a paroxysm of weeping.

I realized then that any thought of loneliness I had ever known was called into question because I was never alone.

Malidoma had prescribed certain rituals for me to do, annually, seasonally, at specific places. One was to take place at the Middle Passage, the Atlantic Ocean. I went to Maine, with a plan to stay at a dear friend's sister's bed and breakfast, which was near the ocean. On my trip there, while relistening to the divination Malidoma had done for me, I prepared for the ritual and contemplated the context of the moment. In the days before, I had been at the first annual TTMDA Summit - East Coast, hosted by Bill Scheidt, Director of TTMDA North Carolina. In this situation, some massive emotional upheavals happened. Now my flight was eight hours late, which had me driving to my destination somewhere around 4:30 a.m. through very rural roads with lots of hills—all uncharted by me.

I did the ritual to the letter. I had to be back at the airport by around 5:30 a.m., so, fully clothed, I slept less than an hour, then got in the car and drove another ninety minutes into the dark of Maine to get to my flight. The power of the ancestors did not fail me; they did not coddle me either.

The severity of all the combined experiences had me wondering if I was in an initiation; *have the ancestors set my journey to do this ritual in such a way as to add massive suffering?* I think so.

Separately at home, I was to find a tree that would be a tree that I would be (if I were a tree). I would pour honey around the tree's base, then sprinkle sesame seeds on the honey. Then I could sit and wait until any living thing began eating it or come back to see if it had been eaten by nature.

I also had to pour libations into the ground to give recognition to the ancestors and ask them to tell me, please, if there were something I was not understanding so I could expand their communication to me.

CHAPTER 14

RHYTHM REVOLUTION/ FUNKADESI/OLD TOWN/ ASM 1996-1999

> "One can say, 'Teach me what you know,'
> but the better request is,
> 'Teach me about what teaches you.'"
>
> — Malidoma Patrice Somé

Beginning in 1996, many fateful things happened.

First, Todd Tesen, a dear friend and member of Stark Raving Ensemble, got married in San Rafael, California. Much of the ensemble road-tripped from Chicago to California. It was an amazing journey seeing some of the most beautiful parts of the United States. This is where I met my now dear friend the filmmaker Josh Fox (*Gasland*, *Gasland 2*, etc). He was a friend of a friend of the theater group, and he came along after getting rejected as an actor for a very important audition. He has since told me that it was that trip that opened his

Me and my bro, the incredible musician, actor, writer, director, filmmaker, and environmental activist Josh Fox 2021 at his beautiful place in Eastern Pennsylvania.

eyes to the beauty and majesty of the land of the United States that would serve as part of the inspiration for his first film, which opened the world's eyes to the evils of hydraulic fracturing, i.e. "fracking." The wedding was amazing; we drummed and danced throughout the night until the night gave up to let the day take the next shift! I flew back to Chicago after. As I approached my seat, I saw a young East Indian fellow with very bright blue eyes and wearing a 1970s Barney Miller kind of jacket. His name was Ved Londhe. He asked what I was listening to. I told him I was a percussionist and I was listening to some of the final edits for my first CD. He excitedly asked me for my headphones. With a smile, he later handed them back, saying how much he dug what he had heard. Then he said, "I play tabla [a set of two hand drums from India]—do you know Zakir Hussain? He's my guru!" Dumbfounded, I looked at him and said, "Yes, I know the most famous tabla player in the world! You are his student?" And so we geeked out talking about lots of good stuff. One thing he mentioned was that one of his best friends was forming a world music funk band that would really be something new and awesome.

When we reached Chicago, Ved and I exchanged phone numbers and planned to stay in touch. Well, when I told my friend Whitfield about Ved, he was super-geeked to meet him. So, we arranged a time for Whit and me to visit Ved's condo and hang out for a while. When we arrived, Ved had a friend with him who played sitar. Those two broke into a jam between tabla and sitar that could have easily been performed at the Chicago Symphony Center. The communication between the players and between the instruments was amazing. The sitar player was Rahul Sharma, one of the founding members of the Chicago-based award-winning funk, world music band Funkadesi.

> "I can't say enough how energizing this band is; there's a lot of funk in the desi!"
>
> — US Senator Barack Obama, after seeing Funkadesi play in Chicago

Around that time, I had been asked by David Blood and Sarina Kates, the folks who started Rhythm Revolution in Chicago, to facilitate a drum circle for them. I had naturally picked up on facilitating drum circles inadvertently on the lakefront when other drummers would sometimes join me, or if I'd come with my posse from the theater group I had started drumming in, Stark Raving Ensemble. If you really opened your senses, you could see, hear, and feel what was necessary in the moment to extract the greatest potential in a group rhythmic interaction. Then Arthur Hull came and did a drum circle at the Guitar Center, then on Clark and Belmont in Chicago. The main thing I learned from him that day was that he had a term for all of these things that would happen in the process of facilitating a drum circle. He had been doing this a very long time and was generally regarded as the grandfather of drum circle facilitation. So now, I had more tools to use in refining my facilitation. At the same time, I was taking private and group lessons in traditional djembe from Yaya Kabo, a Senegalese djembefola and my first African djembe teacher. I created a workshop titled "Ordered Chaos," which would teach effective drum circle drumming as well as some very basic traditional stuff. Each time I did my Ordered Chaos program at that Guitar Center, it was wall-to-wall people, and we felt the power of the collective, intentional, musical focus. It was incredible!

John Yost and I were in the group classes Yaya was teaching at Malcolm X College. He asked if I would co-teach a djembe class at the Chicago Park District where he was a music instructor; we were looking for ways to get more playing time and to workshop the stuff from Yaya's classes. This was my first official time teaching djembe. Rick Neuhaus was in this class at the park district, and at one point, he asked if I would be interested in teaching at the Old Town School of Folk Music. I said, "Sure! What's that?" So he explained it was the largest community music school in North America and had been around since the 1950s. He added that he was taking a djembe class there, but the teacher sometimes didn't show up for class.

> "The Old Town School of Folk Music teaches and celebrates music and cultural expressions rooted in the traditions of diverse American and global communities."
>
> — Old Town School Mission Statement

I would later find out the instructor wasn't showing up because he was starting a new funk, world music band called Funkadesi. He was Baba Meshach Silas, an incredible drummer from Chicago's South Side. I think his priorities were definitely a win-win for the greater good; the band he was forming with bassist Rahul Sharma (whom I had met a month earlier with Ved), Funkadesi, would go on to be one of the most celebrated world

Two years after being hired at Old Town School; one year before dreadlocks; 1999.

music bands in the United States. To this day, I'm proud to sit in regularly with my brothers and sisters in Funkadesi and consider them extended family.

Yaya had been approached about teaching at The Old Town School of Folk Music, but he didn't have his green card yet. When I asked Yaya if he thought I was ready to teach, he was immediately supportive. So, I interviewed with Michael Miles, banjo virtuoso and program manager at Old Town School. I let my djembe geekitude shine, putting an emphasis on knowledge of and reverence for oral history and Mande culture, and he offered me the job. I've been teaching 3-4 djembe classes at Old Town School since 1997. In 1999, Old Town went on a search for a new executive director. I was on the search committee as a representative from the teaching staff.

During this process, we occasionally met with Old Town School's Board of Directors. I had recently started working with an organization called Urban Gateways, a not-for-profit arts institution, and noticed that Old Town School had no presence in the Chicago Public School system. At a board meeting, I asked if they thought it was peculiar that Old Town School had no presence in the CPS school system. They all agreed it was peculiar. I suggested a position be created to facilitate this. They agreed and the outreach coordinator position was created. It was initially offered to me, but they explained that it was an administrative position and maybe I wouldn't want it because what I would want more is to be contracted by the outreach coordinator. Eric Delli Bovi became the first outreach coordinator.

Soon after Eric started, he had been approached by After School Matters, a job training through the arts program co-funded by the City of Chicago, the Federal Government, and a pet project of Maggie Daley (wife of then Mayor Richard Daley). ASM wanted to partner with Old Town School as a source for artists for some of their music and dance programs, and my drumming program would be the first collaboration. So, Eric sat me down and we did the insanely complicated proposal together and submitted it. As a result, I have been employed with ASM since 1999 (it was called Gallery37 back then). To date, my two steadiest W2 paychecks have come from Old Town School and ASM.

> "To provide Chicago public high school teens opportunities to explore and develop their talents, while gaining

2010 - One of my many After School Matters programs in Chicago Public Schools. This was at Douglass High School in Chicago's West Side Austin community.

critical skills for work, college and beyond."

— After School Matters Mission Statement

In ASM, working with teens 2.5 to 3 hours per day, three days a week really gives an opportunity to study those most peculiar beings, teenagers. I heard a story on NPR some years ago about how similar the brains of teens are to those of "insane" people. This knowledge, when interacting with them, gave me huge peace. Don't get me wrong; most teens I've had in my programs were amazing young people, and we did lots of amazing work together. But the ones…well, you know the ones. Reason must use creativity and cunning to deal properly with unreason. I love the Socratic method, especially when guiding teens to whatever truth needs to be understood at the moment. A few can be such brilliant pains in the ass sometimes. I consider it a great gift to be in such a growth-oriented environment with the teens at ASM.

I've almost always done my ASM program in the Austin neighborhood on the West Side of Chicago; it's an area notorious for its violence, especially gun violence. These teens live in some of the worst conditions; often, they are born to addicted mothers, are fatherless, or have gang affiliations, and they are almost all black.

Several of my students have been shot; one was killed by a bullet while defending a neighbor in their home. I hope I'm doing the best I can by going into this area so often and preaching the gospel of the djembe, but it's hard to know. I do know that if they come to my program and keep coming, they are not someplace that may be a lot less safe. Every time I'm with them, I consider that many of their lives are so unstable and unpredictable that what they are bringing to me is the best they can do, and I'm grateful for their presence, for these baby turtles trying to get to the sea of adulthood. I don't know what the solution is to all of this unbelievable gun violence, but I know, as with all disease, it did not happen overnight or for no reason. The history of racism in this country is something I share with my youth in hopes that they can understand more fully why things are the way they are. What we are seeing/experiencing is a result. It's not an unsolvable problem, but *many* things need to change. We can't give up because we can't see the one solution. My heart goes out to all the families of teens fatally shot in Chicago, and all who have been affected by gun violence. And I stay in the game, making sure I'm doing the best I can, knowing it is never enough, being mindful to take a hit of oxygen myself so I am conscious to hand it to others. I feel like this is as good as it gets. Progress in some contexts can only be seen as the sea occasionally swells to produce the shiny, wet back of a huge sea creature—this creature is called hope—very occasionally. For me, in the context of dealing with underserved/under-resourced youth, faith and hope are the things that live between indications of progress.

> "See the light in others and treat them as if it's all you see."
>
> — Wayne Dyer

Djembe is perfect for working with at-risk teens. It is so joyous and engaging from the beginning. When folks are happy, they learn more effectively. When folks are happy, they remember what lightness feels like. Drumming is the practice of connectedness, presence, joy, and so many things! It is one of the greatest gifts to work in this way so much and for so long.

Chapter 15

A Typical Work Week and Typical Gigs

> "The people who make it to the top—whether they're musicians, or great chefs, or corporate honchos—are addicted to their calling…[they] are the ones who'd be doing whatever it is they love, even if they weren't being paid."
>
> — Quincy Jones

Public school, jail, private school, community centers, Old Town School, hospitals, etc.

Every place I go, I do the same things—I play and teach djembe.

Djembe is universal medicine. A typical work week may contain any or all of the following:

Monday

10:30-11:30 Chicago Waldorf School (staff)

12:30-4:00 Montessori School (staff)

Tuesday

9:00-2:00 Residency at a Chicago Public School for 8-10 weeks

3:30-6:00 After School Matters (staff - job training via the arts program; co-funded by City of Chicago and Federal Government, usually held in a school in the Austin Community, usually running year-round)

1:00-4:10 Accompanist and djembe teacher (adjunct professor) for Kimosha Murphy's dance class at the Theatre School at DePaul University (Tuesdays and Thursdays, spring only)

Wednesday

9:30-10:20 Chicago Waldorf

11:30-12:30 Cook County Dept. of Corrections, Div. 11 (via Oppenheimer Family Foundation grant)

1:30-2:30 Baker Demonstration School (via grant that teacher wrote)

3:30-6:00 After School Matters

6:30-8:00 Old Town School of Folk Music (staff) - Mixed Level djembe

Thursday

9:00-2:00 Residency at a Chicago Public School for 8-10 weeks, or Children's Hospitals (via Old Town School grant, drumming for sick kids)

3:30-6:00 After School Matters

1:00-4:10 Accompanist for Kimosha Murphy's dance class at the Theatre School at DePaul University (spring only)

Friday

9:30-10:30 Parent University at Roberto Clemente High School (contract via CPS Office of Teaching and Learning)

11:30-12:30 Parent University at Miles Davis School (contract via CPS Office of Teaching and Learning)

4:30-6:00 Urban Prep Academy for Young Men, Englewood Campus (via Oppenheimer Family Foundation grant)

Saturday

10:00-11:30 Play for Yoga class (trade for free yoga classes)

12:00-4:00 Various workshops in different places in and out of Chicago

Sunday

1:30-3:30 Old Town School (staff) - Advanced djembe

3:30-5:00 Old Town School (staff) - Mixed level djembe

Add in—in random spots—domestic and international workshops, djembe repairs, corporate team building with Sewa Beats USA, https://sewabeatsusa.com/, admin/invoicing/paper/blah blah blah, random gigs with different ensembles, especially Wood Bone and Steel, Kaben Kafo, etc.

Sewa Beats

Kaben Kafo c. 2009 - left to right: Eric Thomas, me, Jason "Wolfy" Wolf, Andrew Elbert, and special guest Grand Master Drummer Moussa Bolokada Conde. Photo by Miro Ledajaks.

Although I've done corporate team building with drumming independently for years, my main work doing corporate team building since 2017 has been with the international training company called Sewa Beats. Doing this kind of work combines my experience in the corporate world with my theater background and drumming. The gigs I do with Sewa Beats are part of the reason djembe has taken me to six continents. I find the work rewarding in very unique ways. As a lead facilitator, I am tasked with being the onsite manager for the gig, which often means

c. 2018 doing lead facilitation at Sewa Beats corporate team-building event.

the logistics of getting hundreds of drums to a facility, loading in, setting up, coordinating rehearsals, and special requests with the client (often having to memorize new details on the spot), executing the program with a team of drummers, and then breakdown and load out. The programs are interactive, so I have to be thinking on my feet all the time, ready to integrate new information on the fly as opportunities arise during the session. This type of work uses more of what I have to offer than anything else I do.

Old Town School

I've been teaching at the Old Town School of Folk Music in Chicago since 1997. Through the school, I do work for/with them in four different ways:

1. **Adult Program:** My three to four classes I teach at the main headquarters of the Old Town School at 4545 N. Lincoln Ave, Chicago have been amazing. This is a place where anyone can take lots of different classes. Guitar classes, Beatles, Grateful Dead, Abba ensemble classes, belly dancing, West African dance, jug band, etc. The people who come to my class are such an amazingly diverse group of humans that I just have no words. On the first day of class, I always have everyone share something about themselves. My students have been plumbers, welders, ballerinas, doctors, electricians, plant medicine specialists, lawyers, and free spirits in all shapes, sizes, colors, and whatnot seeking greater freedom! The one thing everyone brings to the class is vulnerability; they are showing up and opening up. Marriages have resulted from folks who were in my class together; divorces too. One thing I frequently hear from folks after they take my class is that they hear other music differently; music they've been listening to their whole lives.

They can hear everything more clearly as the result of studying djembe music. How is djembe the Healing Drum? When I asked Master Drummer M'Bemba Bangoura if the djembe was used in a healing capacity where he was from, he said no. Other master drummers I trust from Guinea and Mali say the same thing. In some areas it is, but in some areas not so much. Well, M'Bemba added that the way djembe is healing in Africa is different from the way it is healing in the West. I thought this was pure genius. Of course, every society doesn't have the same ills, the same things to heal from—they are so different with occasional similarities!

2. **Outreach Program:** I teach in many different types of schools: public, private, primary, secondary, alternative, and universities. One way I am in Chicago Public Schools is via the Old Town School's Outreach Program, which I was instrumental (pun intended) in creating. I love working with youth. Traveling a path with them in djembe music with all the detail of oral history, geography, history, etc., is always an enlightening experience. I'm frequently surprised when I ask who knows what before I share knowledge. That "current state analysis" thing is really useful, frequently.

3. **Hospitals:** By way of a special grant, I am part of a team of artists from Old Town School who go to children's hospitals in the Chicago area. I bring a few drums and a bag of hand percussion instruments (shakers and bells mostly) and do a session in the common room (play/rec area), then strap on a couple of drums (usually a djembe and a kenkeni) with shakers in my pockets and go to some of the rooms. Some of the patients seem normal. Some are so strapped with tubes and wires that they can only listen as I

play. Some are in isolation, so, depending on their condition, either I wear a gown and gloves as I enter the room, or I play at the doorway. My instruments are wiped down after I leave my gloves and gown in the garbage in the room. I do this gig ten or so times a year, and I have done it for many years. Seeing joy emanate past serious, often chronic illness is a profound thing. It's a humbling thing, playing for sick kids. In COVID-19 times, this program is done virtually.

c. 2017 at Comer Children's Hospital, Chicago.

4. **Referrals Program:** The referrals program is when someone calls Old Town School to hire talent. The most unusual gig was when I played djembe in 20F cold, in the woods, sitting on a chair, surrounded by snow. This gig was for a school outing, and it was me and Bill Brickey. We both played with gloves on and full cold gear. My creativity was challenged by how to keep my hands from freezing while playing. It was a good challenge.

The Cook County Department of Corrections

Isolation takes the love away; it leaves the heart cold. The young men I work with in the Cook County Department of Corrections are a very mixed lot. They have electively enrolled themselves in York Alternative High School, which is a prerequisite to be eligible for my drum program. Most of my guys are in for gun offenses. They are detainees, waiting for their fate/trial to be decided. Some of my eighteen-year-olds have been there for four years, while their case moves at a glacial pace through the bowels of the judicial system. At that age, a significant potential still exists for permanent change away from the world of crime. Some of the most brilliant people I've ever met were in this place. Some were wrongly accused; some were very, very guilty and they knew and admitted it.

One of my best drummers assured me he was only in because he was wrongly accused. After a particularly excellent performance with many dignitaries in attendance, I presented the drummers with personalized certificates of achievement. After this gig, he un-enrolled himself from York and was repeatedly in the SHT (some call it the "hole," "solitary confinement," or "isolation"). This was totally unlike him, for all of his years in CCDOC. I would later learn he had lied to me about his innocence. He was guilty and had beaten someone nearly to death with a gun. Humans are capable of astonishing contradictions. Perhaps if I knew his whole story, I would understand him more fully; perhaps I would see how, based on all things considered, he was doing the best he could. I feel his great performance and me giving him an award for doing such a great job for so long was part of his reaction; I will likely never know.

I got the jail gig because of Ted Oppenheimer, President of the Oppenheimer Family Fund. He called me one day and said, "Taylor, they're drumming in jails in New York. What do you think about doing it here in Chicago? I'll send you the article; what's your address?" His enthusiasm was heartwarming. A retired Chicago Public Schools principal, Ted had been funding my programs via other organizations for decades before we met. We would see each other at recitals and he saw my drum programs in CPS schools. One day, we finally met, and after we were on a first-name basis, he said, "Taylor, I funded a drum program at a school and it sucked! I should have called you!" My response was something like, "Well, let's just be sure that doesn't happen again." Since that time, he has been my single largest funder of my drum programs in CPS. I consider him a friend and trusted elder.

Somebody asked me how many hours a week I work. It's a hard question for me to answer because so much of what I do, I do not consider work.... Okay, some of it is work, but most of it I love.

> "In the Minianka villages of Fienso and Zangasso, the musicians were healers, the healers musicians. The word musician itself implies the role of healer. For the Minianka perspective, it is inconceivable that the responsibilities for making music and restoring health should be something separate, as they are in the West."
>
> — Yaya Diallo, *The Healing Drum*

A Final Note: The Beat Goes On

n 2021, my two African masters transitioned to become ancestors: Grand Master Drummer Mamady Keïta and Elder Master Dr. Malidoma Patrice Somé.

I am thankful that djembe found me; that the ancestors put my life path on a trajectory to meet djembe when the time was right, or maybe "ripe" is a better word. In the twenty-plus years I was with Mamady, I was connected with the greatest depths of the djembe drum as well as a global network of his students and those he calls "messengers of tradition." We have stayed at each other's homes, broken lots of bread together, and had many incredible experiences together outside of the realm of drumming. He was a guru, a friend, a father figure, and an African elder to me. With him I was pushed to physical, mental, spiritual, and psychological levels that left me expanded and changed as a person. Being with him was like looking through a window to ancient knowledge and teachings that transcended the djembe. When he transitioned, I was in nature, surrounded by leaves, branches, plants, and many tiny living things. I found myself speaking to nature, asking the flowers and trees if they had heard about Mamady. Then it felt as if they were asking me if *I* knew; it would make sense to me if nature knew first. He always said that he drew strength from nature and I felt as if he were omnipresent through nature as I mourned. It felt like he was physically closer to me, to everyone.

My relationship with Malidoma was partly informed by his books, in the way we were acquainted, and then through my first divination where my connection was forged with the world of ancestors, which changed my whole life. Reading his books before I met him educated and prepared me to embrace more fully who he was and his unique gift to the global village. It was incredible to meet him as a person, as opposed to being just another participant in one of his workshops, and especially meeting him via connections forged by the djembe (or really by ancestors). I somehow knew djembe would take me to him, and it did. The Blues Brothers joked "We're on a mission from God." Well, after that first divination with Malidoma, I knew I was on a mission from the ancestors; my calling was articulated. I was already living this calling, but I didn't have an awareness or conscious connection to the source of why I was doing what I was doing and why I am who I am. My divine gift to the global village was clarified.

I play djembe because it is how I connect with divinity, with ancestors, and through this lens, I see the world. I see my own awareness and lack of awareness (after the fact, of course!), and I see the same in other people. Djembe brings me joy, pushes my limits, and shines light where there is darkness. It is my greatest hope that everyone finds their passion or that their passion finds them so that each of our divine gifts is shared with our villages and the global village.

Can you imagine a world where we are all doing what we *should* be doing? Modernization has obscured purpose; public education has put standards in place that do not reflect or empower purpose, different ways of learning, and different intelligences, so we must look past those standards. I'm not saying that modernization and public education are bad per se, but if we rely only on those things to form our lives and worldview, something has been lost. If you live in the modern world, it takes work to get beyond the superficial to find who you really are beyond all the domestication, intergenerational trauma, inherited habits, marketing and addictions. In the absence of an intentional effort to delve deeper, you stay on the surface, and whatever current is around you guides you. It reminds me of Peter Marshall's quote: "If you don't stand for something, you'll fall for anything." It is a win-win for you to live a life of purpose filled with intentional acts.

About the Author

Michael J. Taylor (more commonly known as simply "Taylor") is a biracial human who has been a professional performer, teacher, recording artist, speaker, and raconteur since 1994. He specializes in and makes his living playing and teaching the West African Djembe Drum. However, his presentations offer a wide breadth of metaphors and universal philosophy through his own observations and contemplations of life.

After beginning studies in 1999 with Grand Master Drummer Mamady Keïta, the founder of the Tam Tam Mandingue Djembe Academy, Taylor achieved the degrees of TTMDA Certified Teacher (2005) and was the first in the world to achieve the highest degree TTMDA Senior Certified Teacher (2006). Today, he is the Director of TTMDA-Chicago. Through TTMDA, he teaches and performs with and for youths ages 8-108. As the founder and driving force behind Holy Goat Percussion (est. 1995), he imports, sells, and repairs West African djembes and dununs. Samples of his work can be seen on his "djembist" channel on YouTube.

Additionally, Taylor recorded all djembe parts on the Djembeföla! App for IOS, and recorded many of the rhythms for Mamady Keïta's instructional book *Nankama*, with Mamady Keïta and his group Kaben Kafo. With the international corporate training company Sewa Beats USA, he is a lead facilitator, delivering team-building events to corporate clients. He is proud to be, in the words of Grand Master Drummer Mamady Keïta, a "messenger of tradition" in representing TTMDA. He began drumming through theater and has performed and/or taught djembe on every continent except Antarctica so far. In his work as a musician with the djembe, he has put this traditional West African instrument into performance art, storytelling, and contemporary music (jazz, classical, pop, folk, blues, etc.). He also created the DRUMeditation™, a ritual intended to consciously open a portal to the healing and wisdom of the ancestral realm.

Whether as an educator, professional speaker, storyteller, entrepreneur, video/recording artist, corporate team building facilitator, or performer, Taylor brings a unique perspective to his craft. His unique ability to communicate, instill discipline, and promote creativity, combined with his broad range of life and professional experiences allows him to focus on the relationship between the individual and rhythm/drumming. This has led him to an overall philosophy that strives to bridge the gap between all things in rhythm, seeking to find where one's own personal pulse lies in relation to the collective pulse. By way of traditional West African or non-traditional styles, Taylor demonstrates the universality of rhythm in everything he does.

TAKE CLASSES IN THE WEST AFRICAN DJEMBE DRUM WITH M. TAYLOR

Taylor teaches classes in the West African djembe drum in person and virtually. He is an incredibly engaging and thoughtful teacher and brings a unique perspective to his teachings. As a Tam Tam Mandingue Certified Professor, he teaches traditional West African rhythms as well as traditional djembe technique, rhythm exercises, and listening skills. Students are encouraged to explore the far-reaching implications of learning rhythm on how they think, their level of personal confidence, how they feel, and how they reason. The learning of rhythm can be a conduit to understanding the importance of independence/interdependence. Learning your part achieves independence; putting that part in the context of others' parts achieves interdependence.

In his work with children, Taylor has seen how drumming can enliven and educate on a number of levels. Qualities like discipline, patience, focus, and determination translate into reward, community, and "positivity" when children drum. He finds it fascinating seeing kids understand what it is to understand on a deeper level than they are accustomed to. By this he means not only understanding and mastering the pieces of the puzzle, the parts, but fitting them together, making one rhythm, one puzzle, where everyone has a role in the whole.

In his work with the mentally and physically challenged, Taylor has seen how drumming can bring out the abilities of mentally and physically challenged adults and children. Percussion is such a primal thing; its appeal is on a very deep level in the human psyche. He has seen communication/bonding [by way of percussion] on a level with the disabled that most of them were not able to explore in any other mode of communication.

For more information on Djembe classes, contact Taylor at:

www.HolyGoat.com
taylor@holygoat.com
(773) 909-8633

BOOK M. TAYLOR FOR A DRUMEDITATION™!

The DRUMeditation™ is an incredible ritual that is unique for all who experience it. Having had transformative, out-of-body experiences drumming by himself on the shore of Lake Michigan in Chicago, Taylor began to consider that other people, in the presence of this type of drumming, would also feel the same effects. Through decades of experience studying traditional West African djembe drumming with African djembe Grand Master Mamady Keïta and significant readings and interactions with the African shaman, medicine man, and healer, Master Elder Dr. Malidoma Patrice Somé, Taylor has focused his early explorations with djembe for all to experience. He provides DRUMeditations both virtually or live as desired.

In a DRUMeditation™, Taylor sets expectations with participants, does a guided meditation with voice and drum, and summons the ancestors. Then the real journey begins with the rhythmic environments he channels, which open the portal to the ancestral realm.

Taylor finds it very hard to explain this experience, so he prefers to use testimonials to do the job:

"Taylor's DRUMeditation was an experience unlike anything I've ever had. A truly mind-expansive, portal-opening, positive, beautiful experience I look forward to having again very soon."

— M. Matrejek, Creator of the Breathe Discovery Festival

"I have been to many DRUMeditations; every one is different because we are never the same, always changing. Free your mind. Bathe in the sound of the drums; release everything to Spirit. I use this energy to help rebalance myself in this heroic world. You feel the DRUMeditation in your body and it changes you! Blessings, Taylor."

— D. Curtis, Oakwood Farms Retreat Center

"The DRUMeditation put me into a phenomenal, altered state of consciousness where my body moved to the rhythm of the drums automatically in the most healing way possible. I believe the drums provide an important medicine for our spirits, minds, and bodies."

— L. Vasilyeva

"I am no stranger to transcendental encounters, and I can honestly say DRUMeditation was one of the coolest experiences of my life. I can't wait for the chance to do it again!"

— M. Surface

For more information about DRUMeditation™, contact Taylor at:

www.HolyGoat.com
taylor@holygoat.com
(773) 909-8633

BOOK M. TAYLOR FOR STORYTELLING

"Taylor's folktales draw from his experiences with me and his times in Africa. They contain the stuff of folktales of old. They are a wonderful interpretation of African tradition."

— Grand Master Drummer Mamady Keïta

Whether virtual or live, and whether it is one of his original "African-esque Folktales" or a classic African folktale, Taylor breathes life into characters and situations utilizing his skill as a writer, actor, and orator combined with his masterful drumming. Since he began acting in the third grade, Taylor has entertained audiences from 3 to 103 years old. Taylor performs stories that speak to origins, teach morals, and answer questions about why things are the way they are.

For more information about how Taylor can add Storytelling to your event, contact him at:

www.HolyGoat.com
taylor@holygoat.com
(773) 909-8633

BOOK M. TAYLOR FOR CORPORATE TEAM BUILDING

Whether through the company Sewa Beats International or independently, Taylor, an extremely thoughtful and charismatic presenter, brings a wealth of experience from his time as an information technology consultant, computer teacher, and technical writer. He combines these skills with his acting, drumming, and ability to instill discipline and promote creativity to deliver incredible, engaging programs, both virtually and in person.

For more information about how Taylor can help your team, contact him at:

www.HolyGoat.com

taylor@holygoat.com

(773) 909-8633

About M. Taylor Coaching

Are you stuck in life?

Do you desire to pick up a new hobby?

Are you searching for deeper meaning in your life?

Do you want more understanding of who you are on a deeper, philosophical level?

If you've answered Yes to any of those questions, Michael Taylor can coach and guide you through your current life challenges and adversities to help you find your life and soul purpose.

To schedule your complimentary, no-obligation 30-60 minute coaching consultation, text your name and time zone to M. Taylor and he will get back to you to schedule a call.

(773) 909-8633

BOOK M. TAYLOR TO SPEAK AT YOUR NEXT EVENT

When it comes to choosing a professional speaker for your next event, you can't go wrong with Taylor. Combining his own voice with the voice of his West African djembe drum, he engages audiences on numerous levels, telling stories about his unlikely life and sharing his "African-esque" folktales. Whether your audience is 10 or 10,000, in North America or abroad, Taylor can deliver a customized message of inspiration for your meeting or conference. Taylor understands your audience does not want to be "taught" anything, but is rather interested in hearing stories of inspiration, achievement, and real-life people stepping into their destinies. As a result, Taylor's speaking philosophy is to humor, entertain, and inspire your audience with passion and stories proven to help people achieve extraordinary results. If you are looking for a memorable speaker who will leave your audience wanting more, book Taylor today!

For more information about how Taylor can help your team, contact him at:

www.HolyGoat.com
taylor@holygoat.com
(773) 909-8633